Gift of Love

Nora Kay

CORONET BOOKS
Hodder and Stoughton

Copyright © 1997 by Nora Kay

The right of Nora Kay to be identified as the Author of
the Work has been asserted by her in accordance with the
Copyright, Designs and Patents Act 1988.

First published in Great Britain in 1997 by Hodder and Stoughton
A division of Hodder Headline PLC
First published in paperback in 1998 by Hodder and Stoughton
A Coronet Paperback

10 9 8 7 6

British Library Cataloguing in Publication Data
Kay, Nora
Gift of love
I. Title
823.9´14[F]

ISBN 0 340 68964 1

Printed and bound in Great Britain by
Mackays of Chatham PLC, Chatham, Kent

Hodder and Stoughton
A division of Hodder Headline PLC
338 Euston Road
London NW1 3BH

For Bill and Raymond
and for my editor, Carolyn Caughey

Chapter One

The garden was looking tired. It was late summer and the roses were past their best. The long dry spell had taken its toll leaving the grass parched and the earth cracked and grey. A good downpour would do a lot of good but it was dangerous to wish for rain. Once it began it forgot to stop.

Lois wiped her brow and looking about her thought there was little to show for her hard work. Putting down the trowel she went over to sit on the wooden bench below the kitchen window. In her sleeveless blue cotton dress, faded from so many washings and with brown sandals on her bare feet, sixteen-year-old Lois Pringle leaned back, closed her eyes against the strong sunshine and listened to the distant droning of a bee. She must have dozed off and when she opened her eyes the voices drifted out to her.

'Andrew, what are you doing home at this time? Is anything wrong? Are you unwell?'

Lois heard the alarm in her mother's voice and wondered too. Her father was never home in the afternoon; he should have been in his office in Dundee.

'Does something have to be wrong?' The voice was impatient. 'If you must know the painters were in the office over the weekend and that sickening smell of paint was giving me a headache.'

'Didn't you think to open the windows?'

'Harriet, I may only be a humble accountant but please give me credit for some sense. Of course I opened the windows, opened the damn things as far as they would go.' He didn't add that as far as they would go was only about an inch and that the paint wouldn't let them budge.

'Yes, well, people don't always remember to do the obvious.'

Lois smothered a giggle. How like her mother.

'Perhaps not, but I have brought work home with me so I have no need to feel guilty.'

'I should just think not. You give that office more than its fair share of your time.'

'The work has to be done, Harriet, and we older ones are expected to show an example. Is this you on your way out?'

'Not just yet, I've time to make a cup of tea.'

'That would be welcome. I'll have it here then take myself off to the study.'

Lois heard the rush of water as her mother filled the kettle.

'Biscuits, dear, or would you prefer a piece of cake? The sultana is finished and the bought Madeira is quite dry I'm afraid. With me rushed off my feet there has been no time for baking and Lois shows no interest in learning.'

Lois made a face.

'A biscuit will do very well and since you have mentioned Lois this might be a good opportunity to talk about something that is beginning to worry me. No, not beginning, it has been concerning me for some time.'

'Really! And what might that be may I ask?'

'Lois. Where is she by the way?'

'In the garden.'

This was the time to get up and walk away. Lois remembered the old saying that listeners never hear any good of themselves. It was unlikely to be of any importance but if she just crept away she would forever wonder what it was she had missed.

'I can't think what there is to discuss,' her mother continued.

'Can't you?'

'No, I cannot and do remember, Andrew, that I haven't all day. I'm going out.'

'Another meeting?'

'Yes, another meeting and do I detect sarcasm?'

'Not at all, dear, but as I have said before you do too much. It is wise to be able to delegate and you should remember that.'

'Do you? Delegate I mean?'

'I'm learning to.'

'I prefer to do things myself and that way I know they are done properly.'

2

'Yes, well, I don't suppose you'll change and now to what I was going to say about Lois.'

'Are you by any chance suggesting that I am failing in my duty to my family?'

'Not at all. You are a good mother, Harriet, but you do rather favour Marie. No, Harriet, don't interrupt, let me have my say then you can have yours. A mother can have her favourite child, it is quite natural, but what a mother must never do is to let it show. Children soon forget the kindnesses shown to them but they do not forget or easily forgive those they consider have treated them badly.'

'Words fail me, they really do. Winnie cannot possibly feel neglected. As the youngest—'

'Winnie, I quite agree, comes in for a fair share of your loving care. I am not disputing that. Lois, on the other hand, is not so lucky.'

'That is untrue. I do my best for that girl but she is difficult and I'm going to say it, ungrateful.'

'Why on earth should Lois be grateful? Do the other two show any gratitude?'

'This conversation is becoming ridiculous. Do you want more tea?'

'No, thank you.'

'Then I'll empty the teapot.'

'Don't bother, sit where you are until we have this out.'

'Very well, Andrew, since you've brought up the subject, what about you? You show your preference for Lois.'

'I don't think so, but if it is true it is only very recently. Harriet, I am not blind to the way you treat Lois. She is always the last to be considered and taking her away from school when she wanted to stay on was unforgivable.'

'I can't do everything, I need some assistance in the house.'

'But why Lois? She is the brightest of the three and the one to have benefited from extra schooling.'

'I don't recall there being much opposition from you?'

'I know and I bitterly regret it. There were serious problems at work causing me a great deal of worry but even so that is no excuse. Tell me, Harriet, was it spite? Were you afraid of Lois getting the qualifications that were beyond Marie?'

'Now you are being insulting.'

3

'No, I just want this all out in the open. Marie was hopeless at school and desperate to leave. Surely she was much better suited to give you the assistance you claim you need.'

'With Marie's looks and charms she doesn't need to be academic. Few boys are drawn to brainy girls,' she said smugly.

'I disagree but never mind that.'

'For your information, Marie is doing very well in her job and has a real flair for fashion. In fact there is the possibility of promotion.'

'In a small dress shop? Don't make me laugh. What possible promotion can there be other than a bob or two on her wages? Now had she been working in a department store—'

'I would not have allowed my daughter to work in a store. Madame Yvette's, I'll have you know is a high-class establishment and she is just delighted with Marie.' There was a pause, then she added, 'She is so pretty and charming.'

'Who Madame or Marie?'

'Don't be flippant, Andrew.'

'My dear Harriet, surely you haven't been taken in by Madame Yvette? The woman is no more French than you are. That frightful accent is put on to impress the customers.'

'May I ask how you happen to be so knowledgeable about Marie's employer?'

'Office gossip I'm afraid. Madame Yvette, in real life, was plump little Lizzie Robertson. She was at school with the mother of one of my juniors. Bob Fairlie heard them talking, remembered me telling him where Marie worked—'

'And you had a good laugh?'

'We did as a matter of fact.'

'Could we end this conversation here and now?'

'In a minute. All I ask is that you treat the three of them the same. Lois is a nice child.'

'She is moody and difficult and not a bit like the other two. You don't have her all day, I do.'

'In other words I'm wasting my breath?'

'Yes, you are.'

There was a long pause and Lois made to get up, then stayed put when her father spoke again.

'Lois tells me that she is doing well at evening school and her shorthand and typing speeds are good. She is hoping for a job in an office.'

'Not with you I hope?'

'No, I agree that would be unwise but I have contacts that may prove helpful.'

'And what about me or are my needs of no importance?'

'You have Mrs Briggs to do the heavy work and the woman might be prepared to do extra if she were asked. I don't keep you short of money.'

'I never suggested you did. As for Mrs Briggs, to ask that woman to do anything other than scrub floors would be like letting a bull into a china shop.'

'If she is that bad get someone else.'

'Not as easy as you think. Domestic help is becoming extremely difficult to come by and I need someone I can trust. Lois is far from ideal but at least she can be left in the house. Oh, for goodness sake, would you look at the time? I've missed my bus and I pride myself on never being late. This is your fault, Andrew.'

'Don't upset yourself the car is at the gate and I'll run you to where you want to go.'

'The church hall.'

There was the sound of a chair being scraped back and Lois kept out of sight until she heard the car start up. Then she went in by the back door which was open to let the air in and through the scullery to the kitchen. Two cups and saucers were on the table together with the biscuit tin which was open showing the rush her mother had been in. Lois helped herself to a custard cream and poured herself a cup of tea. Nursing the cup, Lois thought back to how barren her childhood had been. If it had been the same for Marie and Winnie she could have accepted that her mother was one of those women who find it hard to show affection. But her mother wasn't made like that. There had been no lack of warmth for her sisters. Was it surprising then that the feeling that there must be something wrong with her had taken root? She had tried so hard to win her mother's love and when she failed, Lois recalled the despair of her anger and the deep, deep hurt. Young as she was some kind of pride had made her pretend that she didn't care. Only she did, she cared so very much – it was her own lonely, private misery.

*　　*　　*

Muirford where the Pringles had their home was a thriving coastal town on the east coast of Scotland not far from the city of Dundee famous for its Jute, Jam and Journalism. The train stopped briefly at Muirford to pick up its passengers. It was an attractive station with a lovely floral display that drew many exclamations of delight. The stationmaster, a portly man with a round smiling face, took full credit. The inhabitants and especially those who made use of the station, were justifiably proud that for the last five years – 1925 to 1930 – the station had won the prestigious award for being the cleanest and the best kept.

Most of the passengers for the first train of the day were smartly dressed businessmen carrying brief-cases and umbrellas who preferred to put some distance between home and their place of work. Occasionally Andrew Pringle used his car for the journey though he favoured the train since it gave him the chance to relax and read his newspaper which he bought at the station kiosk. The local paper was delivered to the house but not until after he had left. This suited Harriet since, had her husband taken the *Courier* with him, she would not have seen it until the evening. That is if he remembered to bring it home.

The house the Pringles lived in was known as Laurelbank and was a detached villa in Greenacre on the outskirts of Muirford. This was a quiet residential district with a close-knit community enjoying many of the advantages of a village. The church, St David's, was within walking distance and each Sunday morning the bells rang out at ten fifty and continued ringing until the service began at eleven. St David's was where the family worshipped and had their own pew for which they paid a half-yearly sum. Sitting for an hour and a quarter on a hard wooden seat was anything but comfortable and Harriet had finally persuaded her husband to follow others' lead and have a cushioned seat that stretched the full length. Individual cushions were inclined to go astray. Since Andrew attended church only occasionally the matter was of little importance to him but it made a big difference to the others. There were fewer grimaces when they got up.

The accommodation at Laurelbank consisted of a good-sized, well-furnished sitting-room and a square-shaped dining-room. Both rooms had a bay window. The curtains in the sitting-room were a deep blue velvet with a matching pelmet whilst the ones in the dining-room were cream and brown and in a floral pattern. Some years ago when the family was very young, a large cupboard had been turned into a downstairs cloakroom with a toilet and washhand basin. This convenience reduced wear on the stair carpet and frayed tempers in the morning since Andrew had first use of the bathroom and the others made do with the cloakroom. Also downstairs was a large kitchen with shelves and cupboards. The tiny scullery had a sink and a draining-board and under it a clutter of enamel basins and a pail. Andrew's study was between the living-room and the dining-room. Upstairs were three bedrooms, a boxroom and a bathroom. The bath was white with claw feet and a cork mat sat on the linoleum which was blue and white. There were shelves beside the window and on one was Andrew's shaving kit.

The front rooms had a lovely view of green fields and beyond that were rolling hills. From the upstairs back windows could be seen slate-roofed houses and in between them a tantalising glimpse of the sea.

Since neither Andrew nor Harriet were keen gardeners – Andrew confessed to not knowing a flower from a weed – it was fortunate that the garden was not over-large. They did have a gardener of sorts, an elderly man who came to Laurelbank twice a week in the growing season and at odd times when a clean-up was necessary. The front garden was smallish and on a slope which made gardening more difficult. Angus McGregor regularly complained about his back and grumbled as he laboured. His work was far from satisfactory which was why Lois had to help. On several occasions Harriet had tried to dispense with the gardener's services but Angus chose not to listen and turned up just as usual. A replacement would have been far from easy unless Harriet was prepared to pay a lot more and as Angus probably knew this, things just carried on in the same way.

Down at the foot of the garden was a clump of berry bushes and most years there was a good yield from them. By the end of the jam-making season the shelves in Harriet's kitchen would be filled with jars lined up like soldiers on parade. Each one had a label showing the contents to be either blackcurrant or raspberry and giving the date of making. In a corner and protected from the birds, was a small bed of strawberries which might produce enough for eating for two or three nights and take the place of a pudding. They were delicious served with a sprinkling of caster sugar and a dollop of thick cream when the dairy could oblige.

To buy strawberries for jam was considered by many housewives, including Harriet, to be ridiculously expensive and picking one's own made good sense. Harriet arranged a day when the girls were to be at home and the weather favourable. They would sit down to have a picnic meal in some farmer's field, occasionally joining like-minded people but more often keeping to themselves. The picking of the berries was left to the young ones. Harriet's back wouldn't take the strain but from where she sat she was able to keep an eye on the Pringle girls as they selected the biggest and juiciest to put in their containers.

Chapter Two

Mindful of her duties, Lois first cleared the table then, getting out a sharp knife, began on the vegetables. Marie and Winnie preferred to take sandwiches with them rather have the rush to get home and back in an hour. Andrew made do with a light lunch in a nearby restaurant.

This meant that at six o'clock or close to it, the Pringles sat down together for their main meal of the day which they ate in the dining-room. The three courses were followed by tea or coffee with Andrew preferring coffee and the others tea. Marie, believing it to be more sophisticated to drink coffee, was trying to acquire a taste for it. Harriet dished up the food in the kitchen and Lois carried the plates through. The clearing up was left to Lois with Winnie occasionally giving a hand.

Lois didn't suppose she was overworked, it was just that she could call no particular time of the day her own. Evening school took up three nights a week which left little time for enjoyment, but she didn't mind since it was the way to get qualifications which would enable her to apply for an office job.

The preparations for the meal complete, Lois dried her hands on the towel and went through to the sitting-room. She would have half an hour with her library book. Sitting down she opened it at the place and with her legs tucked under her began to read. So engrossed was she that the half-hour became an hour and Lois only realised that her mother was in the room when she heard the voice rich with disapproval.

'I might have known. Really, Lois, you are the limit. Is this all you can find to do?'

Lois looked up guiltily and closed the book, forgetting in her haste and confusion to put in the bookmark. Then she felt a spurt of anger.

'Is it so dreadful to come home and find me reading?'

'At this time of day it is,' Harriet snapped. Her feet were killing her and that wasn't improving her temper. 'What about the evening meal? Did you give any thought to that?'

'All taken care of.'

'And, of course, you never look for work, that would never occur to you. There is always work to be done in a house, Lois.'

Then why don't you stay in and do it? It was what Lois longed to say and one day she would pluck up courage to say just that. Or would she?

Harriet Pringle was forty-six, of medium height and quite pleasant-looking when her face wasn't creased in a frown. Despite depriving herself of the sweet dishes she loved, her figure was thickening. Her complexion remained good but her blond hair had darkened to a nondescript colour. She had thick, shapeless legs and suffered badly from swollen ankles which bulged over her sensible brown brogues.

After undoing the buttons of her tweed costume jacket, Harriet sat down on the pale pink sofa and, with one foot, dragged over the stool and put her feet on it.

'That's better. What a relief to be sitting down,' she said with a deep sigh. 'I've hardly been off my feet all day.'

'Why don't you ease off and let someone else do something for a change?' Lois asked as she adjusted the chairback cover.

'This awful heat has a lot to do with my tiredness, we aren't used to it,' Harriet said avoiding a direct answer. 'A light dress and cardigan would have been more suitable but one can never be sure, the weather can be so changeable. As for someone doing something . . .' She shook her head. 'None of them, Lois, would have the faintest idea of how to go about it. They are like children and have to be told everything. Making the tea and preparing sandwiches is about their only strength.'

'That could be because it is all they are asked to do,' Lois almost said, but stopped herself in time. 'You should try explaining to them what it is you want. They can't all be stupid.'

'I'm not so sure.'

Harriet, like a lot of domineering women, didn't think of herself as bossy but rather as super efficient. She fought tooth and nail to get a place on every committee in the firm belief that those same committees would not long survive without her organising skills. If the ladies of Greenacre resented the way Harriet threw her weight about, and most of them did, they had the good sense to keep quiet. No one actually liked the woman but all were agreed that when it came to the bit, Harriet Pringle was the driving force that got things done.

'I forget if this is the day that Winnie goes straight from school to her piano lessons?'

'It is.'

Harriet smiled. Fourteen-year-old Winnie had gained her first certificate a year ago with just three marks short of honours.

'So nice to have a pianist in the family and such an accomplishment for a young girl. We must give her all the encouragement we can.'

The removal of the secondhand piano from the sitting-room into the dining-room had not pleased Harriet one bit but in this her husband had been adamant. He had no objections, he said, to his youngest daughter learning the piano but he wanted some peace when he got home. Scales were the worst and got on his nerves. The sitting-room was where he read his papers and he had no intention of changing his routine and no, he would not go into his study. This was all explained to an angry Harriet who was prepared to stand her ground until Andrew threatened to take himself to his local if his wishes weren't carried out there and then.

That had the desired effect as he expected it would. As a child Harriet could remember how fond of the bottle her father had been and the times she had blushed with shame to see him stagger home. Andrew was a moderate drinker and she wanted to keep it that way.

There were no casters on the piano and it took the five of them, with many stops for rests, to carry it into the dining-room then position it against the wall opposite the sideboard. Somehow it didn't look right, just out of place. Harriet tried altering the position of the other furniture but it still didn't look right and by this time they were all exhausted.

'Evening classes again tonight?'

'Yes.'

'Three nights a week, isn't that rather overdoing it?'

'I don't think so.'

'Dressmaking, now if you were doing something useful like that I could understand it.'

'Dressmaking or sewing of any kind doesn't happen to interest me.' Her mother knew that.

'More's the pity. Think how handy it would be and the savings if you could run up a dress or a skirt. Becky Calderwood makes all her own clothes.'

Lois had seen some of Becky's attempts. 'I know.' She didn't add that it showed, but perhaps her tone of voice said it for her.

'Admittedly Becky isn't very good yet, but she's keen and she'll improve.'

'No doubt she will.' Lois paused. 'Mum, you know perfectly well why I am attending evening school. I want to get some qualifications so that I can get a job.'

Lois dreamed of getting a job, any job in fact just so long as it got her away from the house. She imagined the freedom it would give her and if she saved very, very hard perhaps in time she could leave home altogether. Of course she would be sad to leave her dad and Winnie, Marie too but not so much in Marie's case. No more than idle dreams, she didn't see it ever happening, but if she got a job it would be a beginning.

'What makes you think you will be better off in an office?'

'I don't, but I would like the opportunity to find out.'

'You, my girl, don't know when you are well off.'

Lois thought about her day and the dreariness of it. Up first in the morning to get the breakfast started. Mrs Briggs did the scrubbing and the heavy work but even so there was plenty to do and her mother was doing less and less. If she had fixed hours she would know where she stood and then there was the matter of money. She got pocket money and her clothes were bought for her, but there was no wage packet. She had never had the thrill of opening one yet.

'I don't consider that I am well off and if you want the truth, Mum, I feel exploited.'

'Exploited!' Harriet spluttered. 'Would you mind explaining that to me if, indeed, you know the meaning of the word?'

'I do and I'll explain with pleasure.' Lois was surprised and pleased at the calm of her voice when inside she was shaking. 'It suits you very well to have me at home since it leaves you free to serve on all those committees of yours and attend all the meetings. If I wasn't here you would have to rush home to see to the meals.'

'How dare you speak to me like that, you impudent hussy.' Blotches of angry colour burned high in Harriet's cheeks.

Lois's courage hadn't failed her yet and she wouldn't stop now. If she did she would never have the courage again.

'Yes, I'm daring to speak to you like this because I want you to realise what you have done to me.' She took a deep breath. 'I was doing well at school, my teachers told you that and I was keen to stay on. You, however, had other plans for me and all my pleading was in vain.'

'You weren't victimised, Marie left when she was fifteen,' Harriet snapped.

'That's true. Marie was desperate to get away and you know the reason for that. Academically she was poor and there would have been no point in her remaining at school. She would have had to repeat a year and that would have meant her being with me and that would never have done.'

'Marie has brains, she just didn't use them.'

Lois knew that wasn't true. She was a year behind Marie but even so she had been able to help her with her homework. Marie had struggled to keep up with the others in her class and then when she couldn't she had just given up.

'Marie wanted to leave school the minute she could and what I can't understand is why Marie couldn't have stayed at home.'

Harriet took her time before replying. 'You won't recall because you don't wish to but it so happens that when Marie left school I wasn't so heavily involved in my committees and charity work.'

'No, it is just since I've been at home.'

Harriet overturned the stool then righted it. Raising her face she looked at Lois coldly.

'It is completely out of the question for Marie to be at home.'

'Would you mind telling me why?'

'Marie is holding down a responsible job.'

'No, she isn't, anybody could do what she does.'

'Really, what a dreadful thing to say, but typical of you. Jealousy is your trouble, you have always been jealous of Marie.'

Lois shook her head. 'You couldn't be more wrong.'

'I'm not wrong. You are jealous because Marie is so popular and never without a boyfriend whilst you—'

'I don't get much chance to go out and meet anyone,' she shouted. Her courage was beginning to fail her and Lois felt like weeping.

'You are not a prisoner.'

'Why do you like to hurt me?' Lois burst out.

'What nonsense you talk. You have nothing to complain about, you have a good home—'

'Yes, Mum,' Lois said wearily. 'I share it with Marie and Winnie but what I don't share . . .' She stopped.

'Go on, finish what you were going to say.'

'You've never loved me, never shown me any affection.'

'Have I ever lifted a hand to you?'

'No, but then neither have you to Marie and Winnie.'

'There was never any necessity, they are good girls.'

'And I'm not?'

'You, Lois, are not a very lovable person,' Harriet said cruelly, then wished the words unsaid when she saw the stricken look on Lois's face. But it was too late, she couldn't take them back.

'One day, Mum,' Lois said unsteadily, 'one day when it is too late you are going to be sorry for the way you have treated me.'

'Oh, for goodness sake pull yourself together, you see slights where none are intended.'

It came as a relief to both of them when Winnie came bursting in. In one hand she had a bulging schoolbag and in the other a music case. Both got dumped on the floor and then sensing an atmosphere she looked from one to the other.

'What's the matter?'

'Need you ask? Madam, here, just being her awkward self.'

'Lois isn't awkward, Mum,' Winnie said quietly. 'You never pick on Marie or me, it is always Lois and I just wish you wouldn't.'

'Winnie, my dear, I don't pick on anyone. You aren't here all day and Lois, if she got away with it, would do as little as possible.'

'You're out most of the time and I bet she does plenty. Lois wants to go out to work like Marie and why shouldn't she?'

'I need her at home, that's why.'

'You could have me. I'm a dunce and I would be better at home helping you. In fact come to think about it that is what I'd like to do.'

'Now, now! You are just being a silly girl,' Harriet smiled. 'I want to hear your news, how did the music lesson go? Is Miss Reid pleased with your progress?'

Winnie scowled. The lesson hadn't gone well and Miss Reid had been anything but pleased. 'You are losing interest, Winnie,' she had said, 'and when that happens it is useless to go on.' Winnie knew it to be true but there was no point in trying to tell her mother that. Her mother had set her heart on having a pianist in the family and that was that.

'How should I know?'

'Doesn't she say?'

Winnie shrugged.

'Oh dear, in a mood are we?'

'No, I'm not.'

'I'm sure Miss Reid is pleased, dear. I, myself, can hear how well you are getting on. It is just a case of practice, practice, practice. That is what makes a good pianist.'

'How wrong you are, Mum, musicians are born with a gift, the rest of us are just plodders.'

'You are no plodder, you have a certificate.'

'Oh, Mum,' Winnie said wearily.

'You sound tired and, of course, it is a longish day for you. A glass of milk will keep you going until your father gets home. Lois, go and see to it.'

'I don't want a glass of milk and if I did I'm perfectly capable of pouring one out for myself.'

Harriet sighed and got heavily to her feet. 'That outburst of yours has upset me, Lois. I'm going upstairs to wash and change and by the time I come down I shall expect you to have an apology ready.'

'I'm afraid you won't get one,' Lois said quietly and turning followed Winnie into the kitchen. They heard Harriet's heavy step on the stairs.

'What was all that about?'

'Oh, this, that and the next thing. No matter what I do or say I seem to irritate Mum.'

'I wonder why? She does pick on you, I notice it more now than I used to.'

'It isn't my imagination then?' Lois smiled.

'No. Dad doesn't do it and I can't understand why Mum does.'

'Don't worry about it.'

'I do though, I hate unfairness.'

'That's nice of you, Winnie, but truly it doesn't worry me so much now.'

Winnie nodded but she didn't look convinced. 'She's my mum and I love her but there are times when she has me about screaming.'

'You've nothing to scream about, Mum is all right to you.'

Winnie swallowed the last of the biscuit and reached in the tin for another.

'Put you off your meal.'

'No, it won't, it will just make me fatter.'

'Don't call yourself that. What you are is—'

'Nicely plump.' She made a face and Lois laughed.

Winnie had a round happy face and like Marie took her fair colouring from her mother. Unlike Marie, who had a slim figure, Winnie was small and on the plump side. Harriet called it puppy fat and kept telling her that it would disappear as she got older. Winnie had been hearing that for such a long time that she no longer believed it. Sadly both girls had inherited their mother's shapeless legs.

Winnie gave a sigh of exasperation. 'I just wish that Mum would stop going on about the piano,' she said lowering her voice. 'If only she would try to understand that I'm nothing special and never will be.'

'She's proud of you getting that certificate.'

'Oh, that! Lois, I only got it because the examiner was sorry for me.'

'That's rubbish. No examiner would pass you unless he was satisfied with your performance.'

'Promise me you won't repeat it and I'll tell you something.'

'I promise.'

'I was nervous but then so were the others. We just sat and looked at each other and waited our turn. When mine came I went in and sat down at the piano.' Winnie paused to wipe the crumbs from her navy-blue school skirt. 'I was told to play my piece and I was doing fine or so I thought, when I struck a wrong note. Lois, I was so convinced I'd failed and so disappointed after all the hours of practice I'd put in that I began to cry. I couldn't help it.' She smiled. 'The examiner – he looked a bit like Dad

– gave me his clean handkerchief out of his pocket, patted my shoulder and said I was doing very nicely, just to take my time and play the piece again when I was ready.'

'Which you did?'

'Which I did. Honestly I felt such a fool and would you believe it I made the same mistake again, only this time I didn't stop.'

'Maybe he didn't notice the wrong note.'

Winnie shook her head. 'Lois, of course he did, he must have. An examiner has to have a sharp ear, he couldn't miss a wrong note or he wouldn't be an examiner.'

'In that case you must have done exceptionally well with the rest.'

'You know I never thought of that,' Winnie said looking genuinely surprised, 'but I suppose it was possible.'

'More than possible I'd say.'

'Thanks, Lois, thanks very much, I wish I'd told you before instead of keeping it to myself.' Winnie got to her feet. 'Suppose I'd better get out of this beastly uniform.'

'Don't forget your schoolbag and your music case.'

Winnie was moving away. 'Get them later.'

'Not advisable, Winnie. Mum might fall over them.'

She came back to pick them up. 'Oh, heck, I'd better shift them or I'll be joining you in the dog-house.'

Andrew did little talking at the table, preferring to give his attention to the food. In any case what was said held no interest for him. All Marie seemed able to talk about was that damned shop and who had been buying what. As for Harriet – his scowl deepened – she was as bad encouraging her. A houseful of women was a bit much some days.

Lois had coerced Winnie into helping with the washing-up. Winnie wasn't reluctant to help but it rattled her that Marie got off scot free. Sure to complain about being tired when she was asked to do something but no hint of it when she was getting ready to go out with her latest boyfriend. Why, she wondered, did her mother treat Lois the way she did – at times not much better than a servant. Not something new. She supposed it had always gone on, but what you were used to you just accepted without really noticing. Lois didn't say much but Winnie had the feeling that it was all building up and one day there would be a real showdown.

Andrew was behind his newspaper and Harriet was working at her embroidery. While her fingers made neat little stitches her thoughts drifted to when the girls had been tiny and a lot less worry. Perhaps she was wrong thinking that, for worries there had been. Hadn't she nursed them through those childhood ailments – chickenpox, measles, mumps and most serious of all, scarlet fever. She remembered the broken nights then having to drag herself up in the morning to see to Andrew's breakfast before he set out. Those had been the difficult times with no one to help her. If only her mother had been spared but she had died soon after Marie was born.

She smiled to herself, picturing in her mind Marie and Winnie with their flaxen hair, big pale-blue eyes and chubby limbs. How adorable they had been and everyone had remarked on how lucky she was to have such lovely children. The dark-haired, quiet, skinny little girl with her pale face and her sticklike legs had been the plain one. Now all that was changed. Though it pained Harriet to admit it there was no denying that Lois was blossoming into a beauty with her lovely figure and long, shapely legs.

When heads turned it would be to look at Lois.

'Now then, young lady, what have you to say for yourself?'

'Dad, I know I shouldn't have lost my temper,' Lois said with downcast eyes.

'You upset your mother,' he said sternly.

'Not as much as she upset me,' Lois flashed back, surprised and hurt that she wasn't getting the sympathy she had expected.

'Lois, my dear, there are always faults on both sides and losing one's temper only makes matters worse.'

The evening sunshine slanted into the book-lined study where Lois and her father were sitting in comfortable chairs. Andrew was behind his desk and Lois facing him. Her father was a fine-looking man for forty-nine, clean-shaven and with traces of grey in the thick dark hair. Broad-shouldered and just short of six feet, Andrew, as a young man both before his marriage and after, had been slim and athletic. Now, apart from an occasional game of golf, he took little exercise and like his wife his figure was thickening.

18

Lois had been hoping that her outburst would have gone unreported but she might have known better, Harriet had only been waiting for a convenient time.

'You aren't exactly in your mother's good books.'

'Nothing surprising about that, Dad. I can't do anything to please Mum.'

'Maybe you imagine some of it?' He raised an eyebrow and she shook her head.

You know it isn't imagination, she thought, or you wouldn't have said all that to Mum about being concerned. 'No it isn't imagination, I only wish it were. Even Winnie has noticed and remarked on it.' Lois paused and bit her lip. 'Dad, I'm not prepared to put up with it for much longer.'

'Now you are just being silly, Lois,' he said almost angrily. The hurt look and the trembling lip made Andrew feel murderous towards his wife, but he couldn't afford to show it. He could, however, show a bit more understanding.

'Dad, may I ask you something?'

'My dear child, you don't have to ask.'

Lois took a deep breath and was careful. It wouldn't do to let him know that she had been eavesdropping. 'I don't cause any trouble and I'm certainly no worse than Marie and Winnie so it must be something about me that Mum doesn't like. She must have told you, she wouldn't keep a thing like that to herself.'

Andrew was equally careful, he was treading on dangerous ground.

'Lois, it is a sad but true fact of life that a mother may show favour among her children. A first-born has a very special place in her heart and the youngest comes in for a bit of spoiling.'

'Meaning the middle one doesn't count,' she said with a half laugh, then shook her head vigorously. 'No, Dad, that won't do. Middle children in other families don't miss out. It has to be more than that.'

In those moments Andrew was almost tempted but he couldn't. The day would come but until then he could do no more than reason with Harriet and appeal to her better nature.

'Try to make the best of things, lass, and once you have those certificates I'll use what influence I have to get you fixed up with a job.'

19

'I don't want that,' she said firmly.

'You prefer to do this on your own? Very commendable, my dear, but rather difficult in your case.'

'Why should that be? I'm not stupid.'

'Very far from it but you have no experience and at nearly seventeen an employer would expect more than certificates.'

'And whose fault is that? Just try to remember that I had no choice but to leave school and help Mum in the house.' Then she almost shouted, 'You could have helped.'

'I've failed you, haven't I?'

'Yes, Dad, I think you have.' Lois wished the words unsaid when she saw the hurt in his face. To show him she didn't mean it Lois got up and gave him her lovely smile and for a heartbreaking moment Andrew felt pure pain. How cruel of Harriet to have called this darling child the ugly duckling – he sincerely hoped it hadn't been to her face, but knowing Harriet he thought it quite possible.

Was his wife suffering as she watched the ugly duckling turning into a beautiful swan? Could that be the reason why relations between them had reached an all time low?

'Better get myself back, Dad, no rest for the wicked,' she grinned.

'That's my girl,' he laughed. 'And, Lois—'

She turned at the door. 'You are a very lovely girl, my dear, and I'm afraid you are going to break a few hearts.'

'Me?' Lois said in genuine surprise. 'Not a chance, Marie is the beauty in this family.'

How wrong you are, he thought. He supposed Marie had quite a pretty face but she was so silly. Nothing in her head but fashion and boys, and how annoying it was to see her unable to pass a mirror without looking in it to admire herself.

Allowing Marie to keep her wages was a mistake, he had said so to Harriet. Not that she earned very much but she should be encouraged to save and give a token amount towards her keep. Another thing, she should be giving Lois a hand in the house. For too long he had taken the easy way out and let Harriet rule. That had been his mistake and Lois was suffering for it. Life could be the very devil, he thought glumly.

It was then he began to think about his own life. Where had love gone or had there been much of it in the first place? There were times when he honestly wondered why he had married Harriet. He must have proposed marriage but for the life of him he couldn't remember doing so. More than likely he had just allowed himself to be led to the altar. Filling his pipe, Andrew let his mind wander back and striking a match, he waited until the tobacco caught then puffed contentedly and let the years fall away.

As a young lad the four of them had knocked about together and had met these four girls. As was to be expected they chatted them up and Andrew remembered he'd had his eye on the small, dark-eyed girl with the fringe but he had been too slow off the mark and had ended up with Harriet. Not that there was anything wrong with Harriet's appearance, far from it, she was a nice-looking lass. Come to think about it, a bit like Marie now. The last thing he had intended to happen was Harriet getting the wrong idea and thinking he might be serious. A night out, a visit to the cinema, a goodnight kiss if that was allowed and then a casual remark to the effect that they must do this again some time but that pressure of work made it difficult just now, etc., etc. His mistake as he recalled it, and he was still thinking of it as a mistake, had been calling for Harriet instead of arranging to meet her. Mrs Baxter, Harriet's widowed mother, had answered the door and invited him in. That had been it. The woman, he was convinced of it, had decided there and then that here was a fine match for her daughter, her only child. A newly qualified accountant, a sensible lad with good prospects, Harriet could do a lot worse.

What really clinched it were those high teas that became a regular Sunday treat. Mrs Baxter was a splendid cook, far better than his own mother who had little imagination when it came to food. To be honest he had enjoyed those meals and found himself looking forward to them. Andrew smiled to himself thinking how true the old saying was that the way to a man's heart was through his stomach.

How naïve he had been not to recognise the signs. In a remarkably short time, or so it had seemed to Andrew, Harriet was proudly displaying an engagement ring and from then on the talk was of nothing but the forthcoming wedding. How well he remembered the panicky feeling as his efforts to slow things down were swept aside and his protestations ignored.

His friends, still single and enjoying themselves, had suggested ways of getting out of his predicament but all were unworkable and unthinkable. It would take a brave man to get out of it at this late stage – a braver man than Andrew. When the talk turned to where they would live after the wedding, Andrew grabbed the opportunity for a breathing space.

'That needn't worry you,' Mrs Baxter had smiled. 'Plenty of room here until you find a house that suits you.'

The wistful longing in the voice was not lost on Andrew but he chose to ignore it. He knew that Harriet's mother dreaded being alone and had declared more than once that she wouldn't be losing a daughter but rather gaining a son.

Shaking his head Andrew had looked over at his bride-to-be for her support and surprisingly she had given it.

'No, Mother, that wouldn't do.'

'I wouldn't interfere.'

'We both know that but it is better that we start our married life in our own home.'

'Very well,' Mrs Baxter said, putting on a brave face, 'I was only trying to be helpful but it has to be your decision.'

Relieved that something was going his way, Andrew relaxed and managed a smile for both women.

'You'll have Harriet for a while yet, Mrs Baxter, there is absolutely no rush for us to get married. We can take our time and look around until we find suitable accommodation. Not easy with houses to rent difficult to come by, but something will turn up.'

It struck Andrew that his lukewarm attitude to his forthcoming marriage would have had another girl throwing his ring back at him, but not Harriet. If she was aware of his reluctance to take the big step, and how could she not be, she chose to ignore it.

'Don't be downhearted, Andrew, that needn't be such a big problem.' Mrs Baxter had put her disappointment behind her. If she and Harriet were to live near to each other or at least on a tram route there could be plenty of coming and going. And when the little ones put in their appearance Harriet would be only too glad of her help.

'Why, Mother, what had you in mind?'

Mrs Baxter smiled happily. 'You know the saying that one good turn deserves another? Well, it just so happens that I did someone a favour and this lady's husband has property in various parts of Dundee.'

'You mean a tenement?' Harriet said, not troubling to hide her disappointment.

'That's all I could afford, Harriet,' said Andrew.

'Nothing wrong with starting your married life in a tenement,' Mrs Baxter said sharply, 'your father and I did.' She was annoyed with her daughter. Her disapproving glance held a warning. Mrs Baxter didn't want anything to go wrong at this stage and since she was neither deaf nor blind she was well aware of Andrew's reluctance to tie himself down. 'In a year or two you may well be in a position to afford something better or even think about buying your own home. Always a good investment,' she smiled to her future son-in-law and getting no response added brusquely, 'meantime I'm sure you'll be very happy in a room and kitchen in a good tenement block.'

'If we get one.'

'I can't be sure, Harriet, but I'm fairly confident that when a house becomes vacant you will be offered it.'

Mrs Baxter was proved right. A two-roomed house with a scullery and bathroom did become vacant. It was in Scott Terrace in the west end of Dundee and was one of the more eagerly sought-after tenements since it had a bathroom, was in a quiet respectable area and only walking distance from the park.

Andrew suddenly became aware that his pipe had gone out and that his eyes had been fixed on the wall opposite. Giving himself a mental shake he began half-heartedly on the papers cluttering his desk.

Chapter Three

The days went by with nothing much changing except that her mother was less fault-finding than usual. Lois thought her father must have had something to do with that. She hoped so.

Just as she was taking off her apron the scullery door was pushed wider and Harriet appeared.

'Is that you finished?'

'Yes. Why? Is there something you want?'

'You didn't tell me we were low on milk.'

'I thought there was enough to do.'

'Well, there isn't.' Her glance went to the window. 'The rain appears to be off so this could be a good time to go along to the farm. Better get eggs when you are at it. Make it a dozen and a half and be sure to ask Mrs Roy for brown eggs.'

Her mother was right about the weather, the rain had stopped but for how long was anyone's guess. The black cloud just above looked threatening and Lois, to be on the safe side, collected her old navy-blue school trench-coat from a nag on the back of the cupboard door. The cupboard was a glory hole filled with old coats, mackintoshes and discarded footwear. At spring-cleaning time it was completely emptied and given a good clean out. What was considered too good to throw away found its way back. It had become a family joke just how much did find its way back.

Lois didn't trouble with a hat, getting her hair wet didn't bother her since she was blessed with naturally curly hair which she wore short. Marie's hair went dead straight with even a hint of dampness in the air and this she found a great trial. Every second week she visited the hairdresser's for a Marcel wave and in between she washed her own hair and put in curlers.

Lois had the basket over one arm and the jug in her other hand. A few women shoppers gossiping at the shop door greeted her and she smiled back making some remark about the weather. Greenacre was well served with quality shops and though the prices were higher than in town only a few grumbled and most of these were young mothers with children. The shop windows got barely a glance from Lois, then she was beyond them and level with the church. Close to it was the manse, a large dreary, draughty house that was home to the minister, his harassed wife and their four children all under school age. The only help came from a slow-witted girl who was willing but required everything explained to her several times. The Reverend Alexander Hutchison was a good man, a kind man who gave unstintingly of his time to his flock but was quite unaware that his wife was almost at breaking point. Others saw it but no one thought to interfere, it was a delicate matter after all.

The main street petered out and became a rough stony lane known as the Farm Lane and there Lois had to dodge the many water-filled potholes before coming to the barns and outhouses and then the farmhouse which was part hidden by trees. It was a long low building of grey stone which had been added to with each new generation. The excited barking of dogs could be heard but the animals must have been indoors else they would have been rushing to greet whoever it was. A goose came fleetingly into view followed by another but Lois was wary of them. On one occasion she had discovered a piece of biscuit in her pocket and had held it out. The speed and the shock of having it snapped from her fingers had alarmed her sufficiently to keep her distance in future.

Close to the farmhouse was the dairy and for much of the day that was where the farmer's wife could be found. She was kept busy with a steady stream of customers who liked to buy their milk and eggs straight from the farm. Good money was to be made and Mrs Roy claimed this as her own, which she had every reason to do. She called it her egg money and watched with quiet satisfaction as her savings grew. Of course she knew as everyone did that there wasn't even the remotest chance of her ever being left destitute, but she liked the thought of having her own nest egg. Independence was a fine thing and it meant not being totally dependent on her husband and if he departed this earth before her, on her family.

Mrs Roy, her sleeves rolled up, was emptying the remainder of the milk from one churn into another. She waited until she had finished before looking up.

'It's you, Lois, that's not the rain on again is it?'

'A spot or two, I'm hoping it'll keep off until I get home.' A tabby cat brushed against her legs then with a look of disdain stalked out of the door on silent feet.

'What can I get you, lass?'

Mrs Roy was a cheerful, rosy-cheeked woman in her fifties. She was small and had kept her slim figure but delicate she was not. Moving heavy milk churns was child's play to her and unless it was something exceptionally heavy she declared she wouldn't see anyone in her way.

'Three quarters filled please, Mrs Roy, and a dozen and a half of eggs. Mum said to ask for brown ones.'

Mrs Roy shook her head and sighed. 'Lois, I'm tired telling folks around here that there is absolutely no difference between brown eggs and white ones apart from the colour of the shell. I'll let her have six brown but you be sure and tell your mother what I said.'

'I'll do that, Mrs Roy, but she won't believe it, I know that.'

Lois stood watching the eggs being packed in the basket then the milk ladled into the blue and white jug.

'That should do you then, lass.'

'Thanks.' She got the money out of her purse and waited for her change.

'Better tell you the news or maybe you know it already?'

Lois shook her head.

'I've just heard that Silverknowe is sold. That's a fair while it has been on the market and it'll be nice to see new folk there.'

'I didn't know and I'm sure Mum doesn't or she would have said.' Lois put the change into her purse.

'You tell your mother that it is the Hammonds who have bought it. She'll know who I mean her being a Dundee lass.'

'I'll remember to tell her.'

Lois was only half listening as Mrs Roy went on at some length about the Hammonds. Only when the next customer arrived was she able to make her escape.

'Mum, had you heard that Silverknowe was sold?'

'No, though it was rumoured that someone was interested. Did Mrs Roy say who had bought it?'

'A family called Hammond. She said you would know them.'

Harriet shook her head. 'The name doesn't mean anything.'

'The family belong to Dundee, something to do with jute.'

'Oh, that Hammond. I don't know them but I know of them. They own the Templeton Jute Mills. Did you remember to ask for brown eggs?'

'Yes and Mrs Roy said I was to be sure to tell you that there is no difference at all between a brown egg and a white one, apart from the colour of the shell.'

'She would say that – she wants to keep them for her friends. Did she give you any?'

'Half a dozen.'

'Not making herself short is she? What else had she to say about the Hammonds?'

'Not very much. They won't be taking up residence for quite a long time. I think Mrs Roy said they were coming home from India for good or maybe they are already here.'

'But why come to live here?' Harriet sounded puzzled as she examined each egg for cracks.

'Why not? What's wrong with Greenacre?'

'Nothing, silly. It's just that I recall the Hammonds having a large mansion house in Broughty Ferry which is more convenient for Dundee.'

Lois searched her memory for what had been said. 'Mrs Roy said the drawback to their other house was that they didn't have enough ground to put up a tennis court and Silverknowe has.'

'A tennis court,' Harriet said disbelievingly. 'How often would they get the use of that?'

'We do get some good weather.'

'Two months in the year if we are lucky.'

'Seems they played a lot of tennis in India and want to keep up their standard.'

'We have a perfectly good tennis club here but possibly not exclusive enough for them. In their place I suppose I would feel the same way. What about family? Any mention of that?'

'Two sons.' Lois was enjoying herself, it wasn't often that she was the bearer of news.

'What sort of age?'

'I don't know but one is in the army serving overseas and the other son is with his father in the mill.'

'Married?'

'Mum, I don't know but I don't think so. Mrs Roy made no mention of it.'

Harriet was having a quiet smile to herself. 'It'll be nice having Silverknowe occupied again and particularly when there is a family. Maybe I'll take a walk up to the farm myself next time. Mrs Roy always manages to be the first to hear anything and I'd rather hear it from her than secondhand. And Lois—'

Lois closed the pantry door and turned round.

'Don't be peeling the potatoes, just give them a good scrub with the small brush. It appears we are losing the best of the potato which is next to the skin.'

Harriet was humming to herself and doing a lot of thinking. Young men of good family were none too plentiful and it was so important that Marie made a good marriage. The boys she went out with were nice enough and came from respectable families but they fell far short of Harriet's dreams for Marie. She was eighteen and probably at her loveliest. Harriet's mind was rushing ahead.

On her seventeenth birthday Lois was overjoyed to receive a wristwatch from her parents and a silver chain from Marie and Winnie. This was one of the happy times and, of course, there had been many of those. She wouldn't deny that. She did try to forget about the bad times, but one particular occasion clung to her memory. At the time she had been seven, Marie a year older and Winnie a five-year-old just starting school. The day had begun so well and with such excitement. The sun shone out of a cloudless sky, it was delightfully warm and they were going to Monifieth to have a picnic on the sands. At the last minute Harriet had changed her mind about taking bathing costumes. The girls would just be paddling and they could tuck their dresses into their knickers.

Years later Lois was to decide that that was the day when she finally gave up all hope of winning her mother's affection. Even now, just thinking about it, she could feel the hurt and the awful sense of injustice. Closing her eyes, Lois remembered the feel of the warm sand between her toes and the heat of the sun on her skin. The years rolled away.

Andrew wasn't a picnic person but he had agreed readily enough to drive them to the beach or as near as he could get. He had helped to carry all the paraphernalia so necessary for a picnic and having the car meant that they could take so much more than would have been possible travelling by bus. The arrangement was that Andrew would see them settled before departing for the golf course and return later to drive them home.

Winnie had plonked herself down on the sand and was sucking her thumb, a habit Harriet deplored but she had been told not to make a fuss about it and the child would stop all the sooner. Winnie had been looking at her father.

'Daddy looks funny in those.'

'I'll have you know that these are plus-fours and I don't see anything funny about them,' Andrew said.

'Your daddy suits plus-fours, Winnie, and he only wears them for golf.' Harriet smiled. She was looking summery in a short-sleeved dress with a pattern of red and cream roses and was busy spreading out the travelling rug on the sand. On top of that went a tablecloth. The breeze from the sea refused to let it stay put and giving up the struggle Harriet called to the girls.

'Go and get me some pebbles and hurry.'

'What do you want them for, Mummy?'

'To keep the tablecloth in place. One or two pebbles at each corner should do the trick.'

The girls came back with handfuls and Harriet selected what she wanted.

'When do we eat?' Marie wanted to know.

'Not for a while yet. Play with your bucket and spade or amuse yourself with the beach ball.'

The lovely weather had brought a large number of day-trippers to the sands and there had been a run on the deckchairs. Harriet did manage to get one but by the time she had her purse out and paid for it she had let the man go before discovering she could have done with some assistance to put it up. Andrew had already departed. What was so infuriating was that it looked so easy and was proving to be anything but. By now she was totally exasperated and on the point of seeking assistance when miraculously, the strips of wood slotted into the correct grooves. Smiling with relief Harriet removed her white shoes and sat down with a magazine only to struggle up again to move the chair slightly so that the sun wouldn't be in her eyes. Most of the women round about, young and old, were in their bare feet but Harriet kept on her stockings. The fine sand would get through them and make for discomfort but she would just have to put up with it. There was something terribly common about women displaying their feet, she thought, and her own were not a pretty sight. Perhaps that was the real reason for keeping her stockings on but Harriet wasn't prepared to admit it even to herself.

Comfortably settled or as near as one could be in a deckchair, Harriet read some of her magazine then looked with pride over to where the three little girls were happily making sand pies. How pretty they looked in their little cotton dresses and when they bent down there was a glimpse of matching knickers which looked a lot better than a show of white or navy. Goodness but that sun was strong and she would soon have to cover her arms. The same went for Marie and Winnie, they wouldn't be happy about putting on cardigans but she would have to insist. Being so fair they burnt very easily.

The breeze was pleasant but they could have done without it, Harriet thought, as they sat down to their picnic meal. She had been up early and taken a lot of trouble over the preparations. Harriet had wanted a lovely spread with everything displayed on plates but it wasn't to be. Sand was already on the tablecloth and tiny grains in the cups. The sandwiches filled with meat paste were cut into dainty triangles and wrapped in greaseproof paper. She had baked a Victoria sponge, sandwiched it together with raspberry jam and sprinkled icing sugar over the top. Rather than cut it at home Harriet had brought a knife. A box held an assortment of biscuits but, she thought, it might be as well to keep them for later.

The food had to be taken out of the basket when needed and the girls thought it great fun when they had to rescue the greaseproof paper and chase after paper bags that refused to be caught. Harriet laughed too and made the best of it. Finally the girls quenched their thirst with a drink of orange juice while their mother had tea from the flask.

Some time later the children looked longingly at the sea where others were running in and out and screaming in delight.

'When do we get to paddle?'

'I think you could go now, Marie, your meal should be down. Remember though just to get your feet wet. Next time we'll bring the bathing costumes and you'll have more freedom. Lois, you are to hold Winnie's hand and not let go.'

'All right, Mummy,' Lois answered but she wondered why it had to be her and not Marie.

With their dresses tucked into their knickers the three little Pringle girls ran down to the water's edge then drew back sharply at the unexpected shock of the cold water. Gradually though they advanced a little way until the water lapped round their ankles. It seemed to be getting warmer as they got used to it. Other children were venturing in until the water was up to their knees and Lois longed to do the same. She had long legs but Winnie's were so much shorter and she had been told to keep hold of her little sister's hand. A few hardy swimmers were far out with only their bobbing heads visible.

As the eldest, Marie wanted to show off and with Lois having to look after Winnie there would be no competition. She wouldn't venture far, Marie was afraid when the waves came, but she would turn back before the water reached her knees. The push when it came wasn't particularly hard, just playful or maybe accidental, but it was enough to send Marie off-balance and she fell face downwards into the sea. Thrashing about she screamed with fright and someone lifted her out of the water and carried her to the dry sand. After speaking reassuring words the young man returned to his friends, and Lois and Winnie ran to where their distressed sister was howling her head off.

Harriet heard the screams, but did not at first connect them with her children; then when she did she had difficulty getting herself out of the deckchair and was further hampered by her stockinged feet sinking into the sand. By the time she reached the scene Marie was quite incoherent and Harriet clasped the sobbing child to her bosom.

What was actually said no one could say but Harriet got it into her head that Lois had pushed Marie and all her venom and the fright she herself had got was heaped on the hapless Lois.

'You wicked, wicked girl to do such a dreadful thing to your own sister. Look at her, she's soaked to the skin and shivering and if Marie gets a chill it will be your fault,' she screeched.

Lois was shaking too. 'But I didn't push her, Mummy, I didn't,'

Lois persisted. 'Ask Winnie, I never let her hand go and I wasn't near Marie.'

'Don't lie to me, girl, and don't involve Winnie. There, there! It's all right, Marie darling, we'll get you out of those wet clothes and thank goodness I had the foresight to bring spare clothing.'

Once stripped, given a brisk rub down with a towel, the tears stopped apart from the occasional sniffle.

'There's some tea in the flask, it should still be hot.'

'I don't want tea.'

'To please me you'll drink some,' Harriet said in a wheedling voice.

Lois sat alone some distance away. Her throat felt sore the way it did when she wanted to cry but wouldn't let herself. She couldn't understand why Marie didn't say something. She must know that she hadn't even been near her at the time.

Winnie was giving all her attention to adding shells to the sand castle that Lois and Marie had built earlier. When she got tired of that she came over.

'Mummy, you said we were getting ice-cream.'

'Yes, I know I did and so you shall. Just let me get my purse,' she said. When Harriet returned from the ice-cream van she was holding a slider and two large ice-cream cones. One she gave to Marie, one to Winnie and began on the slider herself.

'What about me?' Lois said in a small voice.

'Bad girls don't get ice-cream. Your punishment, Lois, is looking at us enjoying ours.'

Lois felt her mouth watering as she watched Marie's tongue lick at the ice-cream then the look of bliss as it melted in her mouth. Lois had never wanted an ice-cream as she wanted one now. Winnie's mouth was covered with it and some was dropping on to her dress.

'Mummy, can Lois get a lick of mine?'

'No, Winnie, not even one lick. Yours is melting so eat it up quickly and then get cleaned up. You do make a mess of yourself.'

A wet cloth and a towel were handed round and Harriet was just packing them away when a young woman, trailing a boy of about nine years of age, stopped and spoke to Harriet.

'Has your little girl quite recovered from her fright?'

'Just about,' Harriet smiled. 'I think I got as big a fright as she did.'

'Jonathan?' She raised her eyebrows to her small son. Jonathan squirmed but there was no escape. His mother had that look on her face that meant she would stand no nonsense.

'I didn't mean to push her, my arm just touched her that's all. And it wasn't my fault.'

His mother smiled, the smile of a mother of a well brought-up son.

'Say you are sorry and I'm sure the lady and her daughter will forgive you.'

Harriet forced a smile. 'Accidents will happen I know and Marie is none the worse, thank you.'

Mother and son walked away and Lois willed her mother to look at her but she was already busying herself packing away the picnic things.

'Daddy shouldn't be very long and he'll expect us to be ready.'

Lois waited for the apology that never came. She might, just might, have forgiven her mother for that if only she had given her money to buy an ice-cream. The van was still there and only one little boy was waiting to be served.

In another fifteen minutes Andrew had arrived and Winnie dashed to meet him then pulled him by the hand to their picnic spot.

'There you are, Andrew,' Harriet said smiling, 'and here we are all ready and waiting.'

'Did you all have a good time? Silly question of course you did.'

'Daddy, we were paddling in the sea and Marie—'

'I'm going to tell Daddy, not you.'

'Girls, there will be plenty of time for that when we get home. Just now we must get everything packed away and make sure we don't leave anything behind.'

Andrew muttered about the blasted sand getting into his shoes but he wasn't too bothered. He had played a good game and enjoyed a refreshment and stimulating talk. A little inconvenience like taking off his shoes wasn't going to upset him. Most of the paraphernalia went under his arms and he carried the lot to the car.

Harriet had the travelling rug, her handbag and her own shoes.

The girls had been told to carry their shoes and socks until they were free of the sand then to sit down and put them on but to be careful of the sharp grass that could cut their feet if they weren't careful.

Opening the boot of the car, Andrew pushed his golf clubs to one side to make room for the picnic basket, beach ball, buckets and spades and all the rest of it. That done Harriet got in the front beside her husband and the three girls scrambled into the back. Surprisingly there was little talk on the drive home. The sea air had made them sleepy and only when they reached home and spilled out of the car did the children come to life.

'Buckets and spades at the back door, I don't want sand brought into the house,' Harriet said in a voice loud enough for them all to hear.

'What about my car?' Andrew grumbled, 'looks as though you've brought half of Monifieth beach with you.'

Winnie giggled. 'Silly, Daddy.'

'Never get rid of that stuff.'

'For goodness sake, Andrew, don't make such a fuss about a little sand. I'll take a small hard brush to the carpet tomorrow.'

'Daddy, I fell into the water,' Marie said importantly.

'That was clever.'

'I could have been drowned,' Marie said indignantly.

'But you weren't?'

'But I could have been.'

'Marie, life is full of might have beens and you don't look any the worse for your dooking.'

Marie stormed into the house. She could be dead by now and Daddy didn't even care.

Andrew followed Marie in. 'Any hot water, Harriet?'

'Should be.'

'Enough for a bath?'

'If you aren't too extravagant.'

'Right you lot, I'm having a bath and then I'm going to my study.'

'Very well, dear.'

Winnie was sitting on the floor sucking her thumb.

'Winnie, there are plenty of chairs in this house, kindly make use of one. You are five years of age and not a baby,' said her mother.

'I like sitting on the floor.'

'I'm not concerned with your likes or dislikes. Get up at once.'

With a show of reluctance Winnie got to her feet and took the thumb out of her mouth. 'Mummy, why did you not let Lois have an ice-cream?'

'Oh, yes, Lois, that reminds me . . .'

Lois raised her head. She had been leafing listlessly through the pages of a story book.

'Go and get yourself a biscuit from the tin, dear. Take a cream wafer, you like them best, don't you?'

'No, thank you, I don't want one,' Lois said coldly polite. It wasn't true. She would have loved one but it was no substitute for ice-cream. Young though she was Lois recognised the gesture for what it was. Her mother was feeling guilty and so she should. This was her way of trying to make up but Lois wasn't having any of it.

'Very well you won't get another offer.'

'Mummy, do you know what I would like? A big drink of fizzy lemonade.'

'You'll get a cup of milk, my girl, then it is bed for you.'

'Do I have to get washed?'

'No, we'll give it a miss. You were in the sea so you can't be too bad.' She paused and made a pretence of listening. 'I think that is Daddy out of the bathroom. Run along, Winnie, and ask him if he wants something.'

Winie returned. 'Daddy says what do you mean by something?'

'Oh, give me strength,' Harriet said raising her eyes to the ceiling. 'Something to eat of course.'

Winnie shot off and came back muttering to herself. 'Daddy, said whatever—' She stopped. 'I forget what else he said.'

'Whatever is going,' Harriet finished for her.

Winnie brightened. 'Yes, he did say that. Were you listening, Mummy?'

Harriet shook her head and shoo-ed them out. 'Off you go into the sitting-room and amuse yourselves. I have the table to set for Daddy and I want room to move.'

'Lois, we could play Snakes and Ladders,' said Marie.

'Don't want to,' came the flat reply.

'Why not?'

'Because not.'

'What do you want to do?'

'I'm not playing with you ever again. You could have said something,' she raged, 'you knew it wasn't me that pushed you.'

'I didn't know who it was. How could I?'

'But you knew it wasn't me.'

Marie was frowning. 'Do you think that boy pushed me on purpose?'

'I don't care if he did. You got an ice-cream and I didn't and that wasn't fair.' The words were running into each other. 'When I'm big I'm going to run away and nobody will find me. Well, I might, just might, tell Daddy but only if he promises not to tell Mummy.'

Lois blinked herself out of her daydream. How strange that she should remember that particular day and in such detail.

The all-important certificate in shorthand, typewriting and business routine were now in her possession and Lois was thinking of them as her passport to an office job. She studied the vacancies with great eagerness and began to apply for those she considered were within her capabilities. When her applications were meeting with no success she tried not to be too downhearted but she was being forced to the conclusion that she would require her father's help after all. So much for her hopes of getting a position on her own.

Winnie had had enough of school and was living for the day when she could leave. There was no opposition from her father who saw no reason to force another year on his daughter when she would clearly gain nothing from it. Harriet had battled against this decision until even she was beginning to accept that Winnie, like Marie, was not overgifted with brains. Sadly the piano lessons were not going well either; Winnie had lost all interest, her teacher all patience and losing one lot of fees wasn't going to upset her. She was one of the few qualified teachers and her services were in great demand.

Chapter Four

A letter for her. A letter addressed to Miss Lois Pringle. Lois could hardly believe it. Then she thought it couldn't be what she hoped since it wasn't typed. When she went back to the breakfast table her mother stretched her hand out to take the letters but Lois had her fingers separating them.

'Two for you, Mum,' she said handing over a window-type envelope and a brown one.

Harriet made a face. 'Nothing interesting there.'

'One for you, Dad.' She placed it beside his plate.

'What about the other one?' Harriet asked.

'It's for me.'

'For you?' Harriet raised her eyebrows.

'Could be about a job, Lois, I'll keep my fingers crossed,' Winnie said.

Lois wished now that she had put the letter in her pocket and said nothing about it. Nothing wrong with doing that, was there? The letter was addressed to Miss Lois Pringle and no one had the right to read it unless she chose to allow them. Then again she could have played a game with herself, like guessing the identity of the sender. No one sent her letters so this was quite an event in her life. The writing was quite large with a lot of pressure on the downward strokes. Lois thought that must show strength and determination. Taking her time and refusing to be rushed, Lois used a table knife to slit open the envelope. She drew out a single sheet of good quality headed paper and as her eyes quickly took in the contents she felt her face going hot.

'I've got an interview,' she said striving to keep her voice steady.

'Read it out,' Winnie said impatiently and her father looked up from spreading marmalade on his toast.

'Good for you,' he said.

'Since it is only handwritten it can't be from an office.'

'No, Mum, it isn't, it has a private address at the top.' Lois took a deep breath and began to read it out:

Dear Miss Pringle,

Your letter made me think that you could suit me very well. I am in urgent need of a Girl Friday. By a Girl Friday I mean someone who would be prepared to deal with a varied workload and do so with the minimum of supervision.

If you care to come and discuss this please call at the above address any time between 10 a.m. and 12 noon or 3 p.m. and 5 p.m. on Thursday.

Yours sincerely . . .

It was signed John L. Latimer.

'John Latimer,' Andrew said thoughtfully. 'That name rings a bell. What does he give as his address, Lois?'

Lois looked at the heading. 'Rosewell Cottage, Hillend Terrace, Muirford.'

He shook his head as though that meant nothing, then he nodded. 'I think I have him now.'

'You mean you know Mr Latimer?' Lois asked.

'Not personally, but if he is who I think he is then the man is in great demand as a speaker.' He smiled. 'From what I remember hearing the man can be alarmingly outspoken but witty with it. Some folk appreciate that, others do not.'

'What does he talk about, Dad?'

'Well, now you have me there. He is a champion of the under-privileged and someone who can hold his audience.'

'Andrew, I think I know who you mean though I had forgotten the name. He spoke at one of our meetings, one I was unable to attend and most of our ladies found him insufferable. They complained about him being rude and self-opinionated.'

'Just speaking his mind.'

'Talking nonsense and not prepared to let anyone else have their say.'

Andrew looked amused. 'Harriet, forgive me but I've met some of your committee ladies and it would take more than Latimer to keep them quiet.'

'Now it is you who is talking nonsense, Andrew, our ladies have manners. That man Latimer is just an interfering old windbag. Lois' – she turned round – 'I won't allow it, you can't possibly work for a man like that.'

'I haven't been offered the job,' Lois said quietly, 'but should I be, then I'll most certainly accept.'

'Very sensible, Lois,' her father said ignoring his wife's outraged expression. 'Even if the job isn't to your liking, stick it for a while. You'll find it good experience and remember it is easier to get a job if you are already in one.'

'He sounds all right to me,' Winnie said, 'and I'll bet that working for him would be a lot more interesting than being a dogsbody in some boring old office.'

Andrew laughed. 'And that from someone who has never set foot in a boring old office.'

'If you ask me I think he sounds positively weird,' Marie said as she got up from the table. 'Girl Friday indeed – what does he take you for?'

'I wouldn't know, Marie, but I wouldn't mind at all being a Girl Friday.'

'Knowing you I'm not a bit surprised. I'm off then, someone in this family has to work.'

'Wouldn't call what you do work,' Winnie called after her.

'Winnie, do you see the time?' her mother said warningly.

'It doesn't matter. How often do I have to tell you, Mum, that only those going back after the holidays have to work. The rest of us are just putting in time.'

'You should be one of those going back.'

'Not again, Mum, you never give up do you?'

Andrew laughed. He was taking a later train and enjoying a leisurely breakfast. 'I couldn't agree more, Winnie, the last few weeks are a complete waste of time both for you and your teacher. Still, if Lois gets this job you don't need to go back.'

'You shouldn't be saying that, Andrew, encouraging her to leave before the time.'

'I don't understand you, dear, here is your youngest more than anxious to help in the house—'

'To get away from school you mean. I am not at all sure that Winnie is suited to housework. She could train for something I suppose.'

'Like what?' Winnie said cheekily.

'I don't know, a florist perhaps. The Window Box has a vacancy and that would be a pleasant occupation.'

'Not for me it wouldn't and Nellie What's-her-name worked there for six weeks and she said it was terrible. Her hands were raw flesh from cutting up the stems and forever being in water.'

'Never out of hot water it would be in your case. A florist seems to be ruled out then,' Andrew said getting up.

'Winnie!' Harriet said loudly.

'Yes! Yes! I'm on my way and don't worry, you may be pleasantly surprised and find me better than Lois.'

'That shouldn't be difficult. Mum says often enough that I'm hopeless.'

'You were improving. Winnie, your schoolbag.'

'Don't need it and on my last day I'm going to make a bonfire of all my school books.'

As Lois began clearing up the table she felt almost sorry for her mother, but not enough to throw away her chance. If she did she might never get another.

Andrew spared no sympathy for his wife. She had herself to blame. If she had been a bit more appreciative of Lois she might not be losing her now. On the other hand he was glad Lois was getting out of the house. Like Harriet he didn't see their youngest in the domestic scene once the novelty had worn off. He could see her finishing up as an assistant in a shop but in her case a baker's or a confectioner's. He grinned to himself. Three daughters and they couldn't be more different.

If Harriet would only listen to advice – his advice – life for them all might be a lot easier. Her expectations were too high and she should learn to treat others with more respect. There were many women with families and an unemployed husband who were anxious to make a few shillings doing housework but they expected reasonable working conditions. It was very different before the Great War – then they would have slaved without complaint. If there had been one good thing that had come out of the war it was that women had discovered their worth. Many had held down jobs previously done by men and in a large number of cases they had been more efficient and conscientious, and employers were sorry to see them go.

As soon as she wakened, Lois remembered that this was her big day. She felt a panicky excitement and a great desire for the day to begin. Slipping her legs over the side of the bed she glanced over to where Winnie was sound asleep in the other bed. Careful not to make a noise and disturb her, she padded on bare feet over to the window and moved the curtains to look out and check on the weather. The previous day it had rained, not heavily, just a persistent drizzle. The strong wind had dried up the ground and Lois breathed a sigh of relief. She didn't want to have to bother with an umbrella and wear a raincoat.

How quickly the summer had gone and already the wind was sending the first of the leaves fluttering to the ground. She looked at the path and using her imagination likened it to a threadbare carpet that still held traces of gold, crimson and many shades of brown. Poor old Angus McGregor wouldn't be too happy, he hated the autumn and the endless clearing up. Not like herself, she loved walking ankle deep and hearing the rustle of dry leaves.

If only her stomach would settle and she could rid herself of nerves. It was humiliating. Most girls of her age would be able to take all this in their stride. A little nervousness was to be expected before an interview but that was all. For Lois the forthcoming meeting with Mr Latimer was a momentous event that, if she were successful, could change her whole life.

Dressing quickly she went downstairs to start the breakfast which at the best of times was a rushed meal and eaten with one eye on the clock. Andrew had remembered this and had wished his daughter the best of luck before retiring for the night. Then he had added kindly that she was not to be too disappointed if she wasn't successful, something else was sure to turn up. Winnie had promised to keep her fingers crossed all day – everyone wanted to know how that was to be managed – and Marie, not to be left out, had wished her sister success but seemed amused by it all.

The morning would have been so much better for her interview and she would have had less time to worry. Unfortunately her mother had other ideas. The morning was inconvenient, she said, out of the question and Lois should have known that.

The afternoon wouldn't interfere with the smooth running of the house.

By eight forty-five they had all gone, her father, Marie and Winnie and her mother wouldn't be long behind them. She had, however, found the time to make the double bed she shared with her husband and to tidy the bedroom. When Harriet came downstairs she was dressed for outdoors.

'I'm off then, Lois,' she called from the hall, 'I'll hear how you got on when I get back.'

'Yes, all right, Mum, cheerio.'

Even before she was out of bed Lois had decided to do the minimum of housework, a lick and a promise would do very well. This was her day and she had it all planned. After a light lunch of scrambled egg on toast she would take a leisurely bath and spend time over her appearance. First impressions were important and she wanted to look smart and businesslike.

At half past one she ran a comb through her short curly hair. She didn't use much make-up, her complexion didn't need it, but she put on more lipstick than usual. Then after studying her face in the mirror she took a tissue and removed all but a trace. By two o'clock she was dressed in a plain light-grey flannel skirt and a long-sleeved crisp white blouse with a neat collar. She swithered about what to wear over it. Her lightweight jacket wouldn't be warm enough in the cold east wind and she didn't want to arrive looking frozen. Better to wear her navy-blue coat with the brass buttons down the front and three smaller ones on the cuffs. The first time her father had seen her in it he had saluted her and said teasingly that she looked like a little admiral. Lois didn't mind his teasing, it was her favourite coat and the only one she had chosen herself. Navy court shoes with a small heel and an envelope style handbag completed her outfit.

It would be a mistake to leave the house before half past two, she didn't want to arrive too early. A few minutes after three would be best, she thought, since Mr Latimer had said any time between three and five. Letting herself out of the house Lois locked the door and walked the hundred yards or so to the bus stop and stood waiting. No one else was there. The cold wind was invigorating and whipped the colour into her cheeks. For a little while her spirits lifted and a small smile tugged at her mouth. The bus came and she got on.

After paying her fare and getting her ticket the confidence she had built up disappeared and currents of anxiety shivered through her. What if she wasn't successful and she knew that was all too possible. How would she face them at home? Her mother would have that 'didn't I tell you' look on her face. Her dad and Winnie would be genuinely disappointed for her and Marie – difficult to tell what Marie would be thinking. Probably she wasn't all that interested and why should she be? Really, Lois, you are being pathetic, she told herself, and if you carry on like this you won't deserve to get the job.

'Your stop, Miss.'

Lois gave a start and got up quickly. 'Thank you,' she smiled to the conductor as he stood aside to let her off.

This was a part of Muirford that she wasn't familiar with and Lois looked about her with interest. The tree-lined thoroughfare she stood in was Brownlea Road and on both sides were large houses set well back from the road. High trees and thick shrubs gave them the privacy they demanded and the overall impression was one of quiet respectability. Hillend Terrace was the next turning off Brownlea Road and was narrower. There was no uniformity here, some of the houses were quite small and there was a row of eight semi-detached villas. One stone-built detached house was set apart from its neighbours and Lois was surprised to find that she had arrived at Rosewell Cottage. In her mind she had pictured a small cottage, perhaps not one with roses round the door, but certainly not this. She wondered how it had got its name.

The white wicket gate was in keeping with a cottage, she thought, as she opened it then carefully closed it behind her. Shrubs lined the way along the gravel path that curved up to the front door which was ajar. Taking a deep breath Lois pulled the bell then took a step back when she heard it ring. In a moment or two an inside glass door was opened and a middle-aged woman in an overall pushed the heavy door wider and gave Lois a questioning smile.

'I'm Lois Pringle. Mr Latimer—'

'Come in Miss Pringle. I'm afraid Mr Latimer is out at present, I think he expected you in the morning.'

Lois stepped into a vestibule with coloured glass panels and then into a spacious hall with a circular carpet on parquet flooring.

'I'm very sorry but I couldn't get away then and Mr Latimer

did say between three and five,' Lois said jerkily. Was she too late?
Had Mr Latimer already decided on someone else?

'It's perfectly all right, my dear, you can wait for him in the
sitting-room. He did say he wouldn't be long but if he meets up
with someone . . .' She was opening the door and ushering Lois
in. 'They talk about women gossiping but to my mind we are no
worse than men though, of course, they don't gossip, dear me no,
they talk.'

Lois smiled and sat down on the edge of a leather armchair with
her handbag on her lap.

'I'll put a match to this fire, it's all set.'

'Not for me,' Lois said hastily.

'Another half-hour and I would be putting it on anyway. By
later afternoon it can get quite chilly and in a week or two it will
be fires all day. I won't mind, there's something cheerful about a
fire, as good as company I always think.'

Lois took the chance to look about her. It was a bright,
high-ceilinged room with attractive cornices. A masculine room,
she mused and wondered if Mr Latimer was a bachelor or a
widower. A bachelor more likely since there were no light touches
a woman would have brought and if he were a widower some of
those touches would have remained. The leather armchairs and
sofa showed signs of wear but had a comfortable look about them
and, realising she was sitting on the edge of hers, Lois moved back
to a more relaxing position.

'That'll be a good fire in no time,' the woman said getting up
from her knees, 'and if I'm not mistaken that's the man himself
coming in. Excuse me and I'll tell him you're here.'

Lois heard the voices.

'That's the lass arrived.'

'Sorry, Mrs Wilson, I meant to be back before three but you
know what happens to my good intentions. Where did you
put her?'

'In the sitting-room and I put a match to the fire.'

'Thank you, Mrs Wilson, there's a right chill to that wind.'

Lois was drying her moist palms with her handkerchief and
hastily put it away as the door opened and a tweed-suited man of
middle years with grey hair, bushy eyebrows and a portly figure
came in and smiled to her as she got to her feet.

'Miss Pringle, my sincere apologies,' he said as they shook hands, 'I had intended being back before three.' His voice was cultured and modulated.

'It's all right, Mr Latimer, I only arrived a short time ago.'

'Good! Good! Do sit down. No, not there, come nearer the fire. We'll talk easier if we aren't miles apart.'

Lois had a sudden urge to giggle, she knew it was nerves, but it was all so different to what she had imagined. She took the chair he indicated, put her handbag at her feet and sat primly, leaning slightly forward with her hands folded in her lap and waited for him to speak.

'Heavens! You look nervous, are you?'

'A bit,' Lois confessed. 'I've never been for an interview before.'

'Poor you and you don't know what to expect?'

She swallowed and nodded.

'A little talk to get to know each other, that's all, so relax. I have your letter here,' he said putting it down on the table beside a pipe and a box of matches. 'Thank you for being so honest, I find that very refreshing.'

'I didn't want to give a false impression and I'm very aware that at seventeen I should have some office experience.'

'Frankly your lack of experience is no handicap come to think about it, it could almost be an advantage. This is no ordinary office job as you must have gathered, though being able to type is essential. As to your shorthand I don't see myself making use of it, but then again I may try my hand at dictating for no better reason than to save you losing your shorthand speed.'

Lois was gaining confidence. 'May I ask what the duties would be, Mr Latimer?'

'Many and varied as I said. You would pay my accounts when they are due and check them to see that I am not being cheated. Mistakes are made, Miss Pringle – someone's carelessness – and let me say right away that whether the error is in my favour or not it must be brought to the appropriate person's attention. You would be required to answer the telephone and not to forget to give me the message. Then I would like a filing system introduced, nothing complicated, but rather something that could be understood by a ten-year-old.' He paused as they exchanged smiles. 'My diary has to be kept up to date and I need to be reminded, more than once if I appear not to be paying attention, as to where I should be and when. Following so far?'

'Yes, thank you.'

'In my line of work one receives a number of nuisance letters, begging letters if you like. You will soon recognise them and these go straight into the wastepaper basket. The genuinely needy, Miss Pringle, do not beg, they have too much pride.'

'How do those in need come to your attention?'

'Good question. A neighbour, a friend or perhaps the local minister passes me the word.'

'Perhaps I shouldn't ask this . . .' She hesitated.

'Try me.'

'I was going to ask if charity work is your full-time occupation.'

'Very often it is full-time and a bit more, but this is not charity work in the true sense. Money is not handed out and if it is, it is only very rarely. We try to help people to help themselves. Some, and you would be surprised at the number, haven't a clue as to how to go about applying for a job. They need guidance. A disheartened few who have applied many times become discouraged and want to give up. We encourage them to go on trying. I could go on long enough but that will give you some idea of what goes on.'

'Do you do all this on your own?'

'I work on my own but I am in contact with others engaged in similar work elsewhere in the country. Does that answer your question?'

'Yes, thank you.'

He placed his fingers together and looked thoughtful. 'Perhaps it would be helpful if I were to expand a little and tell you about myself. I am a qualified lawyer but I no longer practise. My parents, bless them, were of the opinion that their son should have a profession to fall back on and to please them I studied law. In the event, having some knowledge of the law has proved to be helpful. That's by the way. Miss Pringle, I am one of those fortunate beings who have been left comfortably off with no need to work for a living. I am not wealthy, not by any stretch of the imagination, but since I do not have extravagant tastes, I should be well provided for in my lifetime.'

'You now help others less fortunate than yourself,' Lois said shyly.

'We all need to give something back, Miss Pringle.'

She nodded and wondered if she was expected to say anything to that but after a pause, when he fiddled with his pipe and put it back down again, he began speaking.

'In my younger days I travelled a great deal and was privileged to see many of the world's wonders. One day I hope to publish a book on my wanderings but meantime my priority is helping the under-privileged, especially the youngsters. Some are homeless and very frightened though they try to pretend otherwise. And would you believe it, the very fact that they are homeless and penniless keeps them from being considered for employment. In time they lose heart and that is when they are drawn into petty crime.'

'I think I can understand that,' Lois said quietly.

'I thought you might. Sadly we cannot help as many as we would like but we try to bring their plight to the attention of those who have it in their power to do something. That is where I come in, Miss Pringle, I do some public speaking and am invited from time to time to give an "after-dinner" speech. It helps to spread the word.' He laughed. 'Not all my efforts are successful. Some ladies' groups have banned me but I'm not losing any sleep over that.'

Lois couldn't help smiling and the reason for her amusement was knowing that one of the groups in question would no doubt be one with which her mother was associated.

Was she imagining it or had a weariness crept into his voice?

'Not the usual office routine and perhaps not to your liking. If you are not interested please say so.'

'But I am,' Lois burst out. 'I'm very interested.'

'That I am delighted to hear.'

Lois flushed. 'Are you offering me the position?'

'I am.'

'Then I accept and thank you,' she said breathlessly.

'And there shows your inexperience.'

Her face fell.

'You are accepting a position, my dear Miss Pringle, without knowing your salary or even your hours of work.'

'As to salary I have no experience so whatever you offer, Mr Latimer, will be acceptable.'

'I won't cheat you and I did make a point of finding out the average wage given to a seventeen-year-old clerkess. There you are, I have it all written out, your wage, your hours of work and your holiday entitlement.'

Lois took the sheet of paper and what she read was very much to her liking. She knew Marie's wage and this was more than she was getting. If she felt a little smug about that Lois felt she could be forgiven.

'Is that to your satisfaction?'

'Yes, it is, thank you.'

'Miss Pringle – by the way, do you like to be addressed as Miss Pringle?'

'No, I don't, I'm not used to it and I would much prefer Lois.'

'Then Lois it is. What a pretty name and quite unusual. Come along and I'll show you where you will be working.'

Lois followed him to the back of the house and into a room that had been made into an office. It had two desks, one with an Underwood typewriter on it and there was a chair pushed under each desk. Another was over at the window. Against one wall was a large bookcase and two filing cabinets and on the floor in front of the cabinets a bundle of papers waiting to be filed. Mr Latimer pointed to a gas fire.

'Heat when you want it, not so cheerful as a coal fire but saves a lot of work. The desk with the typewriter will be yours. I use the other but most of my writing is done in my den upstairs.'

'Did you have someone before me, Mr Latimer?'

'Not a full-time secretary, just someone who came in for an hour or two to help me out. It suited me for a while but not now. When can you start?'

'Right away. Monday?'

'Splendid. I'll look forward to seeing you and I should mention that you are free to make tea or whatever for yourself. Mrs Wilson, my housekeeper whom you met, won't mind at all you using the kitchen.'

Mr Latimer accompanied her to the door and as she made her way to the bus stop there was a spring in her step and she found she couldn't help smiling.

Chapter Five

Lois was surprised, she hadn't expected her mother to be in, but she was and taking it easy. Her stockinged feet were on the stool and she was reading the Births, Deaths and Marriages in the newspaper. Andrew had remarked that he was sure his wife spent more time over the Hatches, Matches and Despatches, as he called the columns, than the rest of the paper put together.

On coming in Lois had popped her head in the door to greet her mother then returned to the hall to hang up her coat on the the hallstand next to Harriet's herring-bone, three-quarter-length coat which she had been wearing when she left the house. She couldn't stop herself smiling when she joined her mother.

Harriet lowered the newspaper and pushed the spectacles up on her nose. They kept slipping down and she would have to take them back to the optician's and have an adjustment made. A nuisance, it meant a journey into Dundee and she could have done without that.

'You look like that cat that got the cream. I take it you were successful?'

'Yes, Mum, I got the job and I'm over the moon. You're wrong about Mr Latimer, he's very nice and I'm sure he'll be very pleasant to work for.'

'Time will tell.' She paused and frowned. 'When are you supposed to start this job?'

'Monday.'

Harriet's eyes bulged. 'Monday? Surely to goodness you don't mean this Monday?'

'Yes, I do.'

'You stupid girl, that is completely out of the question.' The woman was breathing heavily and the newspaper had slipped to the floor. 'You must have known that.'

'Why should I?'

'You have obligations to me which appear to have escaped you.'

'I beg to differ.' The light had gone from her eyes but her voice was surprisingly firm.

'If you know anything you should be aware that every employer is entitled to reasonable notice.'

'Don't make me laugh.' Lois shook her head in amazement. 'I wasn't earning a wage.'

'You had your keep and generous pocket money.'

'Hardly the same and the pocket money wasn't all that generous.'

'You were very well off.'

'I was nothing of the kind. I was a drudge. When did I ever have a day off? Go on, Mum, tell me that?'

'You had plenty of free time.'

'An hour here and an hour there, what good was that?' Lois could feel her anger rising and she tried to keep it under control. Whatever was said she must not weaken. It was true that Mr Latimer hadn't asked her to start on Monday, it had been her suggestion but he had seemed pleased. What would he think of her if she were to change her mind and suggest a later date? That she wasn't dependable? That was exactly what he would think. She must be strong, must hold out and not let her mother win.

'Whatever you say I am starting on Monday and as far as I am concerned that is the end of the matter.'

'Is it indeed?'

Lois got quickly to her feet and walked to the door.

'Come back here at once.'

Lois turned round but kept her hand on the door knob.

'Your father is going to hear about this, my girl.'

'Yes, he is, because if you don't tell him I will. He happens to want me to get a job and will have no objections about the starting date.'

'I am the one being inconvenienced not your father.'

'That's your fault. You've known for long enough that I was looking for a job.'

'That is true but I didn't expect you to get one and you wouldn't have had it not been for that man Latimer. No doubt you were his last hope.'

'I don't think so,' Lois said unsteadily, 'but even if that is what I am I'm grateful to him and I'll do my very best.'

'More than you ever did for me. You never put yourself out.'

Lois had had enough and she was shaking with anger. 'I'll tell you this, Mum, if it wasn't for Dad I would leave home.'

'If wasn't for your father you wouldn't be here.'

Lois stared at her. 'What do you mean?'

Harriet looked flustered. She bent down to pick up the *Courier* and said quickly. 'What I mean, Lois, is that your father will put up with more from you than I am prepared to although that said you are always at your best when he is at home.' Her eyes were cold and unfriendly. 'And now madam, kindly take yourself into the kitchen and get on with preparing the meal. As you will see I did a baking of scones when you were out and they should be cold enough to put away.'

Lois flung herself out of the room then stood behind the closed door with her eyes tightly closed. Her breath was coming in painful stabs and she gave herself a few moments to calm down. Not calm by any means but feeling a little better, Lois went along to the kitchen and with a determined set to her chin began on her tasks. If she clattered the pans more than necessary it was only to give vent to her feelings.

When the family sat down together for the evening meal, mother and daughter hadn't exchanged an unnecessary word. No one appeared to notice, they wanted to know how she got on. Her father was the first to ask.

'How did it go?'

'I got the job, Dad.'

'Well done!' He smiled over to her. 'I had an idea you might.'

'So did I. That's great, Lois,' Winnie said as she helped herself to boiled potatoes. 'Incidentally what is he like this man you are going to work for? Not young and handsome by any chance?'

'No, absolutely not. Mr Latimer would be about ages with Dad I would say.'

Her father smiled. 'Which makes him youngish.'

'Dad, everybody over forty is ancient,' Winnie said dismissively. 'What does he look like, Lois?'

'Sort of portly.' She paused. 'The kind of man it would be nice to have as an uncle.'

Marie made a face. 'I bet he's only paying you sweeties,' she said smugly.

'I'm getting more than you.'

'I don't believe you.'

'Please yourself, but I have it all in writing,' Lois said sweetly.

'Show me then.'

'No, I won't but I'll give it to Dad to read. Here, Dad.'

The page folded into four had been in her skirt pocket and she handed it across the table.

All eyes were on Andrew as he read it and he was looking both surprised and pleased.

'Very satisfactory, my dear. All true, Marie,' he said glancing over to his eldest daughter then back to Lois. 'That happens to be the going rate for a girl of your age but one with probably two years' experience behind her.'

Marie was looking outraged and not far from tears. 'You have no right to be getting more than me,' she said pushing her plate away. 'I don't want that, I'm not hungry.'

'Eat up, dear,' her mother said soothingly, 'and when you consider that you have the advantage of getting your clothes at almost cost—'

'That's right, I'd forgotten about that. I do get more than you, Lois.' She brought back her plate and began to eat.

'If it was me I'd rather have the extra money than get my clothes cheaper.'

'Winnie, I think we can close the subject now,' Harriet said.

'When does Mr Latimer want you to start?'

'On Monday, Dad.'

'That should pose no problems.'

'Winnie?'

'What?'

'No more potatoes. You've had enough.'

'I'm still hungry and you said that potatoes don't make you fat, they just go down to water.'

'Even so.'

'All right,' she said reluctantly, 'I'll leave them but they are just going to be wasted.'

'No, nothing is wasted, they can be fried.'

'You've made me forget what I was going to say. No, I remember now. If I am to work for you, Mum, I want wages. That is only fair isn't it, Dad?'

'I never got a wage, Winnie.'

'That was your mistake.'

'In principle I agree with you, Winnie, but since Lois wasn't given a wage it would be unfair to let you have one.'

'Lois isn't like that. She wouldn't mind, would you?'

Lois did mind but she didn't want to be mean to Winnie. 'You hold out for the rate for the job and get your hours organised too.'

'You had nothing to complain about, Lois, and since you are being paid so well I shall expect a reasonable amount for your keep.'

'Of course, Mum, I'll give you the same as Marie does.'

'Marie doesn't give Mum anything, I happen to know that. You can't deny it so don't look at me like that.'

Marie was looking furious and Harriet didn't look too happy either. Andrew's face had darkened, a sure sign that he was angry. Up to now the conversation had amused him.

'You ruin that girl, Harriet, and it isn't doing her any favours. She should be learning to live within her means and to put a little aside.'

Harriet pursed her lips.

'From now on I shall see to it that both of you give your mother something towards your keep. What that might be I'll decide later. As to savings I would stress the importance of having something behind you but that is for you to decide.' He looked from Marie to Lois. 'Just remember that there might come a time when you will be glad of your savings. Your mother and I won't always be here.'

'You aren't very old, Dad,' Winnie said sounding scared.

'Some folk are cut off in their prime. None of us knows what is ahead.'

'Andrew, I hardly think—'

'They aren't children, Harriet, though at times that is hard to believe.'

'What about me? If I get wages do I have to pay for my board?'

Andrew laughed and his face softened. 'Pocket money for you for a while yet, my pet, then we'll see.'

'Lois go and see to the rice pudding, I don't want it too brown,' Harriet ordered.

They liked it nicely browned which was how it would be but, making no comment, Lois just got to her feet.

'No, let me,' Winnie said getting up and almost overturning the chair.

'No. You can collect the dirty plates and take them through. Put the cutlery together on the top. On top, Winnie, don't leave the knives and forks between the plates as you did last time.'

'No harm done, nothing got broken and only two plates slipped to the floor.'

'Making a mess on the rug, it'll never be the same.'

Not used to getting up early, Winnie was bleary-eyed and making heavy weather of clearing the breakfast table. School, she was beginning to think, hadn't been so bad after all and the hours had been a lot better. Housework seemed to go on for ever and she knew she wasn't getting through as much as Lois.

At the moment Harriet and Lois were both making sandwiches. Lois was preparing her own and Harriet was seeing to Marie's.

Harriet had doubled her efforts to find someone to assist in the house – Winnie wasn't much help – but no one seemed anxious for the job. She thought sourly that it was typical of people today and she would have to resign herself to Mrs Briggs giving her an extra couple of hours and paying a much bigger laundry bill. Really it was too bad of Lois to leave her in the lurch like this and if she would admit it, she was regretting being so hard on the girl. One thing was certain, Mrs Briggs couldn't be trusted with the ironing and Winnie hadn't progressed from simple things like handkerchiefs and tea towels.

Lois was mildly amused by it all. Now, when it was too late, she was being appreciated and she couldn't help being smugly satisfied. Once she would have done anything to help just to get a word of praise from her mother but those days were over. Lois had hardened or perhaps just grown up. She still did what she considered her fair share. She made her bed, Winnie's too sometimes and prepared her own sandwiches. On Thursday evening she did her personal laundry and on Friday it got ironed.

Marie had stopped speaking to her since Lois's refusal to do her ironing, and there had been a stormy scene and floods of tears when the overheated iron had left an ugly brown mark on Marie's best blouse and ruined her silk petticoat.

Harriet was less sympathetic to her eldest these days. Her own life had undergone a change and she was still smarting from having to resign from two of her committees and do a bit more about the house.

Lois was settling into her job and loving it. Going out to work was such a contrast to the tedious life she had known. Her day had a focus, a meaning, and she was doing something interesting and rewarding.

John Latimer was delighted with his 'find' as he took to calling Lois and Mrs Wilson was fussing over her. Lois was overwhelmed, she had never been used to anything like this. In the mornings the housekeeper brought in coffee and occasionally John Latimer would be at his desk and they had it together. When the phone rang Lois answered it and she had become expert at knowing when to make apologies. A warning look and a shake of the grey head would mean he was not 'at home'.

The matter of the sandwiches came up on the Wednesday when Lois went along to the large, well-fitted kitchen to boil the kettle and make herself tea.

'Lass, sit yourself down there,' Mrs Wilson said pulling out a chair from under the table.

Lois sat down wondering what she had done to upset the housekeeper.

'I'm sorry, have I done something I shouldn't?'

'Whatever made you think that? No, no, lass, I just want to say that I am not in favour of sandwiches, all right occasionally, but not every day.' She smiled. 'I had a word with Mr Latimer and he agrees that since I am making a meal for myself in the middle of the day there is nothing to hinder you sharing it.'

Sandwiches would get monotonous and this sounded lovely but she had better not accept. She was flustered. 'That's very kind of you, Mrs Wilson, but I do get a proper meal when I get home.'

'I never doubted that for a moment but this won't be a big meal, just a plate of home-made soup and something to follow.'

'That would be lovely but you must let me pay—'

'For any favour don't be letting Mr Latimer hear you say that. An extra cup of water in the soup and a few extra tatties is about all it amounts to. Have your sandwiches today but starting tomorrow we'll have our lunch together and I'll be glad of your company.'

Lois was happy and as a way of showing her appreciation she had purchased three small house plants and placed them on the sill. John Latimer had noticed.

'Nice splash of colour, gives a lift to the spirits. Did the gardener chappie give you those?'

'No, I bought them.'

He frowned. 'Lois, that was kind of you but unnecessary.'

'Perhaps it was,' she said defensively, 'but I enjoyed buying them and I benefit most.'

'Just so long as you are happy. You must know that you have made a tremendous difference, bringing order out of chaos and I wouldn't like to lose you.'

'Little danger of that,' Lois smiled. She knew when she was well off.

Taking out his fountain pen John Latimer read over his letters then signed his name. 'You are a good typist, Lois.'

'Thank you.'

'Top student were you?'

Lois laughed. 'Far from it. It took me ages to get the hang of touch typing, I never could resist looking down at the keys. There were a few like me and we were made to move to a machine with the keys blanked out.'

'Certainly worked in your case.'

It was hard to believe she had been working as John Latimer's secretary for a month. In that time she had introduced a filing system where none had existed. Invoices, receipts, etc., had all found their way into the cabinet drawers which were full with the overflow on the floor. Getting to grips with it had been slow and painful but she was making headway. Sorting the papers into order was the most time-consuming but, once that was done, it was a simple matter to file them. A great deal of rubbish found its way to the wastepaper basket.

She wouldn't forget the day she was down on her hands and knees beside one of the cabinets when a knock came to the office door. Recognising the three taps as Mrs Wilson's she called for her to come in and when the door opened didn't immediately look up. When she did she was embarrassed to see that the housekeeper wasn't alone. Flushing she got quickly to her feet and smoothed down her skirt.

'I'm so sorry—'

'Lois, this is Mr Napier.' She smiled to the young man. 'He is waiting to see Mr Latimer and I thought it better to bring him here than leave him on his own in the sitting-room.'

'Of course.' Mrs Wilson went out closing the door quietly behind her. 'Please be seated, Mr—' Heavens! She'd forgotten his name already.

'Napier. Tim Napier. Thank you,' he said as he sat down. Before doing so he had waited until she was seated behind her desk.

What on earth was she going to say? He looked relaxed with one long leg crossed over the other. She had seen that he was tall, just under six feet she thought, about the same height as her father. In that brief moment when he stood beside her Lois had noticed that his eyes were light grey and when he smiled the smile reached his eyes. His hair was blue black and she saw his fingers push into it, a mannerism perhaps and he didn't realise he was doing it.

Should she get on with what she was supposed to be doing or make conversation?

'I didn't know Mr Latimer had got himself a secretary.'

'I'm new, just been here a few weeks.' She hoped that piece of information would help him to make allowances.

'Like it – the job I mean?'

'Very much.' Full stop, end of conversation.

They smiled and lapsed into silence. Feeling the need to do something she put her fingers on the typewriter keys only remembering in time there was no paper in the machine.

'Don't let me keep you back.'

'It's all right, nothing urgent.' Lois wondered about his age. Late twenties at a guess and in business judging by the dark, well-cut suit he was wearing and the crisp white shirt and quiet tie.

'Nice office,' he said and wished he could think of what to say. He wasn't usually so tongue-tied, quite the reverse. The girl was a beauty, where had John Latimer found her? Tim wasn't sure if he was glad to see Mr Latimer at that moment or not, but here he was.

'How are you, my boy? Oh, and have you two introduced yourselves?'

'We have.' He grinned. 'Glad to see your filing is removed from the floor.'

'Never been tidier and now what brings you here?'

'Dad couldn't raise you and he suggested I come myself and tell you that there is a vacancy for a bright lad of fifteen or thereabout, one genuinely interested in engineering.'

He rubbed his hands. 'Excellent. Life hasn't been kind to Ned Bell. He's your lad and I'm sure you won't regret taking him on.'

'Send him along tomorrow and Dad will decide when he sees him.'

'Fair enough.' John Latimer was thinking about clothes. The lad needed to be reasonably turned out and there was a fund he could draw on. Only cheap working clothes but better than patched trousers – and shoes, he would need those.

'Mum says she thinks you have forgotten where we live.'

'My apologies, pressure of work I'm afraid, but tell her I'll pay Ashlea a visit in the very near future.' He smiled. 'She's a lovely lady, your mother.'

On his way out Tim was wondering how he could see this girl again. There would be a way and he would find it.

Chapter Six

The family used the back door with the front being kept for visitors. Harriet had repeatedly told them to close the door gently, not to let it bang. Apart from the noise which was annoying, the rough treatment rattled the china and promised one day to dislodge the Willow-patterned plates on display at the back of the kitchen cabinet.

The back door banged shut and Harriet winced but the rebuke died on her lips when she saw the culprit was Marie. A glowing Marie with softly flushed cheeks and sparkling eyes. Straightaway her mother looked at the clock, it was only a little after nine thirty and Marie was seldom home before eleven.

'Hello, dear, this is early for you?'

'I know.' She was smiling broadly and obviously dying to tell her news. 'Mum, you'll never guess who has asked me out.' Marie was breathless with excitement as she flung her handbag on the chair and then stood there with her eyes closed as though in ecstasy.

'Tell me then, don't keep me waiting.'

'Stephen – Hammond – that's who,' she said stretching out the words and waiting for her mother's reaction.

'Stephen—' Harriet said uncertainly.

'Stephen Hammond, Mum,' Marie said impatiently, 'you have to know who I mean.'

'The Hammonds' son! Oh, my dear.' Harriet was positively beaming. Were her secret hopes to be realised without her having to take a hand? 'Someone did mention that there was activity at Silverknowe, but I didn't know the family were in residence. I'm just so pleased.'

Lois and Winnie had stopped what they were doing to give Marie their attention. Winnie had decided to clean out one of the drawers in the sideboard and had come on a folder

63

of old snapshots. The two of them had been in fits of the giggles.

'Where did you meet him?' Lois asked,

'What is he like?' Winnie said at the same time.

'I can only answer one question at a time. First where did I meet him? In the Cosy Neuk, Lois. Joan and I were there when Alastair Cummings came in with this other boy and when Alastair saw us he brought Stephen over to be introduced.'

'Is he good-looking?'

'We-ell, not exactly good-looking, Winnie, but looks aren't everything.'

'Up to now they have been with you.'

'I think lovely manners and a pleasant voice are just as important,' Marie said loftily and got a nod of approval from her mother.

'One would expect him to have excellent manners. The boy would very likely have been educated at one of the top schools. Probably boarding school since his parents were away such a lot of the time,' Harriet said.

Winnie began to gather up the snapshots, then after a smile to herself, handed the bundle to Lois to put in the yellow folder.

'A bit hard on Harry Lindsay. What are you going to do about him?'

'He doesn't own me, Winnie,'

'Of course he doesn't, Marie,' her mother rushed in, 'and you must make that clear to Harry if he looks like being awkward.'

'Wouldn't do to be rash, Marie,' Lois said quietly. Harry was a nice lad and very much in love with Marie. 'You don't know for sure if Stephen will ask you for another date.'

'You can be relied upon to say the wrong things, Lois.'

'That's what I was going to say as well,' Winnie said.

Marie was of the same mind. Harry had been her steady for longer than any of the others. He was a very handsome boy who worked as a teller in the Muirford Bank and was studying hard to increase his chances of advancement. She just wished that Stephen looked more like Harry. Giving up Harry was going to be difficult but it would have to be done. She couldn't throw up a chance like this. As Mrs Stephen Hammond she would be someone of importance. They would have a lovely home with servants and she would never have to dirty her hands. Then travel, that would be possible and mixing with the right kind of people. Not that there was anything wrong with her own family; she supposed they would be in the lower middle class, whereas Stephen's family would be upper middle class. As she thought of a glittering future, Marie gave a shiver of excitement.

'Marie, dear, I'll ask you again. Where is Stephen taking you?'

'Sorry, Mum, I think I was dreaming. Actually it's a foursome. Not what I wanted, and I'm sure Stephen didn't either but he could hardly say so when the suggestion had come from Alastair.'

'Should be able to split up before the evening is over,' Lois smiled.

'Too true. No more questions you are all too curious.'

'Come on, spoilsport.'

'All right, just to brighten your dull lives I'll tell you where we are going.' She paused. 'The four of us decided on the first house of the Regal, then coffee or a drink in the Douglas Hotel.'

Harriet was frowning. Her generation had never frequented hotels and the girls who did were looked down on and labelled 'fast'.

'You will be careful, Marie?'

'Mum, for goodness sake I've been to the Douglas before, nearly everyone has. Don't worry, all I drank was an orange juice.' It wasn't true. Marie did take a sweet sherry but just one and she made it last all evening.

'Marie, did I hear you say the Regal?'

'You did. Perhaps you should wash out your ears, infant.'

'But you've seen it, did you forget?'

'No, I didn't forget.' Marie frowned and waited for what she knew would follow.

'You mean to tell me you didn't tell them you'd seen it?' Winnie said incredulously.

'I didn't because it so happens I don't mind seeing the picture again.'

'That's just not true. You told me it was a lot of rubbish and you even said it was as much as you could to do to sit through the big picture.'

'I did not say that.'

'You did so and Lois heard you as well.'

It was quite true what Winnie was saying, but Lois had no

wish to be drawn into an argument and pretended not to have heard.

'Winnie you have far too much to say for yourself.'

'I'm not making it up,' Winnie said hotly. 'Marie did say it and if she says she didn't then she's telling a lie.'

'Whether Marie said it or not, it has nothing to do with you.'

'Huh! You wouldn't get me sitting through a rotten picture just because a boy asked me out.'

'In your case, chance would be a fine thing,' Marie shot back.

It was the most hurtful thing she could have said and Winnie was close to tears. She didn't know what was wrong with her these days. It seemed that everyone was changing. Her friends, who had always been such fun, were only interested in boys and Winnie felt left out. It had been one of the reasons for wanting to get away from school. The thought of being at home had suddenly become desirable. Winnie didn't see it as hiding, just as a place of refuge until she was ready to face this new and scary life. None of the boys in her year had shown any interest in her and Winnie didn't know whether it was because she gave them no encouragement or – and she thought this the more likely – they didn't find her attractive.

Harriet saw her youngest fighting back the tears and went over to give her a hug and a kiss on the forehead.

'Winnie, you silly little goose, don't take it to heart. Marie didn't mean to be unkind but you know, dear, you can be very annoying.'

Lois couldn't help a twinge of envy when Marie came downstairs, dressed for her date. Usually she was flying out at the last minute but tonight she was giving herself plenty of time.

'You look a million dollars,' Lois said and meant it.

'Pretty good,' Winnie agreed.

'Thanks.' Marie tapped her father on the shoulder. 'What do you think, Dad?'

Andrew lowered the paper he had been reading. 'Very nice, dear, I just hope this young man is worth all the effort.'

'Dad, do you ever listen? I'm going out with Stephen Hammond.' She made him sound like royalty.

'Is he quite a catch or something?' he teased, knowing full well who Stephen Hammond was. Stephen's father, Simon, had applied for membership of the Muirford Golf Club both for himself and his son.

Marie gave up in disgust and Andrew went back to his paper.

Her dress sense had improved and for that Marie could thank Madame Yvette. Gone were the frills and furbelows she had once favoured and instead Marie bought plain dresses that were well cut and hung beautifully. Madame looked well. She was small and dumpy but knew how to make the best of herself. She had an excellent eye for fashion and a reputation for honesty even at the expense of a sale. Word got round that Madame could be relied upon and there was little danger of being sold something that would later be regretted. It brought in more customers and the business that had been started on a shoe-string was beginning to show a handsome profit.

Marie was a good sales assistant, but if she decided to leave Madame knew she wouldn't be difficult to replace. Girls of good families with no academic prospects, would be attracted to the likes of Madame Yvette's, whereas they would turn up their nose at a department store.

For her date with Stephen, Marie wore a slate-blue dress with large white lapels. The calf length was kind to her less-than-perfect legs but nothing could disguise the thick ankles. In the secrecy of her own bedroom, Marie had prayed for slim legs and well-shaped ankles but her prayers had gone unanswered. Magazines recommended exercises and showed pictures of before and after and the tremendous improvement the right exercises could make. Marie had followed each exercise faithfully but after three weeks and no visible improvement, she gave up.

'Marie, the shorter look is coming in, did you know?'

'Of course I knew, I knew long before you.'

'Bad news for both of us.'

'What do you mean by that?'

'Neither of us has good legs. I wish mine were long and nicely shaped like Lois's.'

'There is nothing wrong with my legs, thank you very much. And when Lois was younger she had legs like sticks.'

'Not now though and it is the present that is important. Your fault, Mum, that we got landed with your legs.'

67

No fault of mine, I assure you.'

'Dad?'

'What now?'

'Have you got good legs?'

He grinned. 'Let's just say I wouldn't be ashamed to be seen wearing the kilt.'

'You never do.'

'I did when I was in the Scouts.'

'Now we're going back a bit,' his wife answered with a smile. She did sympathise with her two daughters and had hoped against hope when they were born that they would have better luck but it wasn't to be. Her own mother had been similarly afflicted, it must run in the family. What one can't change, one learns to live with, she had been told. Marie was blessed with a lovely face and a slim, neat figure. Surely one's face was worth more attention than one's legs.

As Marie prettied herself at the mirror, Harriet watched with possessive satisfaction. Pleased with her appearance, Marie lifted the coat from the back of the chair. It was off-white and was her latest buy.

'Just perfect, my dear.'

'Where are you meeting the others?'

'Outside the coffee shop, Lois. I hope Joan and the boys are on time, I don't want to get there first.'

'Why not? Someone has to be first.'

'But not me. You have a lot to learn, Winnie.'

'Don't want to appear too anxious, I worked that out for myself.'

'Mum, why wasn't she drowned at birth?'

'God, what I have to put up with. Can't a man read his paper in peace, not in this house he can't. I'm off to my study and if there is tea going you can bring me a cup but no biscuits.'

'Is Dad watching his weight?' Winnie asked after Andrew had taken his departure.

'He is cutting down on sweet things and it wouldn't do you any harm to follow his example.'

'I try, honestly I do. Some folk are just naturally fat and they can't do anything about it.'

'You'll never be skinny but lose a pound or two and you will look lovely.' Harriet was getting out her sewing. 'You heard your father and I would enjoy a cup of tea myself.'

'My evening off,' Winnie announced.

'No such thing in this house, I never got a whole evening off.'

'You ruined this job for me, Lois Pringle.'

'Oh, come on, lazybones,' Lois said springing to her feet, 'you put the kettle on and I'll get out the cups.'

The tea was made and a cup taken through to Andrew. Winnie picked up the biscuit tin with its faded picture of Glamis Castle and, opening it, offered her mother a biscuit.

Harriet completed the lazy-daisy stitch on the tray cloth and frowned. 'Winnie, you should know better than that.'

'Because of the tin?'

'Yes.'

'But it's only us.'

'It is a lowering of the standards and a common fault of the young people of today.'

A little later Andrew came in with his empty cup and Lois took it from him and put it on the table.

'Are you going back to your study, Andrew?'

'No, Harriet, I've changed my mind. I've read all that is worth reading in the paper so I'll just have a bit of shut eye.'

'Not yet, Dad, I've an announcement to make.'

'My fifteen-year-old daughter has an announcement to make. This I must hear.'

'Looking after this house is only temporary as I think I made clear.'

'Give it a bit longer, you are improving.'

'I knew I would surprise you. The fact is I have other plans.'

'Which we are about to hear?'

'Yes, Dad, I want to work with children.'

'Doing what?'

'Keeping them amused and happy.'

'Who is going to fork out money for that.'

'You'd be surprised, Andrew,' Harriet spoke up. 'A great many mothers just wish they were in a position to have someone look after their offspring. A father sees his children for a small part of the day, very often when they are in bed asleep and look adorable. It's an entirely different story when you have them at your feet all day. Children can be very exhausting, I should know.'

'Were we awful?'

'Three was a handful I can tell you and remember I had no one to turn to. Your grandmother died just after Marie was born and that was a dreadful blow. She would have been such help. As for your other grandparents they died before then.'

'Awful you both being only children. I think I was the only one in my class in school who had no aunts, uncles or cousins,' said Winnie.

Lois nodded.

'The three of us were deprived,' Winnie said dramatically.

'Not necessarily,' Andrew smiled as he put down his pipe, 'some would see it as a blessing. Remember one can choose one's friends but not one's relatives.'

He should have known better, but so often for him it was peace at any price. Harriet had a point, he supposed, when she said that it was his fault that the piano was in the dining-room. She had always hated it there, so out of place, she said. He shook his head and thought back to when it had happened.

'Winnie, are you ever going to lift that piano lid?'

'I might to dust the inside,' she said cheekily.

'Would you not reconsider learning with a different teacher?'

'No, no, and no again.'

'Harriet, for God's sake, how often does she have to tell you? The girl has no interest. Sell it, get rid of it.'

'I won't do that, it is a nice piece of furniture but it has to go back into the sitting-room.'

'Please yourself.'

'No time like the present and it is so seldom we are all at home at the same time.'

'Another time, Harriet, that was a big meal and I don't feel like lugging a piano about.'

'It is almost two hours since we ate. Left to you, Andrew, there would never be a right time.'

'You can't win, Dad, better get it over,' Marie said cheerfully. Life was wonderful and she could afford to be helpful.

'Come on then,' he grumbled.

*   *   *

Perhaps the heavy lift had nothing to do with it, but Andrew was inclined to blame it nevertheless. If not that, what could it have been?

The doctor hadn't dismissed it as lightly as he had expected.

'Not suggesting my number is up, are you?' Andrew said jokingly.

'No, I'm not, but you won't see old age unless you take better care of yourself. Have you had a turn like this before?' Dr Harold Martin, white-haired and sixty-four was looking forward to handing over the practice to his son on his sixty-fifth birthday. He was thoughtful as he put away his stethoscope then turned to his patient to hear his reply.

'A while back I had one but not nearly so severe.'

'That was a warning which you obviously ignored. This is more serious and you'll have to take it easy. Stress plays its part. Any worries at work?'

'No more than usual.'

'Which tells me precisely nothing. How about exercise? Or like the rest of you businessmen are you in and out of the car and forgotten why the good Lord gave you legs?'

'A bit like the pot calling the kettle black. How much walking do you do, Dr Martin?'

'Not a lot I grant you, Mr Pringle, but then I've the excuse of advanced age, you don't.'

'I do play the occasional game of golf.'

'We in the medical profession have mixed feelings about that. Some see it as good exercise and others as too strenuous.'

'Which camp are you in?'

'Too strenuous I would think but then I'm not a golfer. For my money there is nothing to beat a brisk walk. Got a dog?'

'My wife won't have one in the house.'

'Neither will mine. Many years ago we had a Scottie but the beast had to be put down.'

'As bad as a family bereavement?'

'Sadly missed certainly but the reason for no replacement was that it always fell to Mrs Martin to take it out and she'd had enough.' He began writing on his pad then nodded his dismissal.

Andrew finished buttoning his shirt, reached for his jacket and put it on.

'No heavy lifting, but then you wouldn't be stupid enough to do that?'

Andrew thought of the piano and the dead weight it was. 'No. Want me to send in your next patient?'

'If you would.'

Andrew closed the door, heard a bark to leave it open and after doing so told the next patient in the waiting-room to go in.

Going back to the office in the afternoon, Andrew remembered how he had dismissed the first pains and discomfort as no more than indigestion and bought tablets from the chemist. He had thought they helped and perhaps they had. The real, excruciating pain had him gasping. It had happened on the golf course and just after he'd played the third hole. The severity of it as well as the suddenness made him come out in a cold sweat. Charlie Anderson had turned to make some remark and seeing there was something wrong hurried over.

'Andrew, what's the matter?' he asked anxiously.

The stabbing pain had eased and Andrew managed a weak smile. 'I'm all right now, Charlie, just a shooting pain that took my breath away.'

'Better get you back to the club house.'

'I'll manage on my own.'

Two others came over to see what was the matter.

'Honestly, no use spoiling everyone's game.' Andrew was a bit embarrassed. 'You just carry on without me, I'll take a rest in the club before driving home.'

The day had been humid, the kind of weather that saps at the energy and Andrew was putting this forward as a reason for his tiredness and being a bit below par.

'I'll accompany you,' Charlie said. He was a stout man, slightly out of breath but he managed to carry both sets of clubs. 'Maybe you feel all right now but you don't look it.' They began walking slowly towards the club house.

'Had this before, you know, but not so severe. No more than a bad bout of indigestion. Harriet is always telling me to take more time over my food. You know what wives are like?'

Charlie just smiled. He and his wife had a good marriage but

72

he wasn't so sure about Andrew. Harriet, from all accounts was seldom at home whereas his wife was a real home lover.

'Don't want to alarm you but that is more than indigestion. Better see your doctor.' Charlie prided himself on having a little medical knowledge. It was a very little. 'Could be a sign of overdoing it, maybe you need to slow down a bit,' he said repeating words said to him by his own physician, but in his case it had to do with a weight problem.

Andrew fully intended making an appointment with his doctor. The truth was he had been thoroughly scared and the thought of a repeat performance had him coming out in another cold sweat. No point in telling Harriet, she would only fuss and her kind of fussing he could do without. Unfair of him he knew, she would be genuinely concerned. A cool hand on his brow would be soothing, but it wasn't his wife's hand he wanted. Strange how of late the past was intruding on the present.

Chapter Seven

'Stephen, do come in,' Harriet said in her most welcoming voice. 'Marie won't be long.'

Stephen Hammond was a thin, sallow-faced youth with fine sandy-coloured hair and light brown eyes. His father, Simon, had been bald at an early stage and it looked as though the same fate was in store for Stephen. What was attractive about him was his smile which showed his good teeth.

Winnie had wandered over to the window and Lois had just come downstairs.

'You have still to meet Winnie, the baby of the family.'

Winnie moved from the window. 'Hello, Stephen,' she said taking the outstretched hand.

'Pleased to meet you, Winnie.'

'And this is Lois,' the voice was decidedly cooler.

The brown eyes were looking at her with undisguised admiration.

'Delighted to meet you, Lois, and tell me how we have managed to miss each other in such a small place? You and Winnie,' he added.

'I have no idea,' she laughed.

He kept hold of her hand longer than he should and it had been noticed. Other eyes were upon them from across the room.

There was the sound of a door being opened and shut then footsteps on the stairs. Marie came into the sitting-room making as much of her entrance as possible. The nights had turned chilly and some said it was cold enough for snow though it was only the end of October. Marie had managed to look cosy and attractive. Her fine-knit suit was in a warm shade of rose pink with a silver thread woven through it. The hemline was slightly longer than fashion dictated but, as her employer pointed out as tactfully as she could, it was a mistake to be a slave to fashion. The secret of a well-dressed woman was knowing what suited her. Over her suit Marie wore a black coat with astrakhan collar and cuffs. Only on her way out would she button it. The coat had been very expensive – she knew and so did Harriet that Andrew would have hit the roof had he known how expensive. At first Harriet had been unsure and thought black unsuitable for a young girl. Marie, however, had soon talked her mother round, particularly when she knew that Madame Yvette had given the garment her nod of approval.

Harriet was prepared to spend any amount if it helped to bring about a match between Marie and the only son and heir to the Hammond fortune. There was that worrying moment when she thought Stephen had shown too much interest in Lois but then again it might have been her imagination. Stephen was looking admiringly at Marie as well he might. Harriet was all smiles again. Marie, she thought, had never looked prettier.

Marie had on court shoes with a higher heel than she usually wore but she only had the length of the garden to walk. Stephen's yellow two-seater, a twenty-first birthday gift, would be parked at the gate.

'That's me ready, Stephen,' Marie said giving him a radiant smile. She was anxious to get away but mindful of her manners. 'Mum, did you do the introductions?'

'Your mother did, I think I have met the entire family now.'

'You have as a matter of fact,' Winnie said and Stephen looked mystified.

'My young sister means that we have no aunts, uncles or cousins,' she said wearily. 'Mum and Dad are only children and both sets of grandparents have long since departed.'

'Think yourselves lucky. We have a load of relatives, young, old and in-between, who descend on us from time to time. They did when we lived in Broughty Ferry and the excuse now will be to see the new house. Then they'll decide to stay on a bit to make the journey worthwhile. My young sister and I could see them far enough at times, but Mum doesn't seem to mind. Dad does, he mutters about wishing himself back in India.'

They all laughed and then they had gone.

'What did you think of him, Lois?'

'I liked Stephen very much. He isn't a bit stuck-up and he has a good sense of humour.'

'Lost on Marie wouldn't you say?' Winnie's voice dropped. 'She takes after Mum, she hasn't got one either or not much of one.'

Lois wouldn't disagree with that. 'Marie looked lovely.'

'Bet that outfit cost a bomb. Still if it does the trick and Mum gains Stephen as a son-in-law, she'll think it money well spent.'

'Think it could be a love match?'

'No, I don't. Stephen isn't her type but she'll hang on and pretend he is because she fancies herself as Mrs Stephen Hammond. Could be there'll come a day when she regrets breaking off with Harry Lindsay.'

Harriet had come in and must have heard the last part of the conversation.

'What nonsense you talk, Winnie. Marie and Stephen make a lovely couple.'

Winnie shrugged. Her thoughts had turned from Marie to herself. Life was definitely improving. She had started going out with her chums again and discovering that she liked boys after all and, even better, she knew they liked her. Happiness was making her eat less and though she would never be thin – she wasn't built that way – she had managed to lose a pound or two and was pleased with her appearance. Not everyone liked skinny lizzies and plump girls could look equally attractive. Winnie was growing up.

Lois was on her way to the door.

'Where do you think you are going?'

'Out.'

'That was the height of rudeness.'

Lois knew it was and to answer that way was most unlike her but she just couldn't resist it. At long last she was learning to stick up for herself. The bullying had gone on for too long.

'If you must know I am meeting friends.'

'I'm not blind I saw the way you looked at Stephen.'

Lois was almost too shocked to answer. 'I smiled, I believe, and if that upset you then I apologise.'

'Don't get smart.'

'In future I'll make myself scarce.'

'That might be a good idea.'

'In fact, better if I wasn't here at all?'

'My one wish is that some boy would take a fancy to you—'

'But not Stephen?'

'Don't be so stupid. Stephen would never give you a second look.'

'Then why are you so afraid?'

'I'm not. You are impossible and have always been a thorn in the flesh.'

'Yes, Mum, I've always known that and rest assured I'll leave this house as soon as I can and not necessarily to get married.'

Brave words but as soon as she had said them Lois knew the futility – where would she go? With a little money she could go into digs but she couldn't ask her father, he wouldn't approve. In any case she wouldn't want to worry him, just lately he hadn't been looking himself. Probably working too hard to keep them all in comfort. Poor Dad, there were times when he looked worried and depressed.

Tim Napier hadn't forgotten Lois. Far from it: he had taken to haunting the neighbourhood when he judged she would be leaving her work and going home. He didn't know where home was or which bus she would be taking, if indeed she did catch one. Eventually his patience was rewarded when he spied Lois waiting with others at the bus stop. The dark nights were making it more difficult to recognise anyone unless close up but Lois stood out. She was taller than average and there was something about her, a proud tilt to her head, that ensured her a second look.

Not even attempting to disguise his delight, Tim hurried over and Lois, at that moment turned and there was instant recognition.

'We meet again.'

'Hello, Mr Napier,' she smiled.

'Tim, please. I can only call you Lois, I don't know your other names.'

'Lois Pringle. And I'm sorry but I'm afraid it is hello and cheerio, this is my bus.'

'Miss it.'

'I shouldn't.'

'Please, I've been looking for you, you know?'

Lois felt her heart thudding. 'All right,' she said breathlessly.

'I'll drive you home if you will allow me?'

'That's rash,' she teased. 'I could live miles away.'

'The longer it takes the better.'

'Where are you parked?'

'Round the corner in Elm Street.'

The damp chill had everybody stamping their feet and looking pinched and miserable. Lois had been shivering too but not now. It could have been a balmy evening with a glow of happiness keeping her warm.

Under the street lamp it was difficult to decide whether the car was black or dark blue. Tim opened the passenger door for her and she got in then he went round to the driver's seat.

'Where is home?'

'Middlefield Crescent, Greenacre.'

'Lois, I like the name.'

'Mr Latimer said that too.'

'Family name?'

'No, I'm not called after anyone. My father chose it.'

He manoeuvred the car out into the road. 'Job going well?'

'Yes, thank you. Mr Latimer is a good employer and I know I am lucky.'

'He appears to think the luck is on his side.' Tim swerved and uttered a mild oath. 'Wish folk would look after their dogs. I could have struck the beast.'

'Poor dog, probably bewildered by the traffic.'

'Ah, you take the animal's side. You and my friend David would get along well. He's the vet and gives animals the credit for having more sense than some humans.'

'Maybe I wouldn't go that far,' Lois laughed.

There were silences but they were comfortable and Lois was glad it wasn't necessary to keep up a steady conversation. Too soon for her they were almost at Middlefield Crescent.

'Slow down, Tim, we're almost there.' She directed him to the gate and made as though to get out.

'Don't dash away.'

She sat back.

'I wondered if you would have dinner with me one evening?'

Lois felt her face flush. 'I'd like that very much.'

'As luck would have it I have to be in Edinburgh for a few days and I can't say for sure when I'll be back. How about making it for a week on Wednesday, would that suit you?'

'Yes, thank you.'

'Pick you up here at your door – say about seven o'clock. I'll make a reservation at the Welcome Inn, the new restaurant on the Barry Road, know it?'

'No, I don't.'

'You'll like it, I think, and I can certainly recommend the food.'

'It sounds lovely and please don't get out, I can manage perfectly well myself.' She got out and smiled at him before shutting the door.

'Thank you for the lift.'

'My pleasure and don't forget our date.'

'I won't.' As if she would. Her other dates had been with boys but Tim was a man and a very attractive one.

She watched the car until it disappeared round the corner. Her colour was up, she could feel it and just hoped no one would notice and remark.

'That a car door I heard?'

'Could have been.'

'Someone give you a lift home?'

'Yes.'

'Are you going to tell or have I to drag it out?'

'Winnie, I'm serving up the meal,' Harriet called.

'Put out Lois's, she's just come in.'

Lois hugged the thought of her date with Tim to her, and had cast a critical eye over her wardrobe. She had nothing suitable for a dinner date, that much was obvious. A shopping trip was called for and she did have money put by. Madame Yvette's wasn't for her and, anyway, she didn't know if family got discount or just Marie. Probably just Marie. Dundee was marvellous for shops. One of her friends worked in Draffens and had said to try and come in the middle of the day when the shop was less busy. Saturday wasn't the best day, it was always busy, but it was the only time Lois could manage.

Alison, looking smart in her black dress with white lace collar and cuffs, was delighted to see her. She was out to impress Lois with her fashion knowledge and dress after dress was brought out for her inspection. Lois couldn't make up her mind and Miss Dewhurst, the buyer, was asked for her opinion.

'Lucky you to be able to wear practically anything,' she smiled. 'You don't want anything too extreme, no matter how desirable.'

'No, it must do for other occasions.'

'Then I would suggest the coffee and cream.'

'I think I hoped you would say that one,' Lois confessed. 'I love the stand-up collar.'

'Mandarin? Yes, a very attractive neckline.'

'In it you will always feel happy and, another point in its favour, it isn't so very expensive.'

Knowing or suspecting that Harriet continued to slip Marie the occasional ten-shilling note, Andrew took out his wallet and gave a few notes to Lois.

'No, Dad, I have money. I've been saving and I've just bought myself a dress. I'll let you see it some time.'

'Wait until you are in it then I'll give my opinion as to whether it suits you,' he smiled. 'No, no, you keep that,' he said pressing the money back into her hand.

'Thanks, Dad.' Only Winnie knew about Tim, but now she told her father.

'Napier? That'll be the engineering company?' He nodded approvingly. 'Smallish firm with an excellent reputation and expansion very much on the cards, I believe.'

'How do you know that?'

'We accountants get to know quite a lot.' He winked. 'This is going to put you upsides with Marie.'

'Dad, I like Stephen.'

'So do I, but he isn't right for Marie. Your mother has the happy knack of seeing only what she wants to see. She wants the union and Marie is going with the lad for all the wrong reasons. Still it is early days and who knows what might happen.' He sighed and she thought he sounded so tired.

'Dad, are you all right?' Lois said with concern. He didn't look well, his face was grey and there was a puffiness below the eyes.

'I've felt better, Lois. Nothing seriously wrong just lack of energy, a common enough complaint with folks these days.'

'You must take it easier.'

'I intend to, but first I must finish the work I brought home.'

'That shouldn't be necessary, bringing work home.'

'I'm inclined to agree but needs must. Run along now.'

'Mum, know who I saw when I was out?'

'No, how could I?'

'Mrs Hutchison.'

'The minister's wife? Looking as harassed as ever I've no doubt. That woman doesn't seem to be able to organise her life.'

'She had the pram and the three wee ones with her and I thought she looked almost ill. Lucky I was there to grab one of the twins before he ran into the road. Poor soul, you should have seen her, she didn't know whether to shake the wee lad or give him a cuddle.'

Harriet smiled. 'I seem to remember the feeling.'

'I took charge of the twins and walked back to the manse with her. The boys were pulling me in the gate or I don't suppose she would have asked me in.'

'Did you go?'

'Yes.'

'We, in the Guild, shudder to think what the inside of the manse looks like. Those who want to see the minister go to the vestry and not many set foot in the house.'

'Why doesn't someone help the woman, she only has that simple-minded girl.'

'Winnie, I did suggest some time ago that the Guild ladies should offer their services. There is a fund and an understanding that one room of the manse is papered and painted each year.'

'Why isn't it?'

'Our ladies were willing but the minster thought it unnecessary.'

'Well he would, I bet he is never in,' Winnie said indignantly.

'Why are you getting into a fuss over it?'

'Because I think it is a shame and I've offered to go one afternoon a week and look after the children. It will give Mrs Hutchison a chance to go to the hairdresser's or do some shopping.'

'You offered to look after the children?' Harriet said incredulously.

'Why shouldn't I? I wanted to.'

'I should have been consulted, Winnie. You left school to assist me, remember?'

'I do enough and what I do in my spare time is surely up to me.'

'Not if I think you are being taken advantage of.'

'No chance of that. Incidentally, Mum, I'm pretty sure Mrs Hutchison wouldn't say no to a bit of help from the Guild ladies.'

Harriet looked thoughtful. 'Perhaps I could mention it again. The organising would be done by me and the ladies take it in turn to clear out the room for the painter and when he is finished to put the place back in order. It is such a big manse that there is no danger of getting in the minister's way. Personally I see no problems.'

'Nor me.'

'A few of our ladies were anxious not to offend the minister's wife and I have to say in her place I might have been. It is after all admitting defeat.'

Winnie grinned. 'If you were Mrs Hutchison, Mum, you wouldn't let the minister get away with it. You would insist on proper help or is the church too hard up?'

'The minister has his stipend, enough to live on, but it does not allow for luxuries.'

'Not many of those I wouldn't think. Anyway, Mum, do what you can – it is in a good cause.'

Winnie waited until she had been at the manse for a few afternoons before broaching the subject.

'No objections, Winnie, absolutely none. I'd welcome help with open arms.' Elspeth Hutchison smiled. Her light brown hair had been cut short and the style suited her small face. With her health improving there was more bounce to her hair and the hint of a wave was back.

'You look great.'

'Thanks to you Winnie. I really was letting myself go.'

'One afternoon a week isn't much.'

'It means a great deal to me.'

'Mrs Hutchison?'

'Yes?' Elspeth put the baby back in the pram, tickled her under the chin and once she got a smile gave her attention to Winnie.

'You want to tell me that you won't be coming back? Of course I understand a young girl like you doesn't want to tie herself down looking after someone else's children.'

'I wasn't going to say that at all. As a matter of fact I like looking after children. My mum says in a big house like this you need help and if you wouldn't be offended the Guild ladies would be happy to assist.'

'There's much need, the place is a mess.'

'No, but it needs a freshen and I believe the church undertakes to do a room in the manse each year.'

'Alex's fault. The offer was made to him instead of me and of course he said the money could be better spent.'

'The money is there for that purpose. You should put your foot down,' Winnie said hotly then wondered if she had gone too far.

'Alex is a good man, Winnie, and he looks after his flock. No beggar comes to the manse without leaving with something.'

'Fair enough but what about his wife and family?'

'Yes, it is time I stood up if not for myself then for my family. You tell the Guild ladies from me that I would be more than happy for them to come. The manse belongs to the church and should be kept up to a reasonable standard. Don't I sound brave? I'm not afraid of Alex or his wrath, don't think that for a moment. I'm at fault for always giving in to him. That is going to end and I have a feeling that once Alex gets over the shock he'll have more respect for me.'

Winnie smiled. 'That's the spirit.'

'Come, let me fill you up, this is my day for outpourings and you, my dear, are very easy to talk to.'

'Mum says I've too much to say.'

'Mothers always say that. No, Edith, darling, mummy is having a little talk with Winnie. Be a good girl and amuse yourself.'

'Jimmy and Bobby are naughty. They won't let me play with them.' The thumb went into her mouth.

'They are too rough anyway,' said Elspeth.

'Edith, draw me a nice picture, one I can take home with me and pin on the wall.' Winnie stifled a giggle as she thought of her mother's face if she dared do such a thing.

'A house?'

'Perfect.'

'I've only got a yellow crayon.'

'Yellow is my favourite colour.'

Winnie and Elspeth smiled to one another. Edith would be quite happy for a little while.

'When Alex and I got married, Winnie, I had such plans. I was to be everything a minister's wife should be. Always smiling, always ready with a helping hand. Housework to me was something that had to be done but not enjoyed though I did think that when the house was mine it would be different. Not so. The manse was to have an open door with tea and home-made scones available at any time. You're laughing.'

'No wonder. My mother as you know is a manager, but I don't see her tackling that little lot.'

'Then the twins arrived and though we were both absolutely over the moon, I didn't know whether I was coming or going. My mother came for a week to help but that was as long as she could be away from my father. Dad is a semi-invalid and very demanding.'

'What about the other side?'

'Jessica, Alex's sister, is a lovely person and a true friend. She is unmarried and hasn't a clue about babies.'

'What does she do?'

'A teacher and a very good one. Jessica is headmistress in a girls' boarding school in York. Alex says her kind are marvellous in their own little world and I suppose he has a point. She has her rooms in the school and everything done for her.'

'No sisters?'

'Only Angela but she's in Canada. Angela has four boys, no help in the house and manages very well. My grumblings don't get much sympathy. And that is quite enough about me. Tell me about you, Winnie.'

'Not much to tell. I'm very ordinary.'

'That isn't so, but carry on.'

'You've been honest with me and though I've never told this to anyone else I'm going to tell you, but first tell me this. Do you love one of your children more than the others?'

'Yes, I do.'

'Oh!' It hadn't been the answer Winnie expected.

'That said I treat them all exactly the same, never show favouritism. No one, not even Alex would guess. It wasn't what you expected me to say, but it's life dear. We have no control over whom we love most but how we show it is very much in our hands.'

'It isn't like that in our house. Dad is scrupulously fair but Mum doesn't hide her preference for Marie and I come next. I can't understand why it should be but she doesn't like Lois and she certainly doesn't hide it.'

'How strange. And Lois how does she cope with this?'

'Hard to tell,' Winnie said thoughtfully. 'When she was younger she always tried to please Mum.'

'To gain her love?'

'Yes, but it made no difference. Mum was never cruel, don't get the wrong idea, just – I don't know – indifferent I suppose is nearest.'

'That is a form of cruelty,' she said softly. The baby whimpered and Elspeth bent over the pram and lifted the baby out. 'There, there, my pet,' she said soothingly and cuddled her close. 'You and Marie take after your mother in appearance and Lois after her father.'

'That can't have any bearing on it?'

'One wouldn't think so but then there is nothing so complex as human behaviour if I can put it that way. If Lois is coping don't let it worry you.'

'I don't know if she is. Lois is changing.'

'She is growing up. You are a very attractive family, Winnie, and I know you won't mind me saying that Lois is blossoming into a real beauty. Could it be that your mother sees this and is jealous for her first-born?'

'Surely not, that would be unforgivable.'

'Edith, is this for me?' she said taking the sheet of paper and wondering which was the right side up.

The crayon-stained finger pointed. 'That's smoke coming out of the chimney.'

'Yes, I knew that.'

'It's the bestest one I've done.'

'I'm honoured,' she said giving the child a kiss. 'And now I must go.'

Chapter Eight

Tim was very special, her first real date and she wasn't going to tell her mother or Marie. There would be time enough for that if Tim asked her out again. If he didn't she would be dreadfully disappointed but she could cope with disappointment better on her own. Pretending not to care and putting a brave face on it would be an ordeal and a humiliating one.

Her father and Winnie knew about Tim but they were different. She could trust them, she hoped, to say nothing about it until she gave them an opening. As for her new dress, that was a secret and not even Winnie had seen it. They shared a bedroom and had their own wardrobes but neither of them would have dreamt of going through the other's clothes without permission.

It should have been so easy to slip out of the house without attracting attention. She had done it often enough. All that was necessary was to put her head round the door to say she was going out and that she had her key to get in. Lois had reckoned without a bored Winnie who had been deprived of her weekly magazine. She had been quite desperate to read the next instalment of the serial and the wretched newsagent didn't know what had happened to her copy and he didn't have a spare. She would get it tomorrow without fail.

Harriet was luckier. She was happily behind the *People's Friend*. Annie S. Swan was her favourite writer and until recently the *Friend* had been the only magazine allowed into Laurelbank since it was the only magazine according to Harriet that recognised proper values.

With school behind her Winnie had rebelled and other magazines began to find their way into the house. Harriet declared them rubbish and said she wouldn't open one. Winnie wasn't so sure. How come she knew so much if she didn't read them?

'Lois, what time are you going out?'

'Not for a while yet.' She gave her sister a warning look but Winnie chose to ignore it.

'Have you told them?'

'Told us what?' Marie drawled.

'Lois has a big date.'

'You mean Lois is actually going out with someone interesting?'

'Very, very interesting,' Winnie said, purposely avoiding Lois's eyes.

'Yes, Winnie, I would go along with that.' The voice came from the depths of the armchair and Harriet's head jerked up.

'How do you know that? Have you met him?'

'Not yet, Harriet, but I look forward to that pleasure.' Andrew was teasing but Harriet wasn't amused and neither was Lois. Andrew, however, was enjoying himself. For once Lois was in the limelight. 'Lois, what is the lad's first name?'

'Tim,' she said shortly.

'Tim Napier,' Andrew said nodding his head with satisfaction. 'Harriet, it may have escaped others but you know about the Napier Engineering Company.'

'Of course I do.'

'Then you must know that the company is going from strength to strength and making the newspaper headlines. Not just our local paper but throughout the rest of Scotland.'

Marie never read the newspaper so it all went over her head. Harriet knew most of what was going on but she could only give her husband limited attention. She had stopped reading, it was difficult to concentrate and one matter and one matter only was concerning her. She was totally absorbed in the romance between Marie and Stephen. They were a couple, everyone saw them as that so surely, surely it couldn't be long before they announced their engagement.

Harriet watched for signs and waited with a feverish impatience while at the same time trying to rid herself of the nagging worry she couldn't explain away. Why had Marie not been invited to Silverknowe to meet Stephen's parents? Laurelbank had become almost a second home to their son.

Lois didn't hurry on her way downstairs. She was feeling acutely embarrassed and suddenly the dress that had seemed so perfect in the shop was less so now. Did she suit the style? Were the colours right for her? Most of all was she overdressed? In those agonising moments before she opened the sitting-room door, Lois envied Marie and wished that she had even half of her sister's self-confidence. When she did open the door and go in Lois looked directly at her father sprawled comfortably in his chair. He must have seen that look as a silent plea for help and was quick to respond.

'Lois, my dear girl, you look absolutely lovely and that dress could have been made for you. Was it?'

She smiled. 'No, Dad, this is just off-the-peg and needed no alteration.'

'That's what comes of having a model figure,' Winnie said admiringly.

'Young Napier had better be taking you some place special.'

'Tim said he was booking a table at the Welcome Inn,' Lois said breathlessly.

Her father nodded. 'Heard talk of it in the office. A fairly new establishment somewhere on the Barry Road and gaining a reputation for good, imaginative food and excellent service.'

'Has Stephen taken you there, Marie?'

'No, he hasn't, Winnie, but we'll try it some time,' Marie said lazily. After buffing her nails she held up her hand for inspection. Turning to Lois she said, 'Where did you buy that? I quite like it.'

Winnie moved along the sofa to let Lois join her. 'The dress? I got it in Draffens.'

'Really? I *am* surprised that a shop like Draffens didn't advise you as to the correct length.'

'But they did.'

'By they I suppose you mean your friend Alice. Isn't that where she works?'

'Yes.'

'Lois, you can hardly expect a junior to know very much.'

'Just for your information, Alice is far from being a junior, she has had two promotions,' Lois said indignantly. 'And another thing, she asked the buyer for her opinion.'

'Ignore her, Lois. Marie doesn't think anyone but herself and Madame Yvette knows about fashion,' said Winnie.

'You know nothing so do everybody a favour and keep quiet.' Marie turned back to Lois and gave her a kindly though condescending smile. 'Don't worry about it you'll be sitting most of the time and apart from the length, the dress is quite fashionable.' She paused. 'I do like the neckline.'

'What is wrong with the length?'

'Stand up.'

Lois did so.

'Too short, I'm sorry but it is and it spoils the effect. A shame really.'

'As a mere man I'd say the length is absolutely right. Fine by me, anyway.' His eyes twinkled. 'Since Lois and I are the only two in this family to have good legs where is the harm in showing them off?'

'Couldn't agree more, Dad, and I'm honest enough to admit it. If I had legs like Lois you wouldn't get me hiding them.'

'No need to hide yours,' her mother said sharply.

'But there is. I wish I looked like Lois,' Winnie said wistfully.

'Winnie, don't be silly.' Lois smiled to her young sister. Winnie could never see her own good points. 'You are very attractive and that isn't just my opinion.'

'Thanks Lois, you mean well but the mirror doesn't lie.'

'The way you look at yourself in it, it does.'

'That is true, Winnie dear, you make the mistake of picking on your less than perfect points. You have a lovely skin that many would envy.'

'Maybe I have, Mum, but the bad points outnumber the good.'

'Oh, well, if you are determined . . .' Harriet shrugged and gave her attention once again to Marie. 'When is Stephen coming?'

'Couldn't say, he'll just arrive,' Marie said carelessly.

Andrew hadn't quite finished. 'Harriet, I think you would agree with me that we have been blessed with a good-looking family and with our middle daughter turning out to be a stunner.'

His wife stared. 'What on earth has come over you? You aren't usually so free with your compliments.' When had he last paid her one, she thought resentfully. Her eyes went to Lois. 'If you want my opinion I like the colours though coffee and cream are more suitable for the older woman. The style is – quite nice, but as to the length I have to agree with Marie that the longer skirt is more elegant.'

'Perhaps it is more elegant, Mum, but long skirts are no longer fashionable and didn't you say, Marie, that you would rather be dead than be out of fashion?'

Marie opened her mouth to protest but the sound of a car drawing up ended the conversation and Winnie got up and dashed to the window.

'It's not Stephen, it's a dark blue car.'

'That will be Tim, I'll get my coat.'

'No, lass, don't go rushing out, take your time. I'll go and bring the lad in. No use him sitting out there,' Andrew said getting smartly to his feet.

This was her father acting completely out of character and he was doing it for her. She didn't want it, but since there was nothing she could do about it Lois just resigned herself.

Andrew returned with Tim and as he came into the room his long slow smile was for her. It was as though he knew she was uncomfortable and was trying to put her at ease.

'Meet the family, Tim,' Andrew said heartily as he drew him over to where Harriet was sitting. 'This is my wife.' They shook hands.

'How do you do, Mrs Pringle, I'm delighted to meet you,' Tim said courteously. Then he was being introduced to Marie and Winnie.

In those moments Lois felt so proud. Tim looked so very handsome in his well-tailored light grey suit and he was obviously making an impression. Marie's mouth had dropped open and Lois knew that she was wondering how on earth her sister had managed it. Harriet was equally taken aback, but better at hiding it. Here she was expecting a shy young boy who wouldn't have a word to say for himself and instead there was this young man with the relaxed easy manner she admired so much. A handsome lad and she was recalling a little of what Andrew had been saying about the Napier Engineering Company. Plenty of money there and Tim must be the owner's son, perhaps he was an only son.

What should she do? Harriet was torn two ways. She couldn't bear the thought of Lois making such a good match but on the other hand she wanted to encourage Tim to come to the house.

Marie had been immediately attracted, she had seen that and just of late Marie had seemed bored with Stephen. Maybe Stephen wasn't the greatest catch after all.

The truth was that Harriet was finding this young man utterly charming and was finding herself smiling foolishly.

For her part Marie was comparing this tall, very assured and incredibly handsome young man with Stephen and Stephen was suffering badly in the comparison. To say she was stunned wouldn't be too great an exaggeration. He wasn't so very young, she thought, probably middle twenties or even late twenties and that was a definite advantage. He had everything she wanted in a man and from what she gathered there was plenty of money.

When their hands met Marie felt a small delicious thrill and Tim got the full benefit of her most dazzling smile. He had met Marie's kind before and was amused. The occasional date with girls of her type had been fun, but that was where it ended. Lois was his kind of girl. The two sisters couldn't be more different. One so fair and the other so dark. The youngest was a little dumpling and looked just fresh out of school.

To hasten their departure Lois had lifted her coat from the back of the chair and Tim, taking it from her helped her on with it. Then they moved to the door.

Tim smiled. 'Good night and thank you for inviting me in, Mr Pringle, it was a pleasure to meet you all.'

'You will be made welcome at any time, Tim,' Harriet gushed. 'Take care of my lass.'

'I'll do that, Mr Pringle, never fear.'

Once outside Tim took her arm and Lois said apologetically, 'I'm sorry you were let in for that. I tried to slip out but Dad of all people stopped me.'

'Don't apologise. I wanted to meet your family just as I want you to meet mine, but all in good time. I won't rush you.'

'Thank you,' she murmured.

'Fathers of young daughters, I am led to believe, can be very possessive. You are a lovely girl, Lois, and very young and it was only natural that Mr Pringle would want to check on me and hopefully I passed the test.'

'You did.' She didn't add with flying colours though she could have.

'Even on such a short acquaintance I would venture to say that you are your father's favourite.'

'How can you possibly tell?' She was as amazed as she sounded.

'The expression on his face when he looks at you as though you were very special,' Tim said as he opened the car door and held it until she was settled. Then he went round to the driver's seat, got in and switched on.

'You didn't see that expression on my mother's face,' Lois said and then wished she hadn't. What had made her say it?

'No,' he said, then checked the mirror before moving out and into the road. 'I would say your sister, Marie, scores there and young, chubby Winnie is the baby and loved by you all.'

'Don't call her chubby, she is very sensitive.'

'She suits it, the chubbiness I mean.'

'I know, but try telling her that.' Lois's face softened. 'Winnie is a darling, impossible at times but still a darling. Oh! That car that passed, the yellow one, did you see it? That belongs to Stephen, Marie's boyfriend.'

'Saw the tail end. A most attractive girl your sister.'

Lois felt a sharp stab of jealousy and was immediately ashamed.

'Yes, she's the beauty of the family.'

'No, she isn't, you are that. Marie is pretty and appealing. She knows how to flirt and a lot of men are suckers for that.'

'Are you?'

'At one time I might have been, but I have more sense now.'

Lois wondered if that were true.

'I can see by your face that you don't know whether to believe me or not,' he teased.

'I don't as a matter of fact, after all I hardly know you.'

'We'll soon change that.'

They didn't talk all the time but the silences were comfortable. When Tim was concentrating on his driving she watched the strong, capable hands on the wheel. The journey took less than forty minutes, then Tim was slowing down and swinging the car off the road. There was a parking area at the back and a number of cars were already there.

'We aren't the first,' he said as he opened the passenger door.

'My father had heard of this place. Someone in his office was here recently and was full of praise for the food.'

'Word gets round and most of the tables had been booked when I phoned.'

Taking her arm they strolled round to the front of the building and Lois looked about her with mounting excitement. She had occasionally had a meal out, a family celebration in the local hotel, but nothing like this. The Welcome Inn was well named, it looked very inviting.

Many years ago the restaurant had started life as a coaching inn and the new owners, astute businessmen, were anxious to retain its antique charm but not at the expense of comfort. Not easy to achieve but they had managed to marry the old with the new without ending up with something ridiculous. Money had been borrowed and risks taken in the firm belief that cash spent now and the job done professionally would eventually bring in rich dividends. If the first few months were anything to go by the Welcome Inn was destined to be an excellent investment.

The attractive entrance was lit with hanging lamps that glowed a dull red and an assortment of colourful plants covered the shelves. They were greeted by the head waiter, smartly dressed in his evening suit, who gave them a welcoming smile.

'Do you have a reservation, sir?'

'Yes. Napier.'

A pen went through a name on the list, then at a snap of his fingers a young, fresh-faced, narrow-hipped waiter hurried over and took charge of Lois's coat.

'If you would be so good as to follow me.' The head waiter smiled. 'And it is my duty, my painful duty, to remind tall gentlemen to watch their head.'

Tim ducked as they went down a few steps and through a narrow opening, then along and into the dining-room where a lighted candle was on each table. Here the head space was more generous but even so Tim's head just cleared the rafters by very little. The chairs were pulled out for them and they sat down. Once seated the large, stiffly starched white napkins were shaken out of their folds and placed over their knees.

'Thank you.' Lois smiled as she accepted a leather-bound menu. Tim was given the other together with the wine list also leather-bound and with gilt corners and a tassle. That done, the waiter departed.

'I've already mentioned David to you,' Tim said leaning across the table and speaking softly.

'Yes, you have.'

'He's six two and the warning to duck came too late. What a wallop he gave himself and the language.' He grinned. 'Just let me say I couldn't repeat it to you.'

'No wonder, a crack on the head is no way to start the evening.'

'He got over it. It was after all the waiter's fault and he was full of apologies. Almost fell over himself to give us extra special service. The meal was absolutely splendid and all was forgiven until David wakened up next morning with a lump on his head the size of an egg.'

'Poor David, he won't forget to duck next time.'

'How true and now we had better study this menu.'

After a few minutes Lois looked up. 'This all seems very wonderful but I am going to have to ask you to advise me.' She didn't add that she was a bit out of her depth but he probably knew that.

'All will be explained in a moment. Both David and I needed some of it put in plain English but let me say first how lovely you look and I am not the only one who thinks so.'

She frowned. A compliment was very welcome but he didn't have to overdo it. 'Not a soul has noticed me,' she said.

'Yes they have, You are coming in for a lot of admiring glances from other tables. I see them, you don't.' He smiled at her embarrassment but was touched too. 'The most delightful part for me is that you are so unaware. Let it remain that way and now food and you want my advice?'

'I don't want to make an expensive mistake and choose something I don't like.'

'Hang the expense but the chances of choosing the wrong dish are almost impossible. That is what I think, but then again I can eat anything.'

'So can I.'

'In plain language, Lois, the choice is between pork, lamb, beef or fish. The whole lemon sole I can personally recommend if you are a fish lover. Then there is the Tay salmon, that is always a treat. The beef is as stated, Aberdeen Angus and one can't do better than that. The pork is wrapped in pastry and, though I haven't had it myself, others I know have and found it thoroughly enjoyable.'

'You must eat out a lot?'

'Yes, I plead guilty to that.'

'I think I am going to have the pork, I've never had it with pastry.'

'Chance to try it then.'

'What are you having?'

'The roast beef and Yorkshire pudding, I think. Sounds fairly ordinary but believe me the beef is cooked to perfection and the rich gravy is out of this world.'

'You make it sound almost irresistible but I'm going to stick with the pork.'

'Fine, we've got that settled now how about a starter?'

'Something light – grapefruit and orange I think.'

He nodded and picked up the wine list. 'What about wine? Have you a preference?'

'No.'

'Meaning you'll take anything?'

'Meaning I don't know anything about it. At Christmas we had white wine and I pretended to like it but I didn't.'

'What was wrong with it?'

'Tasted like vinegar.'

'Surely not!' He smiled. 'Leave the choice to me – a good wine complements a meal.'

'So I've heard.'

Tim gave the waiter the order then sat back.

'This is all very lovely,' Lois said, and her gaze was taking in the fashionably dressed women at the other tables.

'Meaning the decor or the diners?'

'Both.'

'All very pleasant, a nice atmosphere?'

'Yes.'

What was wrong with her? Lois thought desperately. Why couldn't she carry on the conversation? Laughter rang out from other tables and people were talking softly but animatedly. And

Tim was looking at her, waiting for her to say something and she couldn't think of a thing.

'You must find me very dull,' she burst out.

'Why should I?'

Her hands were moist and she kept them under the table. 'I don't exactly sparkle.'

The first course arrived before Tim could answer that. He had chosen leek and potato soup. Lois lifted her small spoon and began on the fruit. Tim took a few spoonfuls of soup then put down his spoon and they both reached for a piece of the crusty bread.

'Lois, I am going to ask you something that might make you angry. I hope it doesn't, but I am going to risk it.'

'I hope it won't make me angry but I won't know that until I hear it.'

'Most girls would envy you, think you lucky to be blessed with looks and intelligence yet you don't appear to appreciate them.' He leaned forward and their eyes met. 'Why have you such a low opinion of yourself?'

'I didn't know I had,' she replied stung.

'You keep apologising for nothing. I don't know, of course, but I would say that someone has taken away your confidence and perhaps hurt you badly.'

She swallowed. 'Does it show as much as that?' The evening that had promised so much was going all wrong. She was spoiling it for both of them.

'Only a little.'

'It must be more than a little when you've mentioned it.'

He saw the hurt in her eyes and Tim was cursing himself. All he wanted was to help Lois but stupidly he had gone about it in the wrong way. He should have waited until they knew each other better.

'Sorry Lois, tact isn't my middle name.'

'It's all right, I'm too sensitive.'

'Is that all right?' he asked meaning the starter.

'Very nice, thank you.'

'Take more crusty bread, it's made on the premises. Nothing is brought in.' Tim was talking to help her relax.

Lois hadn't eaten the other piece. Unaware of what she was doing she had crumbled the bread between her fingers. The lump in her throat was making it difficult to swallow but she forced the fruit over. Then almost defiantly she reached for a piece of the warm bread, spread it with butter, and ate it.

Tim watched her but kept silent. The girl had been badly hurt and would need careful handling. Something was very far wrong at home or elsewhere and if he were patient perhaps he would learn what it was.

They both smiled, glad of the distraction. Two waitresses, dressed like serving girls in Victorian times, came to collect the plates. They wore long, black skirts, very full and with a high-necked frilly white blouse and leg-of-mutton sleeves. Over the skirt was a tiny starched apron and perched becomingly on their head a lacy cap.

Lois had recovered; she was herself again and captivated by the waitresses.

When they had gone, Lois said, 'Tim, they look enchanting and just right.'

'In keeping with the surroundings?'

'Absolutely and thank you so much for bringing me here.'

'Thank you for coming,' he answered and they both burst out laughing. Then Lois became serious. 'I'm all right, Tim. I really am all right now. Please forgive me.'

'Nothing to forgive – I was clumsy.'

'You deserve an explanation.'

'Not unless you want to give it.' He hoped very much that she would.

'I think I have to.' She took a deep breath. 'This goes no further – it is just between us?'

'That goes without saying.'

She nodded. 'I just had to be sure.'

'You have my word.'

There was an interruption when the wine waiter arrived, showed the bottle to Tim who looked at the label and nodded. The cork was drawn with a great show of expertise and a little of the wine poured into the glass for Tim to taste. Lois had a great desire to laugh. What a carry on! She almost wished that Tim had found something wrong just to see what would have happened. Tim, however, was perfectly satisfied and the waiter three quarter filled their glasses then took the bottle away but left it within their sight.

'What was amusing you? I saw your lips twitch.'

'I was wondering what would have happened if the wine wasn't to your liking.'

'Another bottle would have been brought to the table.'

'Ask a silly question.'

'Not at all, it wasn't silly. Not many find fault and a few do just to show off.'

'Is another bottle brought to the table?'

'Oh, yes, the customer is always right even though he isn't,' Tim grinned. 'No one loses out, the wine isn't wasted. And now back to what we were talking about.'

'I'd rather not, it isn't important.'

'It is to me,' he said gently.

She sighed. 'I'll start by asking a question. When you were a lot younger what was your relationship with your parents?'

He looked surprised. 'Very good, couldn't fault them though there were times when I thought them too strict. They weren't, of course, there was an acceptable standard and I had to be made to understand that.'

'And I take it you had a lot of affection from both parents?'

'I suppose so. Much as you have yourself I imagine.'

'Then you imagine wrong. My father loves me, always has, but not my mother, not ever. No, don't interrupt, Tim, you asked for this so just listen, please.'

'Sorry.' He picked up his glass and drank some of the wine.

Lois decided to do the same. She took a sip then another. 'This is good,' she said sounding surprised.

'You won't insult it by likening it to vinegar.'

'I wouldn't dare,' she laughed.

'Lois?'

'Yes, all right. You were quick to notice that Marie is Mum's favourite.'

'I was equally quick to notice that you were or rather are your father's.'

'Yes, I accept that.'

'Your mother loves your sisters but not you?'

'That's the way it is.'

He shook his head. 'No, Lois, it isn't the way it is. Your mother couldn't help but love you.'

'Wrong! Wrong! Wrong!' People at another table looked over and

101

Lois flushed and lowered her voice. 'She has never loved me not even when I was small. It wasn't that she couldn't show affection. There are some folk like that, I know, but she isn't. Marie and Winnie were for ever being cuddled.'

'Lois, no mother would completely withhold affection from one of her children, it wouldn't be natural.'

'You don't believe me,' she said flatly.

'I didn't say that or at least I didn't mean to.'

'You meant it all right.' He heard her bitterness.

Tim's eyes were kind. 'Perhaps you are making more of it than you should,' he said softly and touched her hand. 'Could it be, Lois, that your mother was trying to even things up when you were children? After all your sisters could have resented the way your father showed his preference for you.'

'But he didn't,' she protested. 'Dad was always scrupulously fair, he treated the three of us exactly the same. What I got they got. Dad, you have to remember was out working for a lot of the time.'

'Yes, fathers see much less of their children.'

'Mum always gave in to Marie and Winnie but not to me. I'm sounding childish I know but I happen to be telling the truth.' She gave an impatient toss of her head as though she had had enough and wanted the conversation to end.

Tim didn't want it to finish there. Lois was going to be important to him and this thing festering inside her had to be dealt with. He was sure that she was nursing a grievance that had no foundation unless in her imagination. Unfortunately it was deep-rooted, dating from her early childhood, and removing it wouldn't be easy.

'I'm sure you are, the truth as you see it.'

'Meaning it is all in my imagination,' she said resignedly. 'Well you just go on thinking that, Tim, but I know better.'

'If your mother's hostility to you was so pronounced your father must have seen it?'

'He did, I know he did, but he found it easier to ignore.'

'You aren't a child, you don't have to put up with it.'

'I know that, but it takes money to leave home.'

'Don't do that for heaven's sake. I meant you could take a stand.'

'Apart from the financial side I wouldn't want to hurt my

father and he would be terribly upset. I would miss Winnie too,' she added.

'But not Marie?' His eyebrows went up.

Lois felt annoyed. Why did he have to bring Marie into it?

'A little, yes, I would miss her a little,' Lois said shortly, 'but a separation wouldn't greatly upset either of us. Do you mind if we stop talking about this now?'

'No, just as you wish and thank you for telling me what you have.'

'I wish I hadn't.'

'Don't. It is always better to talk troubles over with someone sympathetic.'

'I wouldn't have said you were sympathetic, quite the reverse in fact.'

'You are going to be important to me. I hope you are?'

She smiled and nodded.

'That's good and that is why, my dearest, I want this problem sorted out.'

'If only it were that easy. My mother won't tell me why she dislikes me, but she doesn't deny it.'

'Don't think we have been forgotten. Most people who come here like to spend the entire evening over their meal. That is why there is such a long time between courses.'

'All the more enjoyable for having to wait.' She smiled.

'You have some experience in the house you told me. Does it extend to cooking?'

'Only plain fare – it was all I was taught. Mum thinks she is a good cook and I suppose she is, but she doesn't have much imagination. We all know what to expect on certain days of the week.'

'My mother enjoys cooking but she doesn't get the chance to be imaginative. Dad goes in for plain food and I don't see him changing now.'

They leaned back in their chairs as their glasses were topped up, then came forward only to part again when the main course arrived. The waiter put down their plates and the two serving girls waited, one with two kinds of potatoes and the other with a selection of vegetables.

For a few moments the food got their full attention, then Lois spoke.

'This, Tim, is delicious and the pastry mouth-watering. Aren't they lucky to have such a wonderful chef?'

Tim was pleased. Lois was completely relaxed now and there was a lovely flush to her cheeks. Perhaps the wine had something to do with that and he would have to watch. She wasn't used to it.

'That wine is quite strong, Lois, so go easy. I don't want you arriving home—'

'Drunk and disorderly,' she grinned.

'I doubt if you would get to that stage, but I'm not risking your father's wrath.'

'Point taken. No more wine. You'll have to drink the rest.'

Lois would always be grateful to Tim for those happy times. He was loving and caring and demanded no more of her than she was prepared to give. She was very sweet and innocent and he would do nothing to hurt her.

As for Lois, life had taken on a whole new meaning and the irritations at home bothered her less. Occasionally Tim and she went to the theatre in Dundee when it was something that appealed to them both. Other times it was the cinema where they held hands and when suspense or excitement got too much for her she would clutch him and then remain for the rest of the evening in his arms. At the Welcome Inn they got the special attention reserved for regulars and at other times they drove into the country, found a quiet place to park and sat and talked.

Harriet had invited Tim to Laurelbank for a meal and there he had met Stephen. The two young men got on well and Marie was in her element flirting openly with Tim, but careful not to completely exclude Stephen. All this alarmed Harriet and she determined to have a serious talk to Marie. A further annoyance was to learn that Tim's parents were anxious to meet Lois. His mother hadn't been too well but as soon as she was better a date would be set.

'Marie, do sit and pay attention, this is important.'

Marie was bored, she wasn't seeing Stephen and a night at home with her parents was the end. Lucky Lois to be out somewhere with Tim. Winnie was out and that was all to the good. They had never really got on but if anything she was becoming a bigger pest than ever. Lois wasn't so bad and Marie began to think a foursome, Tim and Lois, she and Stephen, might be fun. If she was to be completely honest with herself Stephen was becoming just a little bit boring. Everything was boring to Marie these days.

'What is important? Important to you is not important to me,' but she sat down beside her mother. 'Where is Dad?'

'In his study.'

'For how long?'

'Long enough for us to have this conversation. Hasn't Stephen made any mention to you about meeting his parents?'

'No.'

'I can't understand it, I really can't.'

'I can. I think I can. I'm not their choice for their little boy.'

'This is not funny, Marie.'

'It isn't funny for me either.'

'Stephen loves you. I mean he's told you that?'

'Of course,' she said scornfully.

'Then what is holding him back? He's over twenty-one.'

'Stephen likes things the way they are, he is in no hurry to get married.'

'Or engaged?'

'Or engaged.'

'But that is unfair to you,' Harriet bridled.

Marie shrugged.

'You don't seem concerned, I have to say.'

Marie's control finally snapped. 'Mum, you have an awful lot to learn.'

'Have I?'

'Yes, you have. You were mad at me for throwing myself at Tim, as you put it.'

'No wonder. I saw Stephen's face and he wasn't amused.'

'That was the whole point. I wanted to make him jealous.'

'And did it? Make him jealous, I mean.'

'Oh, yes, Mum. Stephen was furious.'

'But Tim and Stephen get on well, or so I thought.'

'They do but that isn't the point. Lois doesn't have much to say and Tim and I were doing most of it.'

'And the outcome?' Her mother smiled.

'The meeting with his parents will come, but probably not until after the engagement.'

Harriet's eyes popped. 'Marie, you clever, clever girl. You mean it, an engagement before long?'

'Wait and see.'

'Oh, my dear, I couldn't be more pleased.'

'You mentioned that Stephen and Tim get on well?'

'Yes, what of it?'

'A foursome might be rather fun. We could go dancing, not here but in Dundee or Forfar.'

Harriet didn't think it a good idea at all. She didn't want complications and she was well aware that Marie was attracted to Tim. Tim liked her but she was sure that was as far as it went. To show her disapproval would be a mistake, it would only encourage Marie. Harriet was learning slowly and painfully when to hold her tongue. So all she did was smile and shake her head.

Chapter Nine

That year the winter was as cold as anyone could remember and many of the side roads in Greenacre were blocked with snowdrifts. Folk were glad of the dross in their cellars or bunkers to back up their fires so that they could leave them to burn all night in the slim hope that the water wouldn't freeze in the pipes. The most wanted man was the plumber and he was in constant demand.

For the children unable to get to school it was a magical time. There was the fun of snowballing and the thrill of sledging. Not all were fortunate enough to own a sledge but mother's scrubbing board made a good substitute and it was truly amazing what the youngsters of the village could find to sit on and slither down the slopes.

On a bright morning the snow was a brilliant white that dazzled the eyes and the trees had a fairytale look with every branch and twig thickly covered. By evening the whiteness had dulled to a slate-blue, but when morning dawned everything was white again and still no sign of a thaw.

During this exceptional spell of weather, the Pringles, with the exception of Harriet, took it in turns to keep the paths and the pavement in front of the house clear. They moved mountains of snow, or so it seemed, using the garden spade and the short-handled shovel kept in the coal cellar. After that came a determined effort with the hard-haired brush which cleaned the ground but made it dangerous under foot. Harriet was nervous of slippery surfaces and made free with the salt until it ran out and no further supplies were available.

As so often happens in adversity the dreadful weather conditions were drawing people together and folk who normally wouldn't have passed the time of day with a stranger now stopped and spoke. A few trains were running but the timetable was suspended and passengers stamped their feet, blew on their hands and waited with commendable patience for the signal that would herald the next train. Andrew had discovered an ancient pair of wellingtons in the glory hole and took to wearing them and carrying his shoes in his brief case. The galoshes he had worn in previous years were of little use with the snow more than ankle deep in most places.

John Latimer had been adamant that Lois shouldn't tackle the journey until there was an improvement in travel conditions but like so many others she set out each morning dressed for the weather. When a bus did come she used it until it failed to negotiate a hill or got stuck for some other reason. Then it was Shank's pony for the remainder of the journey. To arrive at all, no matter how late, was an achievement and one was hailed like a hero and overwhelmed with offers of refreshment.

Everybody grumbled but cheerfully and when the thaw did come there were mixed feelings. Suddenly what had been a beautiful winter scene had turned to slush and the trees dripped miserably. The dry cold had been healthy but this dampness chilled people to the bone. Bronchitis and other chest complaints plagued the elderly and doctors' waiting-rooms were filled with sufferers.

The cheerful faces became pinched and glum as flooding became the next problem.

The harsh winter had already given way to an indifferent spring when tragedy struck. There was no warning and the end came with a brutal suddenness that was almost unbearable. Andrew had suffered a heart attack in the office and was dead before the doctor arrived. There had been nothing different that morning when he set out and he hadn't complained to his colleagues of feeling unwell. The chief partner, Philip Rodgers, elderly and frail, was in a state of shock. He had gone along to Andrew's office to have a word with him and found him slumped over his desk. A doctor had been summoned and had arrived within minutes of being called – but it was too late.

Harriet, pale and anguished, had refused all offers of help and had made the necessary arrangements herself. Everyone marvelled but felt uncomfortable too at her cool efficiency. Some said it hadn't sunk in and when it did she would go to pieces, but they were wrong. Marie and Winnie wept uncontrollably and at one point

Marie had been on the point of hysterics. Harriet had slapped her face and the shock of such treatment from her mother had quietened her down. She started to sob quietly.

Lois went about the house as white as a ghost but she shed no tears. Had she been able to, it might have eased the raw pain that was tearing at her inside. Only her eyes, dark and shadowed, showed her deep distress.

The funeral had been well attended, Andrew had been liked and respected. Colleagues, friends, golfing companions and neighbours gathered at the cemetery to follow the cortège, Tim and Stephen had both attended the funeral then gone directly back to work. At the house tea and sandwiches were prepared for any who chose to return. Not many did and the leftover sandwiches were eaten the next day. Harriet, pale and composed, had accepted the sympathy offered with a quiet dignity that had impressed Lois. The widow wore black but had said it was unnecessary for the girls and that she was sure their father would not have wished it. Provided they wore quiet colours like navy or grey – Marie had a black coat – their outfits would be perfectly acceptable. Harriet didn't mention that the expense of new clothes was something she wanted to avoid.

Andrew's affairs would be in order, she was sure of that, but she wouldn't know how they were to be placed until the estate was settled. There was little doubt in her mind that their standard of living would have to change but by how much was the question. The house was hers, there was no problem there and somehow she would manage to keep it going. Lois would have to give more towards her keep and Marie must be made to understand that she couldn't expect so much in future. Winnie might need to find employment but not just yet and when she did then Harriet would have to do a bit more about the house. She viewed the prospect with dismay. It wouldn't be easy but no matter how difficult, she would not economise on Marie's wedding. That had to be a day to be remembered and her savings would go on that. Then she thought about Andrew. He wouldn't be there to give his daughter away and there was no one else, no one she could call to mind to fill that role. For the first time the tears came and taking the pillow from Andrew's side of the bed, Harriet wept into it.

Both Lois and Marie were taking three days off work. Lois could have had longer but she wanted to go back to work. Going about the house they were mostly silent and when they spoke to each other it was in whispers. Lois and Winnie had taken over the household tasks and were just left to get on with them. Marie followed her mother around the house as if afraid to let her out of her sight.

'Mum,' Marie turned her blotchy face to her mother. 'What are we going to do without Dad?'

'We'll have to manage and you, Marie, will have to buck up. Tears won't bring him back.'

'I know that, I don't have to be told.'

Marie did feel some shame. She would miss her father but she had never considered herself close to him. Her real worry was how they were going to manage financially without her father's salary coming in.

Harriet knew her daughter very well. 'Darling, I know what is going through your head and there is no need to feel ashamed. We have to consider the future.' She paused and frowned worriedly. 'Right now I can't say how we will be placed but economies will certainly have to be made.'

'Like what?'

'The laundry bill for one thing. We'll have to stop sending clothes to the laundry and do them at home.'

'You won't have Dad's washing.'

Harriet looked at her sharply but Marie didn't seem to think she had said anything out of place. For those moments Harriet had been shocked then she decided that Marie, quite a change for her, was only being practical. Andrew's shirts had after all been a large part of the weekly laundry.

The empty chair at the table upset them all and Harriet had removed it to the other side of the room. They kept to the usual routine and after the meal had been eaten and the table cleared they went through to the sitting-room.

Winnie asked the same question as Marie.

'Mum, what are we going to do?'

Harriet was rearranging an ornament as though she needed to be doing something with her hands. None of them seemed able to sit down and relax.

Mrs Pringle shook her head, her face was grey and Lois, watching, saw her own grief mirrored in the other's face. In those moments Lois realised that Harriet had loved her husband though she had never seen any outward display of affection. This was a side to her mother that Lois had never seen and she had a sudden overwhelming desire to put her arms around the older woman and give what comfort she could. Instinctively she moved forward, her arms opening ready to embrace and for a startled moment their eyes met, then abruptly Harriet turned away. Marie and Winnie were near and she put an arm around each and drew them to her.

If the action was meant to alienate Lois, to keep her apart, it had succeeded. Stunned by that single act of cruelty and feeling like a wounded animal that needs to hide, Lois had rushed upstairs to her room and shut herself in. She had to get away, she just had to. If she could have gone tonight she would but there was no place to go. Tomorrow she would do something, anything. With her father gone there was nothing for her here. Winnie would miss her just as she would miss her young sister, but Winnie would understand. Where she went didn't matter, all that mattered was getting away. As far away from Laurelbank as she could, she would turn her back on her old home.

Sleep that night was slow to come, there was so much going through her head. She lay awake until daylight filtered into the room and by morning her mind was made up. Mrs Wilson was her best hope, indeed her only hope; she hadn't been able to think of anyone else who could be of assistance. Surely what she was asking wasn't too much? A room and the use of scullery or kitchen where she could prepare her own meals. Thank goodness she was provided with a good midday meal which would save quite a bit. Lois felt a little cheerier and managed to act much as usual at breakfast.

John Latimer was deeply concerned about Lois and did all he could to help. Only time would ease the pain of loss but work would keep her mind off it. He left typing but with instructions that she could take as long over the letters as she wished. There was no hurry. Mrs Wilson was even more concerned. Everyone grieved for a loved one, that was as natural as breathing but this was so much more. There was something far wrong. It wasn't her place to ask and she wouldn't make the mistake of trying to get it out of the lass. The best she could do was to encourage Lois to eat instead of picking at her food as she had been doing this last while.

'I'm so sorry, Mrs Wilson, this is lovely but I have no appetite just now.'

'That's all right, no need to apologise. Forcing yourself to eat food you don't want would do more harm than good. In a day or two you'll feel more like it but meantime we'll have a cup of tea.'

They sat together in the kitchen drinking tea and not saying very much. Then the housekeeper patted her knee and said kindly, 'Lois, life can be very cruel and this is a very great loss you have suffered.'

Lois lifted her chin and stared ahead. Her lips drooped in a small and rueful smile and the sadness there wrung the housekeeper's heart.

'I adored my father, Mrs Wilson, he was very special to me.'

'Of course he was, I can understand that but you must be brave. You and your sisters will have to help your mother—'

Something in the stricken face stopped her and Mrs Wilson was shocked at the hardness in the voice when Lois spoke.

'My mother doesn't want my help, that is the very last thing she wants. My sisters', yes, but not mine.'

'Lois, dear—'

Lois gestured wildly almost upsetting her cup. It rattled in the saucer then settled. 'You don't understand, how could you? I don't understand it myself.' She swallowed painfully. 'I've been trying to pluck up courage all morning to ask if you . . .'

'Ask me what?'

'I have to get away from home, Mrs Wilson, I just have to. I'm not looking for a great deal or at least I don't think I am. A room and the use of kitchen or scullery where I can prepare a meal. I am domesticated, I can say that for myself. A room without attendance shouldn't cost too much, I can't afford a lot. Would you know of someone?' She was pleading.

'No one I can think of this moment.'

'No, of course not, I'm expecting too much. Please forgive me and forget about it. I know' – her face brightened with the beginnings of hope – 'an ad in the newspaper, why didn't I think of that before?'

'Just stop there, lass,' Mrs Wilson said sternly. 'You've sprung this on me without giving me a chance to think. Maybe I can help, but I need a little time.'

'Please, I shouldn't have asked, I had no right.'

'You had every right and what harm is there in asking? I'm fond of you, lass, and I'll do what I can. That doesn't mean I approve of what you are contemplating and you must promise me that you won't be hasty and do something you may regret. Do I have your promise?'

Lois nodded. The tears that wouldn't come when her father died were coming all too easily now. Little kindnesses brought a lump to her throat and at this moment she couldn't trust herself to speak without breaking down.

'I don't know the circumstances and there is no reason why I should, but you are a sensible lass. Whatever it is you have to put up with, another week or two won't make much difference.'

Lois didn't altogether agree with that, but she accepted there was sense in what Mrs Wilson was saying.

The housekeeper busied herself cutting an iced sponge into six and put a piece on a plate for Lois then got another plate from the dresser and took a piece for herself.

'That won't take much eating.'

'Thank you, Mrs Wilson, you are very kind.'

'It would be a sad day if we couldn't give a helping hand when it is needed.'

'Do I really have a chance of getting a room? In this district I mean?' The blue eyes were bright with unshed tears.

'Depends on you and what you are prepared to put up with.' The housekeeper smiled as she ate her sponge and saw that Lois was eating hers. She got up to fetch the teapot and top up their cups.

'Just about anything. Beggars can't be choosers.'

'You are not reduced to that.' She was silent, then nodded her head slowly. 'There is someone I have in mind but I'm not sure if it would work out.'

Lois's face lit up. 'You have someone in mind? What is she like?'

'Sharp-tongued and difficult.'

'I wouldn't mind that. I would be doing for myself and I wouldn't get in her way.'

'Would, would, would,' she smiled. 'Don't get carried away.'

'One more would.' Lois laughed. 'I would be careful to use the kitchen only when I was supposed to.'

'Lois, she isn't as difficult as I am making out and I happen to like her.'

'I shall too I'm sure. Do you really think she would consider me?'

'That I would have to find out.'

'You will put in a good word for me?' Lois said anxiously. 'Maybe she'll think I keep late hours just because I'm young.'

'Lois, it is quite possible that she will consider you too young in any case. You are, you know, very young to be leaving home.'

'I know and I can't blame people for thinking all the wrong things,' Lois said wretchedly. 'You aren't too sure about it yourself.'

'I must confess to not being too happy but I wouldn't put you down as an impulsive creature.' Mrs Wilson smiled kindly. 'So let's just say that you have a genuine grievance and you feel the need to get away for a while.'

For good, Lois thought, but she smiled and nodded. It was better to agree.

'You can rest assured I'll do my best for you if for no other reason than to stop you putting an ad in the newspaper. That can be a risky business especially for a young lass.'

Lois laughed. 'Mrs Wilson, I'm not as green as I look.'

'What you are is too trusting for your own good.'

Lois thanked Mrs Wilson and went back to the office and after clearing the dishes and tidying the kitchen Mrs Wilson put on her coat and hat. In case she decided to do some shopping she took her basket and her purse. The lady she had in mind didn't live far away and soon Mrs Wilson had reached the home of the spinster lady, Miss Rebecca Watt. Mrs Wilson and Miss Watt had met, strictly speaking, by accident. It had been one miserable January day when the roads were slushy with dirty wet snow and underneath lurked the menace of black ice. It had been foolish to venture out, Miss Watt knew that but she decided to risk it. Life was full of risks she told herself and this was a very small one. Step out, don't think about falling and you won't. Who had said that? Only the sure-footed surely. Miss Watt followed that advice and all went well to begin with. It was on her way back from the library where she had collected three books that she lost her footing, the heel of her shoe had come in contact with a lump of ice. Miss Watt fell, knees down making huge holes in her thick lisle stockings but still clutching her string bag and safeguarding the books which could have got soaked. Willing hands helped her to her feet, but it was Mrs Wilson who did that bit more and insisted on escorting her home and making quite sure that she was all right. The friendship had started then, they didn't meet regularly but every four weeks or so Mrs Wilson would receive a neatly penned note asking her to take tea on a specific afternoon.

'I do hope this is not inconvenient,' Mrs Wilson said as the daily woman showed her into the sitting-room where Miss Watt had been reading.

She put down the book and smiled. 'Not at all, I'm delighted to see you.'

'I really came to ask—'

'All in good time, Mrs Wilson, it's hot in here isn't it? Too hot for you I know but it is the way I like it. Take your coat off.'

'I'm not staying.'

'Long enough to tell me what you've come for.'

Mrs Wilson had to laugh at that. She took off her coat and put it over the back of her chair and went to sit in the chair at the other side of the fire from Miss Watt.

Mrs Wilson said what she had come to say and when she came to the end looked at Miss Watt who had remained silent and looked thoughtful. Then she sighed. 'Only eighteen and leaving home. Now why would she be doing that?'

'Problems.'

'Haven't we all? What kind of problems does this young woman have?'

'That I wouldn't know. I didn't enquire since it is none of my business,' Mrs Wilson said tartly.

'Could be mine though if she were to be living here.'

'That's true but I know Lois and you won't find a nicer girl.' She paused. 'From what I gather the trouble arose after Lois lost her father.'

'Recently?'

'Very recently. They were very close and this has been a dreadful blow for the girl. She and her mother never got on.'

'Mmmm. She works for John Latimer you say?'

'Yes, that is how I know her.'

'Is he satisfied?'

'More than satisfied. He considers her a find.'

'Does he now? Bonny is she?'

'As a matter of fact she is.'

'There you are then – a pretty face, that's all a man sees.' She sniffed. 'Have you time for a cup of tea?'

'No, thank you I have a bit of shopping to do on the way back.'

'Won't press you, not my way. What kind of job does this girl have with Mr Latimer?'

'Types his letters, the usual office work,' Mrs Wilson said vaguely as her eyes went to the grandfather clock sitting in the corner of the room. Miss Watt had noticed, she didn't miss much.

'Ten minutes fast, has been that this long while. To alter it would upset the chime or so I am led to believe. Very well, since it is for you I'll see this girl but no promises.'

'I wouldn't expect any. Just remember all she wants is a room and the occasional use of the kitchen.'

Miss Rebecca Watt looked very severe with her straight, thin grey hair scraped back and secured in a tight little knot. She was sixty-four years of age, tall and thin and enjoyed reasonably good health. Her features were sharp and she had a tongue to match but even so there was a kindliness and in times of trouble she would be a good friend to have. She hadn't always got on with her own mother and had some sympathy with Lois. The death of Miss Watt's sister, Sophie, two months previously had come as a shock and her sudden death was deeply felt. Although they had never been close they had been there for each other. The large family house became the property of the spinster sisters and being large they were able to live their independent lives.

Rebecca was reserved, studious and liked her own company. Sophie was smaller, gentler and liked company. They each had their own sitting-room. Sophie entertained friends in hers and Rebecca shared hers with her Siamese cat, her books and an assortment of newspapers and periodicals that kept her up-to-date with world affairs. If she felt particularly strongly about anything Rebecca would write to the editor of the newspaper. Occasionally she would praise a line he had taken but more often she would be disagreeing. Her views would be explained clearly and at some length and when a much reduced version of her letter appeared in print she would be furious and further angered if a sentence taken out of context altered the whole meaning.

Glenburn, her home, could have done with the services of a housekeeper or at the very least a live-in maid and some casual help. As it was a woman came in each day to clean the house and give instructions to another who did the heavy work.

It shouldn't have worried her, but it did. Rebecca feared the dark and was ashamed of her weakness. Sleep seldom claimed her before the small hours and she would lie awake watching the shadows on the ceiling and listening to the strange noises, the creakings and the groans that were so much part of an old house. No doubt the same happened during the day but went unheard. What after all is there to fear when daylight is streaming through the windows? Darkness is the time when fear takes hold and imagined terrors fill the mind.

Rebecca was gradually coming round to having a young girl in the house. She could see the advantages in so far as her own life was concerned. A resident housekeeper would make more demands since conversation at some level would be expected, and the woman could be a gossip. Rebecca shuddered at the thought. A young girl on the other hand would have no interest in an elderly woman. Two people under the same roof that is all it would be. When Sophie had been alive Rebecca had slept reasonably well and even when she didn't the night sounds didn't alarm her.

'Miss Watt won't be the easiest person to get on with.'

'I know, you've told me that.'

'I want to make sure you understand.'

Lois smiled. 'I won't blame you if it doesn't work out, if that is what you are afraid of.'

'It crossed my mind.'

'It is going to work out. I'm very lucky to be getting a room in Miss Watt's house and I'll be very careful.'

'In that case I'll cease worrying.'

'Please don't worry and I'm very grateful to you.' Lois took a deep breath. 'No matter how difficult Miss Watt proves to be she won't have the power to hurt me.'

'And you have been hurt, I can see that,' Mrs Wilson said gently.

'Yes, very badly hurt.' She paused, swallowed and began again. 'When I was younger I had no choice, I just had to put up with it.'

'And now you are doing something about it?'

'That's right I *am* doing something about it.'

It did surprise Mrs Wilson that Lois should be so unhappy at home but she was inclined to think that the girl was too sensitive, too quick to take offence. Over-sensitive people took to heart what others could shrug off and leaving home was a drastic step. On the other hand if things had got this bad then a short separation might be good for mother and daughter. A cooling off time to let them get things in perspective. There would be faults on both sides, there always were, but if they could bring themselves to talk about them the chances were that it could be sorted out. It made Mrs Wilson feel thankful that her own relationship with her mother had been so good. They had been friends as well as mother and daughter.

Not one who did much walking herself, Mrs Wilson encouraged it in others. As for herself she got enough running up and down stairs, reaching up, bending down and forever on the go. Office workers were a case in point, cooped up all day and sitting most of the time. Unless they did something about it, in the years to come they would pay the price. Lois was quite prepared to take the risk but gave in to pressure. Once lunch was over she was all but pushed out of the door to stretch her legs and get some fresh air into her lungs. These walks had certainly familiarised her with the immediate neighbourhood. Miss Watt's house, Glenburn, was number 36 Brownlea Road. A narrow lane led from Hillend Terrace to Brownlea Road and although she didn't recall seeing Glenburn she knew where she was going.

Giving her attention to the numbers, Lois walked along Brownlea Road until she came to number 36. It was hardly surprising she hadn't seen the name since it wasn't in evidence anywhere. The number was faded but at least she had been able to make that out.

Later Lois was to learn that years ago there had been a wooden sign attached to the gate but it had become unstuck and no one had bothered to have it replaced. There was no need. The postman, the grocery delivery man, the milkman and anyone else who mattered, knew that number 36 was Glenburn and that Glenburn was the home of the two spinster ladies, Miss Rebecca and Miss Sophie Watt. Sadly the gentle Miss Sophie had departed this world.

Lois stood in front of the house just looking at it and felt a flutter of excitement that this might be where she would be living. Glenburn was one of the smaller residences in this genteel neighbourhood though that didn't make it small. Lois counted seven chimney pots and seven chimney pots would mean seven rooms with a fireplace and she rather thought there would be one or two without. The stonework had darkened to a dull grey but it didn't detract but rather enhanced the house's appearance. The solid oak door was reached by rounded marble steps.

Lois had opened the gate and walked along the gravel path breathing in the air that was thick with the sweet smell of freshly cut grass, a smell she particularly liked. Through the shrubbery Lois made out two figures and a barrow. One man was doing the work, hoeing the ground while the other was leaning on his shovel and taking it easy. It was a peaceful scene on this quiet afternoon in late May with only the twittering of the birds and the distant hum of a car or a bus. The tramlines didn't come out this far.

Lois wore a light summer skirt and a lime green blouse with a white cardigan. She tried not to be nervous, told herself she wasn't, but so much depended on making a good impression. This was nothing like going for an interview for a job, yet to Lois it was just as important. A new, independent life could be ahead or a continuance of an existence that was becoming intolerable.

Working for John Latimer had given her much-needed confidence and in him she had found a friend. Once when she had been unaware of his scrutiny and he had seen the sadness in her expression, he had said quietly. 'Always remember, Lois, that no matter how long and hard the road we travel we do arrive at the end of it a wiser and stronger person.'

Lois was recalling those words of wisdom. Was she becoming wiser and stronger, she hoped so. Forcing herself to relax she put a smile on her face and gave the door knocker two sharp raps. She waited and waited and was about to follow those with another rap when the door opened and a flushed face appeared.

'Sorry if I kept you waiting. There are times you need two pairs of hands in this house,' she grumbled.

'I heard that Mrs Barlow.'

Lois looked in bewilderment from one to the other. Mrs Barlow was obviously the cleaning lady with her dark green overall and a dustcap on her head. The other lady was tall and thin with a long, sallow face and a sharp intelligent look in her grey eyes.

'I'm Lois Pringle.'

'That much I gathered since Mrs Wilson said to expect you this afternoon and I am not in the habit of entertaining young women.'

Lois smiled uncertainly. She was still on the doorstep.

'Do come in.' Then to Mrs Barlow. 'The steps could do with a wash wouldn't you say?'

'And when would I get the time to do that?'

'I accept it is not one of your duties. Where is Whatever-you-call-her?'

'One of her bairns is sick.'

'One of her bairns is always sick.'

'She'll try and come in tomorrow but I wouldn't bet on it.'

'Come along Miss Pringle we'll go along to my sitting-room.' Then over her shoulder, 'Employ someone else, Mrs Barlow, you have my authority.'

'As if I would dream of doing that. The poor soul needs the money and when she does put in an appearance she works hard.'

Miss Watt shrugged her shoulders as if giving up. Lois had an urge to giggle but kept her face straight as she followed the woman along the passage. Mrs Barlow shut the door with a bang and returned to her duties.

The hall and passageway were carpeted but it seemed faded like the wallpaper. Gleaming brass candlesticks and ornaments were crowded on a hall table and against the wall was a hallstand with an assortment of walking sticks and umbrellas. An ancient, dirty beige raincoat hung over a knob and a black felt hat was over another.

Miss Watt turned the brass knob of the door and ushered Lois in. Her first impression was of how old-fashioned it all was. There was a prickly horsehair sofa, lace antimacassars and a bearskin rug in front of the fire.

'Sit yourself down,' the woman said showing Lois where she could sit then sat down herself in a large plush chair. Her feet went on a beaded footstool and once comfortable she smiled at Lois. 'You will have to excuse that small exchange. Mrs Barlow is a gem though, of course, I would never say that to her face. She loves to grumble and contrary to what you might think I do not overwork my staff. I say staff which is rather ridiculous when I only employ Mrs Barlow and that woman with the sick bairn as well as two gardeners. Much of the house is unused so there isn't a tremendous amount of work.'

Lois nodded.

'Move back if the heat is too much for you.'

'This is fine but I'll take off my cardigan.' She slipped it off and put it over her knees. The room was very hot.

'Old bones have to be kept warm and though I am not all that old I do feel the cold and the sun will soon be away from this side of the house.'

It was like stepping into another age, Lois thought, as though life had gone on but the house had remained as always. Miss Watt hadn't moved with the times either. The dark grey skirt that reached almost to the ankles showed a glimpse of black patent leather boots. A high-necked blouse hid most of her scraggy neck. The blouse was ochre-coloured and had a cameo brooch pinned to it.

Lois hadn't noticed the Siamese cat until, disturbed from its slumbers it stretched and yawned then padded over to its mistress. With a graceful thump it landed squarely on her knees and Rebecca Watt scratched its fur and let it settle.

'Well, what do you think? You've had a good look round.'

Lois flushed. 'I'm sorry if I was rude.' She bit her lip. 'It wasn't intended.'

'I'm sure it wasn't.' She paused and there was a hint of a twinkle in her eyes. 'So far so good is that what you were thinking?'

Lois burst out laughing. 'Better than that.'

'Very different to what you have been used to?'

Lois wasn't sure as to how she should take that so she was careful.

'This is a lovely old house, Miss Watt, with a lot of charm. I come from a comfortable home but much smaller.'

'Yet you are prepared to leave it?'

'For personal reasons, yes, I am prepared to leave it.'

'Young as you are, you appear a sensible girl and I suppose you've thought this over very carefully.'

'I assure you I have.'

'Miss Wilson has acquainted you with my requirements?'

'Yes, she did. You want someone in the house overnight but otherwise you do not wish to be disturbed.'

'That is going a little too far I think. I value my privacy but I am not unapproachable.'

'My wish is to be independent, Miss Watt, and all I require is a room and the use of the kitchen to cook myself a meal. I would only use it sparingly—'

'Use what sparingly?'

'The – the kitchen,' Lois stumbled. 'I wouldn't overdo it and I have my main meal of the day with Mrs Wilson.'

Miss Watt pushed the cat down from her lap and smoothed her skirt.

'No problems there that I can see.'

'Miss Watt?'

'Yes?'

'Before this goes any further I should like to know what would be the charge for the room?'

'Not very much.'

'That is too vague, Miss Watt.' She smiled. 'Your not very much might not be the same as mine.'

'Shall we say . . .' Miss Watt pondered and then named a sum that was ridiculously small.

'I can afford more than that. The only reason I asked you to be precise was because I have to live within my means.'

'Very sensible of you, but I'll be quite satisfied with that.'

'Thank you, that is very good of you.'

'As a rule I don't talk about myself or my family, but if we are to live under the same roof you should be told a little. I am difficult, tetchy is how I heard myself described and I wouldn't dispute that. My sister, you did know that I had lost my sister?'

'Yes, Mrs Wilson told me. You must miss her.'

'I do, I miss her more than I ever would have thought. Sophie was a much nicer person than I am. We were chalk and cheese. Sophie liked company and I have always been a loner, perfectly happy with my own company. We had little in common and were seldom in each other's company yet when she was taken it was like losing part of myself. It took death to make me realise that Sophie had been an important part of my life. My dear, there must be a lesson there somewhere.'

There was such sadness in the voice that Lois felt a lump come into her throat.

'Mrs Wilson told me a little about you but only because I insisted on knowing why a young girl should be leaving a good home.'

'What is a good home, Miss Watt?' Lois asked.

'The answer to that should be where one is happy and contented.'

Why? Why? Why? Lois closed her eyes for a moment. Why couldn't people just accept her without demanding an explanation? She wasn't the first person to leave home and not the youngest. Miss Watt wasn't exactly demanding an explanation other than what she had already given, but she wasn't completely satisfied either.

'I'll try to explain. I was reasonably happy when my father was alive. We got on well and I know he loved me. My mother has no time for me and I don't know what I have done to deserve that. She would never give me any reason.'

'That was very wrong of her. Was she ever cruel to you?'

'Not in the sense I think you mean, but a form of cruelty for all that. My sisters came in for a lot of love but there was never any for me.'

'There is a reason for everything and one day, my dear, you will find out what it is your mother holds against you.'

'I think I am past caring.'

'Your father could not have been unaware of this.'

'He knew, it distressed him, but I don't think there was anything he could have done.'

Miss Watt wasn't so sure, but enough had been said on the subject and she got up stiffly. 'We'll go upstairs and I'll let you see what would be your bedroom. It was my sister's but all the bedding and her personal belongings have been removed. I thought it better to have that done right away and I'm glad I did. Mrs Barlow, sensible woman that she is, suggested the room could do with a freshen up, new wallpaper and paintwork done. It was an ideal time with so much taken up to the attics. I'm the last of the line and when I am called it is going to fall to some stranger to clear out the attics and believe me that will be some task. My mother wouldn't part with anything – you know the saying, keep something for seven years and you'll get a use for it. If that still holds after seventy-odd years, upstairs will be a treasure trove for someone. Will this do?'

Lois's eyes shone. 'Do? I think it is absolutely lovely.' And it was. The bed with its pink bedspread was too big to be a single and too small to be a double.

'That is a three-quarter bed,' Rebecca smiled anticipating the question.

'I didn't know there was such a thing.'

'Not very common or perhaps not very popular and I can't understand why. Some single beds, unless they are against the wall, are so narrow that one could very easily fall out.'

'You have one yourself?'

'Yes, I have one myself.'

The wardrobe was huge and there was a dressing-table with a triple mirror and a stool set before it. There were two winged chairs with soft cushions and pretty floral curtains at the window.

'If you've seen all you want we'll go downstairs. You go ahead I have to take my time. Once I could run up and downstairs just like you although running was frowned on in my day. Open that door facing you.'

Lois opened it.

'Go in.'

Miss Watt followed her into the room. 'My sister and I had our own sitting-rooms because Sophie liked to entertain and I preferred being on my own. You can have your friends in and perhaps I should ask if you have a boyfriend or should I say young man?'

Lois thought about Tim. She hadn't seen much of him of late and that had been her fault. Tim had done his best, but she had felt herself to be poor company and had declined most of his invitations. That was about to change she hoped. She did feel more able now to pick up the threads and Tim would have to be told about her leaving home.

'I wouldn't be inviting Tim here Miss Watt.'

'No reason why you shouldn't if you are prepared to obey the rules. I don't think I am being unreasonable when I say that you are at liberty to entertain your friends in the sitting-room but and I must emphasise this, no male friend to be in the house after ten thirty.'

'The only person I would ask into the house would be my young sister.'

'Just as you wish.'

'When may I come, Miss Watt?'

'As soon as you like. See Mrs Barlow about the arrangements. I'll talk it over with her and once she is fully in the picture you will find her very helpful.'

'I don't have to ask,' Mrs Wilson smiled, 'I can tell by your face that all went well.'

'All went very well. I like her, I really do.'

'Which means she must have taken a liking to you.'

'I hope so. Has Mr Latimer been in?'

'Briefly.'

'Oh dear, I hope he isn't annoyed with me.'

'Why should he be annoyed?'

'I've been away a long time.'

'You asked permission.'

'I know but he probably thinks I should have gone in my own time.'

'Which would not have suited Miss Watt. Stop worrying.'

Lois left Mrs Wilson and went to the office. Her work was well up-to-date but Mr Latimer had left some letters for her to type. On the top was a note. 'Hope you were successful. No hurry for these apart from the top one. J.L.'

She typed the letter and two others then tidied her desk and left. One minute she was desperate to be home with her news, then in the next she was dreading it. Silly really. She should be looking forward to this with satisfaction. Her mother couldn't stop her leaving home even if she wanted to. She was old enough to be in charge of her own life and she would tell her that if she put forward any objections.

A sprint to the bus stop was wasted, the bus moved off before she could reach it and she had to cool her heels for fourteen minutes before the next one arrived. She hurried from the bus to the house knowing that Winnie would be holding back the meal until she arrived. It was two main meals in the day but Winnie knew to give her a small helping.

Had Lois not been in such a hurry and glanced down the street she would have seen and recognised the car and been prepared.

Chapter Ten

She went in quickly closing the door behind her. Laughter was coming from the sitting-room which must mean they had taken their meal without waiting for her. Lois didn't much care, she wasn't very hungry.

Opening the door she was taken aback to see Tim and Marie sitting together on the sofa and enjoying some private joke. Her mother was nearby and she too looked amused. As Lois was to find out later it was all perfectly innocent but keyed-up as she was it didn't look that way to her.

Tim got quickly to his feet. 'Lois, we didn't hear you coming in.'

'That much I gathered,' she said icily.

Marie tittered and her mother muttered something about helping Winnie.

Tim could see that something had upset Lois but even so there was no excuse for that. What on earth had he done? Damned if he knew.

'I came straight here after work because I thought we could go out and have a meal. I was sure your mother wouldn't mind if I took you away,' Tim said coldly.

Before Lois could answer Harriet had come back into the room.

'Tim, dear, I've just checked in the kitchen and Winnie assures me there is plenty to go round so please do stay and share the meal with us.'

Not if I can help it, Lois said to herself. It was the very last thing she wanted. She needed to apologise to Tim and explain her odd behaviour.

'No, Mum, thank you but no.' It was very firmly said.

'Tim can speak for himself,' Harriet said tartly.

'It is really very kind of you, Mrs Pringle, but Lois and I have a lot to say to each other—'

'Do your talking after the meal.' Marie wanted Tim to stay, he was good company. 'We'll promise to leave you in peace and where, tell me that, are you going to get served at this time? It is too late for high tea and too early for dinner,' Marie said knowledgeably. 'And,' she added for good measure, 'you aren't dressed to go anywhere special unless you change.'

Lois hadn't given a thought to her appearance.

'She's dressed to go anywhere,' Winnie stormed at her sister. 'Lois can wear anything and get away with it which is more than you can.'

'What a cheek!'

'Girls! Girls! Tim, do excuse them. Three girls together can be the limit. A brother would have helped to calm them down but sadly I wasn't blessed with a son.'

Tim had Lois firmly by the arm.

'Thank you very much, Mrs Pringle, you have been very kind and I do apologise for holding up the meal and Winnie –' she looked over – 'that was an excellent cup of coffee.'

'Was it? I'm glad, I don't get much practice and Mum that is the last of the Camp coffee.'

There was a small silence. Andrew had liked his cup of coffee but Harriet had thought there was little point in buying another jar since they all preferred tea. Marie had tried and failed to acquire a taste for coffee though she pretended to like it when she was dining out.

'Yes, dear, I know and I'll see about it and Tim if I can't persuade you to stay this time you must come some other evening.'

'Thank you, I'll be happy to do that.'

Lois couldn't help but see the look of envy on Marie's face. It made her feel sorry for Stephen, he deserved better.

When the door was closed Tim hurried her down the path. 'Come on, darling, I'm starving and I hope you are too.'

'I might be if I thought about it.' She wasn't hungry but she thought she would manage to eat something.

'Then think about it.' He laughed. 'And don't worry, Marie is quite wrong, there are plenty of places very willing to produce a meal at any time.'

'Some place quiet. I'm sorry I should have taken time to change.'

'Nonsense you look cool and pretty.'

The place Tim chose was well off the beaten track and was two small cottages that had been made into a tea-room. As well as afternoon teas they served cooked meals on request. It meant waiting but it was worthwhile when it arrived.

Tim made no reference to her odd behaviour until they were seated then he leaned over the table and took her hands in his. There were no other customers and the elderly waitress bustling about paid them little attention.

'Now what was that all about?'

'I'm very, very sorry,' she said sheepishly.

'I should think so too. What a way to treat me. There I was waiting for you to come and when you did—'

'Tim, I apologise and I apologise again. There was a lot on my mind – actually if you really want to know – I was going to get in touch—'

'You were? I'm very glad to hear it,' he said softly and pressing her hand.

'Then seeing you there I was so taken aback. I mean it was such a shock to see you sitting beside Marie and laughing together as if—'

'As if what?'

'Nothing.' She hung her head. 'I thought, you see, that you'd come to see Marie and not me.'

'For an intelligent girl you can be very silly.'

She nodded.

'Lois, my darling little idiot, get this into your head once and for all. I am in love with you—'

'Are you? You've never said that before.'

'Of course I have and I've shown it in dozens of ways.'

'You've never said the actual words before,' she insisted.

'Then I am saying them now.' His voice dropped but the words were clear, 'I love you, Lois, today, tomorrow and for ever.'

A lovely smile came over her face. 'Tim, you are a dear.'

'Is that all you can say? How about you saying those words to me?'

'I think I love you, Tim.' She saw his face cloud. 'I'm almost sure I do,' she added and wondered what was holding her back from a total commitment.

'Then I suppose I'll have to be content with that meantime. As to Marie, to put your mind at rest, I like her and I like Winnie and there is no harm in liking is there?'

'None at all.' She paused. 'Tim, I have something important to tell you.' She broke off and they both leaned back as the waitress arrived with the cutlery and began to set the table.

'I'm all ears,' he whispered when they were alone.

'This is not the least bit funny, it's serious. I'm leaving home, I've taken a room, renting one, in a large house owned by a Miss Watt. It's only a stone's throw from the office which makes it very convenient.'

'You can't do that, Lois.' Tim sounded horrified.

'Why can't I?'

'Because – look, Lois, be reasonable. I gather you and your mother are not hitting it off just now—'

'You have a short or perhaps convenient memory,' Lois said coldly. 'I told you before that we have never got on.'

'I know that and I hadn't forgotten. Lois, you aren't the only one, it happens in other families too.'

'I doubt it.'

'It does and those concerned learn to live with it. It is a case of ignoring what you don't want to hear.'

She shook her head in bewilderment. 'I'm wasting my breath, you will never understand. My mother appears to you to be a perfectly reasonable person and she is – to everyone but me.'

'And what has Mrs Pringle to say about you leaving home?'

The waitress arrived with their meal – grilled lamb chops sprinkled with chopped parsley that looked very appetising. They were served with potatoes and vegetables and the dishes left on the table should they wish more. A jug of water arrived with two glasses.

'Not another word, Lois, until we eat this. Another five minutes and I think I would have collapsed in a heap on the floor.'

Lois laughed and the tension was broken. The chops were tender and she surprised herself suddenly finding her appetite.

'Everything to your satisfaction?' The stout woman in the white apron who may well have been the cook came to ask.

'Delicious,' Tim said. 'Lovely,' Lois added.

Tim helped himself to more potatoes. 'Now that we are both feeling better tell me what Mrs Pringle had to say to this.'

'She doesn't know. I was all prepared to tell her this evening—'

'Ah! And I put paid to that?'

'Yes, I'm afraid you did.' Had it not been for you it would have been all over, she thought and wished it were.

'She is going to be very upset and shocked too.'

'If she is upset it won't be for the reason you are thinking. My contribution to the household expenses will be missed and the assistance I give in other ways.'

'I never thought you could be so hard.'

Lois didn't like to hear herself described as hard. She didn't think she was; in fact she was sure she wasn't.

'Since you disapprove so strongly I can hardly ask for your assistance.'

'That was uncalled for,' he said stiffly. 'Of course I'll help you in any way I can. All I was doing was trying to talk some sense into you but I accept that I have failed there. I truly believe that you'll rue the day as the saying goes.'

'Maybe I will and maybe I won't but this is my life, Tim, and I have the right to make my own decisions.'

'Fair enough and now tell me where I come in?'

'Transferring my belongings if that isn't too much to ask?'

'Nothing is too much to ask if it is going to help, Lois,' he said quietly, then they both looked up with a smile to decline a pudding.

'Tea and perhaps home-made scones and pancakes?' the woman suggested hopefully.

'Lois?'

'No, thank you.'

Tim smiled. 'I'll take the bill when you are ready.'

'Thank you, sir.' She turned away.

Tim leaned forward. 'Tell me, Lois, when is this move or is that not yet decided?'

'This weekend.'

'As soon as that?'

'The sooner the better.' Lois fell silent thinking of what lay ahead.

It was going to be uncomfortable for them all. How would they take her news, sprung on them like this? To wait until tomorrow with a sleepless night between was too much. She had to get it over tonight and Tim would understand. Poor Tim was having to do a lot of understanding and she wouldn't blame him if he was getting rather tired of it.

She wiped her lips with the napkin and put it on her plate. 'Tim, would you mind terribly if I asked you to drive me straight home?'

'No, I wouldn't because I saw it coming. This is weighing on your mind and you want it over?'

'Yes, I do and, Tim, I promise to be better company after this.'

'Of course you will and, incidentally, my mother wants to meet you and she suggested I bring you on Sunday, but I take it that is out of the question?'

'I'm afraid so but do thank your mother and tell her how sorry I am. Perhaps another time if she is kind enough to ask me.'

'Of course, she'll understand and I'll explain without telling her you're flying the nest.'

'I won't mind if you do.'

'All the same I won't.'

'You really expect me to go crawling back?' He heard the anger in her voice.

'No, Lois, you won't crawl, but you may still want to go home and if so don't let pride hold you back from admitting you made a mistake.'

What was the use? she thought despairingly.

Tim dropped her at the gate and she went in by the back door to find Harriet alone in the house.

'You are back early,' her mother said looking up from her sewing.

'Yes, I wanted to come home, I have something important to tell you.'

Harriet felt her heart drop like a stone. This was it. Tim had proposed and Lois was to be engaged before Marie. How was she going to bear it?

'Mum, don't you want to hear what I have to say?'

'What do you have to say?'

'I'm leaving home.'

'You are what?'

'I'm leaving home, I'm going to live elsewhere.'

Harriet's first feeling was of such relief that she had to check the sigh. There was no engagement and come to think about it, had it been that, wouldn't they have both come in? As for this nonsense about leaving home she would soon settle that.

'So you are considering leaving home?' She raised her eyebrows.

'No, I have been considering it for a long time but now I have done something about it.'

Harriet was taken aback and momentarily lost for words. She folded up her sewing and put it in the needlework box, the small activity giving her a chance to recover.

'You have somewhere to go?'

'Yes.'

'When do you propose removing yourself?'

'This weekend.'

Harriet lost some colour. 'This weekend,' she repeated.

'Yes. Tim will help me transport my belongings.'

'As a matter of interest might I be told why this is happening now? Is there any significance in the timing?'

'No. I just feel I have had enough.' They were talking calmly, no raised voices. To an onlooker they could have been discussing the weather. Lois was amazed at how calm she sounded when she was anything but. Her hands were held tightly together to stop them shaking and her stomach was churning with nerves. Why she should be in this state she didn't know.

'I see.'

'A long time ago I stopped wondering why it was that you disliked me so. I've just come to accept it.'

'That is ridiculous, all in your imagination.' Her face had gone paler.

'No, I didn't imagine any of it.'

'You don't care whom you hurt.'

Lois gave an incredulous laugh. 'That's rich coming from you.'

'So I am to blame am I?'

'Yes, who else could I blame? You are the one who has made my life miserable. Once you get over the shock you'll be happy not to have me around.'

'Putting aside questions of gratitude and family feeling there are going to be a few eyebrows raised.'

'Then let them be raised.'

'This won't do your reputation any good.'

'I don't follow, perhaps you should explain yourself.'

'Very well. Your two sisters are perfectly content at home.'

'So they should be, you look after them very well. You mean, of course, that people will think that I should be contented too?'

'Yes. If I were you, Lois, I would think about that, it deserves serious consideration.'

'I can't believe you are pleading with me to stay?'

'Hardly, but I do feel some responsibility for your welfare.'

'You amaze me, Mum, do you know that?' Her eyes flashed. 'You have never been concerned with my welfare, in fact you wouldn't shed a tear if you never saw me again. If I'm missed at all by you it will be for the money I brought into the house. Marie doesn't part with much and she's always got away with it. Maybe that will have to change. With Dad gone,' her voice wobbled, 'you could be a bit strapped for cash.'

'I'll manage or rather we'll manage.' Harriet's head went higher and it was that small proud gesture that was nearly Lois's undoing. She would have welcomed anger, she had expected that. How absurd to feel like crying and Lois got up quickly and went over to the window to look out at the familiar scene. Soon she would be looking out at another garden and that too would in time become familiar.

'Yes, I expect you will,' Lois said quietly without turning round. Then she walked out of the room.

'Lois, come back please,' her mother called after her, 'I don't think we have quite finished.'

Lois came slowly back into the room.

'Sit down, no point in standing.'

Lois sat down in the chair and waited.

'No one would believe you if you suggested to them that I treated you badly.'

'I know that, you have been very clever. Dad knew though and he tried in his own way to make up for it by giving me more attention and you resented that. Marie never notices anything because she is so taken up with herself but Winnie isn't so blind.'

'You have had a good Christian home.'

'Far from it. You ruined my childhood and though it is unchristian to say it I can never forgive you. I have lived in a comfortable house but it was never a home to me because the woman who calls herself my mother deprived me of my rightful share of her love.'

'I never ill-treated you. How dare you suggest I did.'

'Not in the physical sense but you virtually ignored my existence which is as bad or perhaps worse.'

'Marie and Winnie would never speak to me like this.'

'Why should they? They had nothing to complain about. You have been a good mother to them. I didn't ask much, just to be treated the same.' Lois smiled. 'You are not a violent person but even if you had been the marks of physical cruelty fade and are gone but the scars of mental cruelty remain. I have battled with those and I am winning. In years to come you may have cause to regret all this because I would have been a good daughter to you and if you had ever been in need I would have come running.'

'I don't need you. I have Marie and Winnie.' She was breathing heavily. 'And now are you quite finished?'

'You called me back and since you did I'll have my final say. If I am blessed with children of my own they will be treated exactly the same. No favouritism. We are all human and it may be that deep down I will find I have more love for one child than another. That will be my secret and no one will ever be the wiser. My children will be happy because I will make sure they are.'

The door opened noisily and Winnie came in. Harriet was glad of the interruption. Lois's wounding words had gone deep especially as every word she had spoken was the truth.

'Winnie, I did not hear that lock click,' she said severely.

'I know I left the door open for Marie. She's just coming. What were you two discussing? It sounded very serious.'

'It will keep until Marie comes in,' Harriet said in clipped tones.

'Nothing wrong is there?' Winnie asked anxiously.

'All in good time, dear.'

'What is all in good time?' Marie said, making straight for the mirror and patting her hair into place.

'Did Stephen muss it about?' Winnie grinned.

Marie didn't bother to answer.

'Get your coats off both of you then come and sit down,' Harriet said tiredly. 'Did you have a nice evening, Marie?'

'All right, I suppose.'

'Is that all?' Winnie opened her eyes wide. 'Getting tired of poor Stephen are you?'

'If you think he would ever look at you, you have a hope.'

'Stop it. I'm getting very tired of the way you two behave.'

'Sorry,' Winnie mumbled. She sat down and a moment or two later Marie did the same.

'Lois has given me her news, now she can tell you yourself.'

Winnie sprang up and gave an astonished Lois a bearlike hug. 'You are engaged? Tim popped the question?'

'No, Winnie, I am not engaged, it is nothing like that. I'm leaving home, that is what this is all about.'

Marie laughed incredulously. 'You leave home, what a joke. Where on earth would you go?'

'Never mind that,' Winnie said sounding distressed. 'You don't mean it, Lois?'

'I'm afraid I do, Winnie.'

'But why?'

'Because I am not happy living here.'

'I've never made you unhappy?'

'No, and I'm going to miss you.'

'You aren't suggesting I am to blame?' Marie said looking bewildered. 'Honestly Tim and I were just larking.'

'I know that, Marie. I snapped because I was on edge and if Tim hadn't been there you would have been told at the table.'

'If it isn't Winnie and it isn't me—'

'It's Mum. We need space between us. We'll get on better apart.'

'Oh, I see, a temporary estrangement,' Marie said with a knowing nod of the head.

'No, not temporary, once I go I won't be back.'

'Not even to visit,' Winnie said tearfully.

'No, but I hope you will come and see me.'

'Where are you going? Is it fixed?' Marie wanted to know.

'Yes, all fixed. I've got a room to rent with a Miss Watt. She has a large house in Brownlea Road which is very near to where I work.'

'You are going to live with a spinster lady,' Marie said scornfully.

'In her house but we are unlikely to see much of each other. Her sister died recently and Miss Watt wants someone in the house.'

'To keep her company?'

'You couldn't be more wrong. Had she wanted a companion she would have advertised for one. She likes her own company and that suits me. I can come and go as I please.'

For a moment Marie was envious. No one to ask questions of where one had been or where one was going. Then she thought of doing for herself and knew the life wasn't for her.

'She'll be back, Mum. I give her a month then she'll come crawling home. That's what you are thinking too, isn't it?'

But Harriet was strangely silent.

'I won't be back, Marie.'

'Lois, change your mind, please, just for me,' Winnie pleaded.

'I can't, Winnie, and you of all people should understand.'

'What should she understand?'

'Winnie knows how it has been with Mum and me. She's more observant than you.'

'Thanks very much. And I'm not so blind as you like to think. You didn't like it because I am Mum's favourite but what about you? You were Dad's.'

'And me, am I anybody's?'

'You don't count, infant.'

'Perhaps I was Dad's favourite, Marie, but he never made it obvious, he wouldn't have done that. Dad was kind and he would never have willingly hurt anyone. Mum, on the other hand, made it crystal clear that she had no time for me.'

'Mum, why do you let her get away with saying that about you?'

'It's true, she can't deny it.'

Harriet's face was expressionless as she looked at Lois.

'Enough has been said. Lois has made up her mind to go and as far as I am concerned she has made her bed, now she can lie in it.'

Lois burst out laughing and they all looked at her.

'I'm sorry,' she said smothering her mirth, 'it was just the mention of a bed that did it. I'm getting a three-quarter bed.'

'What on earth is that?' Winnie asked.

'It is not so very unusual,' Harriet said. 'Some folk find a single bed too narrow and double bed too big that is why three-quarter beds were introduced. They weren't a success, not in the trade, and very few are made today. And now, Lois, before I retire to my bed perhaps you would be good enough to inform me of your arrangements,' she said coldly.

'Certainly. Tim is coming over on Saturday afternoon to take my clothes and the rest of my belongings to Brownlea Road.'

'Fine. I'll make a point of being out of the house at that time.'

'Thank you, that would be best,' Lois said gratefully.

Lois had never been so glad to get to her bed. She wished that it was all over and she was settled in Brownlea Road. She was dead beat, the events of the evening had left her drained. Winnie wouldn't give her peace, she was too upset to be silent and asked the same questions over and over again. Eventually Lois feigned sleep and only opened her eyes to the darkness when she heard the deep, steady breathing from the other bed.

Lois wasn't the only one lying awake. Through the wall Marie was tossing and turning. Her own life wasn't going smoothly and there was no one she could turn to and, even if there had been, what could she have said? Her mother would be horrified and take steps to remove the threat if she even suspected. After the bitterness of their quarrel Harry Lindsay had kept his distance. He had called her a gold-digger to her face and taken up with other girls but he had quickly tired of them. Marie, with all her faults, was the girl he loved and he was sure that she loved him and not Stephen Hammond.

Harry was a bank clerk, an intelligent boy two years older than Marie and he was ambitious. The light burned late at night while he studied for the exams that would lead to advancement. If Marie became engaged to Hammond he would put in for a transfer, he had made up his mind about that. Edinburgh would be his choice and promotion might come all the sooner if he managed to get into the head office. Meantime he hadn't quite given up his chances with Marie.

As for Marie she had got to the stage that when she came out of the shop she had a look to see if he was lurking about in some entry waiting for her. She knew he was deliberately tormenting her and she had stormed at him and pretended to be annoyed when secretly she was pleased but anxious. Anxious that Stephen or her mother would find out. Stephen was becoming tiresome. He was too ardent and pretending something she didn't feel was becoming a strain. Marie wondered for how much longer she could go on this way. It wasn't that she found Stephen repulsive, far from it, but the remembered excitement of being with Harry kept intruding. Still, she kept reminding herself, wasn't it a small price to pay for a life of luxury and the Hammond name?

Chapter Eleven

Marie worked all day on Saturday and Harriet had gone out after lunch leaving Winnie and Lois in the house. Winnie was doing her best to be helpful but breaking down in tears every little while.

'Winnie, I'm only going to be a bus ride away, I'm not going to the other side of the world.'

'It won't be the same.'

'I know that,' Lois said softly, 'but nothing stays the same. The three of us are grown-up and maybe before long you'll want a change yourself.'

'Some hope of that. Marie will get married to Stephen and you to Tim and I'll be left here with Mum.'

Lois sat down on the bed and drew Winnie over beside her.

'I can't advise you and I wouldn't even attempt it in case it turned out to be the wrong advice. What I am doing feels right for me and you'll know when the time comes what is best for you.'

'You're not only my sister, you're my friend.'

'That isn't going to change, why should it?'

Winnie nodded, gave a sniff and used the back of her hand to wipe her eyes. 'Believe it or not, Lois, but Mum is very upset about this.'

'I'm glad, it might make her think back.'

'Can't you forgive her? She could be sorry and not able to say so.'

'No, Winnie, if she is upset at all it isn't at me departing – she'll miss the money coming in that's all.'

'Are we going to be hard up?'

'Not exactly hard up, at least I don't think so, but you might have to be more careful.'

'No extravagances?'

'That's right.'

'Perhaps it is time I looked for a job.'

'Would you like that?'

'I might, but what kind of job could I get?'

'Nothing unless you make some effort.'

'Meaning I'm lazy?'

'Meaning you need to take yourself seriously.'

'I'd still like to work with children,' Winnie said thoughtfully.

'Then start looking. Mum is perfectly capable of looking after herself and she can resign from some of those committees and do a bit more in the house. It wouldn't do her any harm to sacrifice something.'

'She won't though.'

Lois got off the bed. 'On your feet, Winnie Pringle. Come on, there's work to do. I haven't emptied my wardrobe yet.'

'Some of my clothes can go in.'

'That's right, you can spread yourself.'

A few minutes after two, Tim arrived with a large suitcase and a Gladstone bag.

'Tim, how very thoughtful of you. You know this, you're wonderful,' she smiled and they kissed lightly.

'I know and I'm glad you know it too.'

'It was completely out of character for Lois to be demonstrative in front of anyone but she was just so happy to see Tim. She threw her arms around him and hugged him.

'All that for bringing a suitcase and a bag,' he teased. 'Had I known I would have piled a lot more into the car.'

'This will do very nicely, thank you.' She had needed to feel his strength, his strong, comforting arms around her. Without Tim she would be very much alone.

Perhaps Tim knew that. 'Seriously, are you all right?' His eyes were anxious.

'Yes, I am, I'm fine, just a bit excited. I've got butterflies in my stomach.'

'You'll get over that. How is the packing going and is your assistant pulling her weight?' He hadn't meant to use the word weight and waited for a cutting reply. But Winnie ignored it or hadn't noticed. He saw her forlorn expression.

'Winnie has been marvellous – I don't know what I would have done without her. Tim, I'm so glad you brought that case and bag, I seem to have masses of stuff I'd forgotten I possessed.'

'Dump what isn't worth taking.'

'Typical of a man. I couldn't do that. Everything seems to have some – some—'

'Some memory?'

'Yes. I remember the little trinkets Dad gave me and the birthday gifts from Marie and Winnie.'

'You don't have to bother with those,' Winnie said.

'I want to take them.'

'Much room where you are going?'

'Plenty of it. There is a huge wardrobe, twice the size of mine and lots of deep drawers.'

'No problem then. Pile them into the car and sort them out in your own time.'

Sharing a bedroom with Winnie when they were younger had been fine. They were company for each other, but space was becoming a problem. It would be lovely, she had to admit, to have a room to herself and Winnie, once she got over the parting, would appreciate the extra space.

'Winnie! Winnie! Winnie! Don't stand there looking like a wet Sunday, make yourself useful and take that down to the car,' Tim ordered putting a cardboard box of books in her arms.

'Typical, I get the heaviest.'

'Of course.' He patted her bottom. 'Move, sweetheart.'

She laughed. 'I'll be away to a shadow. Is this the last?'

'Just about,' Lois said smiling to both of them.

Winnie came back into the house. 'Lois, I'd like to see where you are going to live. May I come? Mum won't be back until evening and I'm not doing anything.'

'I don't think—' Lois began.

'Of course you must come. Not much room I admit but if you don't mind sitting with something on your knees we'll manage.'

'I won't mind that not one little bit,' she said happily.

'And Winnie?'

'What?'

'Put something pretty on, I'm taking you both out for dinner.' He wiped his brow as if exhausted. 'We deserve it I think.'

Winnie positively glowed. 'Thanks, Tim, thank you very, very much.' She would put on her new pale green skirt and green and white blouse. Marie said accordion pleats with her hips was a mistake but she didn't care, she felt good in it.

When Winnie went upstairs to change Lois looked at Tim gratefully. 'I felt awful leaving her on her own and that was just so kind of you.'

'Well, the poor kid looked so miserable.'

At last everything was packed away in the boot and on one side of the back seat. Winnie didn't have anything on her knees after all and she was glad about that. She didn't want her new skirt creased and Tim had whistled when he saw her and said she looked great.

'Would you mind waiting in the car for me. I'll only be five minutes.'

'Why? What have you forgotten?'

'Nothing, Winnie, I just want to say goodbye to Laurelbank,' Lois said awkwardly.

'On you go, darling.'

She smiled. Tim understood.

Lois went back indoors and looked about her. Memories came flooding back and her throat felt tight. This, in all probability, would be the last time she would set foot in her old home. The good memories, the happy times would go with her but the others would remain behind. She must make sure they did.

Last night before sleep came she had gone over her life and tears had squeezed slowly out of her eyes as the more painful of the memories surfaced. She must put on a brave face but Lois was finding it hard and rather frightening to prepare herself for the next phase. There was no turning back. She had chosen this way.

Now she was looking at the past, at her father's chair. No one had dared sit in it when he was alive and no one did now that he was gone, no one in the family that is. It wasn't a shrine – it was Dad's chair, shabby and stained with tobacco marks. Harriet had wanted to replace it but Andrew had been adamant that it remained. Lois's lips twitched as she looked at the pink sofa. Her father had hated it, calling it a monstrosity that shouldn't have been given house room. Harriet had been tempted by the bargain but later had regretted her purchase. It had been a bargain that had turned out to be anything but. Nevertheless it was a good sofa, well made and with strong springs. It could be re-covered but by the time that was seriously considered, the bright pink had faded to a rather pretty shade of rose pink and they were all used to it.

Her father had not been a handyman, he hadn't the patience for it, but Harriet had been all for him trying his hand at wallpapering the sitting-room. In the end it would have been cheaper and easier on tempers to get in the decorator. All might have gone well if only Harriet had chosen a plain wallpaper or one that did not require matching. Unfortunately she had got carried away with a lovely patterned paper and did not foresee problems.

Andrew, frustrated and wearied of it all had exploded in temper, his language was not fit to be heard by the family and the girls were kept well out of the way. Harriet was handy with a brush and made a good job of the paintwork. The wallpaper was badly matched, but no one commented, no one dared. His wife had the furniture rearranged to hide the worst parts. If Andrew had been spared a decorator was to be engaged in the spring to paper and paint the sitting-room. Lois wondered if her mother would ever get around to it or if when Marie got married she would move to a smaller, easier to manage house with Winnie.

'Goodbye, Laurelbank,' Lois said softly and picking up her coat she went out, locked the door and made sure it was secure. Then she ran down the path to the car.

'That's the worst over, darling,' Tim said giving her knee a squeeze.

'Yes, I think that is the worst over.'

Tim started up the car. 'Tell me this address again.'

'Miss Watt, Miss Rebecca Watt, 36 Brownlea Road.'

'Muirford,' Winnie added. 'Do you know how to get there, Tim?'

'Yes, Winnie, I do, I know the district. A very good friend of mine has a veterinary practice in Oakfield Road which I understand is quite near.'

'Tim, Miss Watt has a cat, a Siamese.'

'Then the beast might well be known to David. His customers or clients or whatever they call themselves, are mostly elderly women and children.' He grinned. 'When it comes to hamsters and tortoises he is an expert.'

'Remember our tortoise, Lois? It didn't live long.'

'And we wept oceans, I remember that.'

'Small children arrive with their pets and put all their faith in David.'

'Quite a responsibility,' Lois murmured.

Tim waited until he had manoeuvred a sharp bend then he added. 'The worst part of his work, he says, is when he has to put a much-loved pet to sleep.'

'He sounds very nice this friend of yours, I look forward to meeting him.'

'Must arrange that. Is this spinster lady one of those finicky types who cannot bear to see anything out of place?'

'No, she is not like that and don't describe her as a spinster lady.'

'Why not? She's unmarried. How about unclaimed treasure, is that better?'

'Worse.'

Winnie spoke from the back sea. 'If I decide against getting married I would call myself a bachelor lady or bachelor girl.'

Tim hooted with laughter.

'Well, you have to agree it is better than old maid or spinster. They sound like somebody on their last legs whereas a bachelor sounds young and carefree.'

'So often the case, Winnie.'

'Men are so smug,' Lois laughed.

Lois had a set of keys for her new home, though she didn't expect to use them. Mrs Barlow's hours were flexible to suit both she and her employer. Sometimes she took Saturday afternoons off but not this one. She would be there to welcome Lois.

She had the front door open and stood in her green overall but minus the dustcap. Lois hurried along the path towards her.

'Mrs Barlow, do you want us to go round the back?'

'No, why should you do that? This is easier. You have help-ers I see?'

'My sister and Tim.'

'Your young man I take it?'

Lois blushed. 'Yes.'

'Bring everything up,' Mrs Barlow called to Tim and Winnie. She had a very carrying voice.

When they arrived Lois made the introductions.

'Where would you like me to put these, Mrs Barlow?' Tim asked. He picked up two cases and waited for instructions.

'Upstairs, I'll lead the way and I needn't go empty-handed.' She took up the Gladstone bag and had a good look at it. 'My father had one of these, held such a lot and they never go done. Last a lifetime and more.'

Mrs Barlow left them saying Lois had enough help and she would see her later.

'This is huge,' Winnie said gazing about her. 'It's old-fashioned and sort of grand.'

'Gracious living and big enough for a dance,' Tim said surprising Lois and twirling her round the room while managing to avoid the boxes.

'Stop it, Tim, you'll have me dizzy.'

'Out of condition, too much sitting in the office and not enough exercise.'

'Speak for yourself, I'm as fit as you are.' She flopped into the chair. 'Tim, if you want away, please go. Winnie and I will soon sort out this lot.'

'I'll take you at your word. When shall we say? Six thirty, seven, or later?'

'Between half past six and seven would be lovely.'

'Don't know where we'll get in but I'll see what I can fix up.'

'Lois, I think Tim is marvellous and I just hope you appreciate him. Sometimes I wonder if you do.'

Lois looked at her sharply. 'Why do you say that?'

'I could be wrong and maybe you do appreciate him. You don't fall over people the way Marie does and that's good but maybe you should show your feelings more.'

'I can't help the way I'm made.'

'No, and it's same with me. Do I empty these boxes?'

'Yes, please. There is a cupboard I can put the empty boxes in for the time being. Tim can take away his suitcase and bag.'

'Is this bedroom and sitting-room combined?'

'It could be but Miss Watt wants me to make use of the sitting-room her sister had.'

'You mean they didn't sit around together?'

'Not because they didn't get on, they did, but they were very different. The one who died was fond of company and Miss Watt prefers her own. She isn't anti-social but she told me she likes her books and does a bit of writing.'

'With her cat for company.'

'Yes. I don't know whether it is a he or a she but it had a very disdainful look on its face when I saw it. I don't think it took to me.'

'Give it time. Mrs Barlow seems nice enough.'

'She is. Hasn't she got lovely hair? Last time I saw her it was hidden by a dustcap.'

'Yes, I noticed, a sort of bronze colour and those waves have to be natural.'

'I'm sure they are.'

'A waste.'

'Why?'

'I bet she doesn't appreciate having such gorgeous hair. You don't appreciate your good appearance but then I suppose you don't notice, you just get used to it.'

The owner of the beautiful hair came in.

'My, but you haven't been long in squaring things up,' she said looking about her approvingly.

'I've still some tidying up to do.'

'No hurry. Miss Watt would like a few minutes when you're ready.'

'I'll wait here,' Winnie said.

'No, you've to go along too. I'll make a cup of tea, you'd like that?'

'No, thank you, Mrs Barlow, Tim is coming to take us out for a meal. He's coming some time after six thirty.'

'You can still drink a cup of tea. Miss Watt has had hers and I'll put a tray in what is to be your sitting-room. Moving house is thirsty work.'

'Come in,' Miss Watt called. She was on her feet when they went in. 'Welcome to your new home, my dear.'

'Thank you,' Lois said, suddenly shy.

'And you'll be the young sister?' she said to Winnie.

'Yes, Miss Watt, this is Winnie.'

'You don't look like sisters but then Sophie and I didn't look the least bit alike either. My mother used to say that if we hadn't been born at home she would have been convinced there had been a mix-up.' She smiled. 'Not very likely but then again not impossible. Nurses have been known to make mistakes. Do sit down both of you.'

They sat together on the horsehair sofa.

'Lois takes after our Dad, Miss Watt, and Marie and me – I mean Marie and I take after Mum.' She flushed crimson.

'Me or I, honestly does it make the slightest difference just as long as we make clear what we mean?'

Winnie smiled with relief. She was beginning to like this old lady. She wasn't nearly as forbidding as she appeared.

'Lois is the brainy one. Marie is—'

'Winnie?' Lois said warningly.

'It's all right I was only going to say that she isn't very bright like me, but in her case it doesn't matter because she's pretty.'

Miss Watt threw back her head and laughed. 'How refreshing to hear sisterly candour. Sophie and I, when we were young, could be uncomplimentary to each other but that said we would not have allowed anyone else to make disparaging remarks. Now there are a few matters to settle to save confusion later.'

Lois wondered what this was about.

'Regarding food—'

'Miss Watt,' Lois put in quickly, 'I'll buy what I need and everything will be left clean and tidy in the kitchen.'

'I don't doubt that, but it wasn't what I was going to say.'

'Sorry.' Lois bit her lip.

'No, my dear, I just want to explain the situation. Buying food for one is very wasteful. Actually it is two counting Mrs Barlow but still we buy more than we need and some of it has to be thrown away which is criminal and so many people going hungry. I can't help them poor things, other than not be wasteful. Don't buy bread or milk and that goes for potatoes and vegetables too. Use what is there. In fact all you need buy for yourself is meat and fish. Occasionally not even meat if I fancy a roast of beef. I eat little but I do like food in the house.'

'Thank you.'

'As to laundry, this is collected weekly. Mrs Barlow will keep you right. All this should have come from her but she was of the opinion that it was better coming from me. Where was I? Ah, yes, all linen and towels go to the laundry. You will be required to do your personal laundry but that is all. That deals with that I think, but do ask if you are unsure.' She paused. 'Mrs Barlow comes in daily and has the run of the house as you may have noticed. She isn't happy at the thought of me being in the house alone overnight and I am not too happy about it myself. Having you will make a difference and I am sure we shall all benefit in one way or another.' She smiled. 'I think that is everything so off you go both of you. That's Her Nibs scratching at the door, she'll be offended. I never, or hardly ever, shut her out.'

Winnie opened the door and grinned. The beautiful fawn-coloured animal positively exuded indignation and ignoring the strangers made straight for her mistress as though to demand an explanation.

'You can keep your Siamese, I'd much rather have a tabby.'

'So would I.'

'The manse has a tabby and after a slow start I'm accepted. Enough about the cat. I'd say you've landed on your feet. Heavens! I wouldn't mind coming here myself. No bus fares and hardly anything to buy for food.'

'I don't like taking too much.'

'That would be silly if it is just going to waste.'

'I know, but I'll try and make up for it in some other way.'

'Where are we going?'

'My sitting-room.'

Winnie giggled. 'This is all getting too much for me.'

'I've not seen it properly,' Lois said opening the door. 'Nice isn't it?' she said almost proudly.

'I'll say. You can do your entertaining here.'

'Won't be much of that.'

'Me and Tim. Is that tray for us?' she said pointing to a set tray.

'It will be. Mrs Barlow said she would make tea.' Lois let Winnie deal with the tray and pour the tea. It gave her a chance to look about her. She went over to the mantelpiece and picked up one of the ornaments. It was a black, slender cat with its front paws together and a wise rather supercilious look on its face. It seemed both sisters had a fondness for cats.

'That's the tea out.'

'Yes.' Lois had a look out of the window first. There was a well-kept lawn and rose trees then steps down to a lower garden.

'Come on, I want this before it gets cold.'

'Thanks,' Lois said accepting the tea and a piece of home-made sponge cake.

'I'm acting mother, you don't mind?'

'Bit late if I did. No, of course I don't mind.'

'I'll be able to tell Mum that you are all right.'

'Yes, you will and Mum will be so relieved to hear it,' Lois said sarcastically.

'Don't, Lois, it isn't like you and Mum has her good points you know.'

'I'm sorry and of course she has.'

'I feel a bit like piggy in the middle. I love you both and I just wish I could make things right between you.'

'No chance of that, Winnie. Don't blame me, you know yourself how hard I've tried.'

'It's all beyond me,' she said, reaching for another piece of sponge.

'Go easy on the cake.'

'Mrs Barlow said to eat up.'

'I didn't hear her. And eat up doesn't mean eat everything up. Tim is taking us out, probably for a slap-up meal and he'll expect us to do justice to it.'

'Never fear, I will. This just fills up a corner.'

It was a Saturday evening and all the popular restaurants had been fully booked. A couple might have been squeezed in but three was out of the question. The Beveridge Hotel, a mile out of Muirford, had been the last hope and the fact that the person at the other end didn't have to check the bookings but replied promptly that a table was available gave Tim cause for concern. On the other hand he had promised and surely the meal would be reasonable. Years ago he had gone to the Beveridge with his parents for a family celebration and recalled it then as dull and dignified. If it hadn't changed they weren't exactly in for a riotous evening.

'Where are you taking us, Tim?'

'A place which will require you both to be on your best behaviour.'

'But where?' Lois persisted.

'The Beveridge Hotel.'

'Have you been there?'

'Yes.'

'Before my time?'

'Well before I knew you. I was with my parents.'

'So long ago you were in short trousers,' Winnie grinned.

'More likely I was in my first longs. I can't recall the meal but at that age I would have eaten anything – in fact I must have been a bit like you, Winnie.'

'The cheek of some people.'

'Kidding apart I really am sorry I couldn't get a table elsewhere but it was hopeless.'

Lois knew that Tim would have gone to a lot of trouble and Saturday nights were always busy. 'I'm sure it will be very nice.'

'We can only hope. The hotel does have a reputation for catering to the tastes of the older generation, retired majors and their ladies, that kind of clientele.'

'Sounds just my cup of tea,' Winnie said.

'All will be well, Winnie, if you remember that hilarity will be frowned on.'

Lois laughed and recognised that she and Winnie were gripped in that strange excitement that could quickly change from high spirits to deep depression. Tim probably recognised it too and was trying to keep everything light-hearted.

Winnie suited her plumpness and her skin had a lovely soft bloom, a cream and roses complexion.

Lois had changed into a dress and bolero. The dress was primrose yellow and the bolero was yellow but with a pale blue stripe. The colour was perfect with her blue-black curly hair. She really was stunning, Tim thought proudly and wondered how long it would take her to realise she was beautiful. In some ways she was mature, but she was too trusting and for a lovely young woman there were so many dangers. He just wished she was still at home with her mother.

'Here we are,' Tim said driving through the wide entrance and scattering the gravel. A few cars were to the side of the hotel and parked alongside. The once prestigious mansion house had been built for one of the jute barons and when the jute trade suffered a decline it was sold to a company that eventually received permission to turn it into a hotel.

The trio left the car and walked to the front and into a very large, spacious hall lit by a splendid chandelier. The wooden floor had a high polish which made it look dangerous and Lois and Winnie took care as they crossed it.

'Just as well they don't have rugs down,' Lois said sotto voce, 'or I'm sure there would be a few accidents.'

'Gracious living at its best,' Winnie said sounding awed, 'and would you look at that?'

In years gone by the great hall had been heated by a log fire but the fireplace had been removed and the space left was filled with colourful plants and trailing greenery. The gleaming brass box nearby held sweet-smelling logs that were there purely for decoration.

'It's so quiet,' Winnie whispered.

'Told you it would be. What do you bet there isn't a soul under seventy? Some may have dozed off.'

Winnie clapped a hand to her mouth and Lois giggled. Tim was a scream.

'May I help you?'

They hadn't heard anyone approach and they turned as one.

The head waiter as he turned out to be was of medium height but carrying too much weight which showed in his florid complexion. He was immaculately dressed and had the haughty manner of an old-fashioned manservant.

'Yes, I should think you could. I have a reservation in the name of Napier.'

He nodded gravely. 'Follow me, please, and allow me to apologise on behalf of the management for any inconvenience—'

'What sort of inconvenience?' Tim said sharply.

A look of pained surprise crossed the man's face. 'Surely you must have noticed, it has been well advertised in the newspapers and elsewhere that we are under new management and the main dining-room is being refurbished.'

'No, I didn't, but then I've been abroad.'

Lois and Winnie turned away to hide their faces.

'We are using a smaller room at the back but I can assure you and the ladies that you will be very comfortable and the food will be to our usual high standard.'

He looked and sounded so pompous and Tim was poker-faced – how did he manage to keep a straight face? Winnie and she were having a hard time keeping in their merriment.

When they reached the temporary dining-room they were shown to their table. Three faces hid behind their menus until the head waiter had taken himself off.

'Tim Napier you'll never go to heaven. What was that about being abroad?'

'An excuse for not reading the local news.'

Everyone wasn't old but nobody apart from themselves was young. Most of the ladies were dressed up to the nines. It was a way of displaying their jewellery. Some ladies sat alone and were perhaps residents. A few bewhiskered men concentrated on what they were drinking and largely ignored their wives who sat bolt upright in the manner they had been taught.

In sharp contrast and a welcome sight was the saucy young waitress who came to take their order. Her lace cap was set jauntily on her head and catching Winnie's eye she grinned mischievously.

'Made up your mind what you want to eat?'

'I think so,' Tim said. 'You do seem to cater for the elderly. I'm amazed we are allowed in.'

'Trying to change our image and Lord knows we need to.'

'Going to take a while to do that.'

'Oh, I don't know. You're here and that's a beginning and now would you mind giving me your order, the staff are not supposed to chat.'

She was telling the truth if the head waiter's face was anything to go by.

They gave their order and whatever the head waiter said to her it earned a toss of her head and a more pronounced wiggle to her hips.

'Can't see her lasting long, in fact I'm surprised she got the job in the first place,' Tim said.

'Just what I was going to say.'

'The bit about changing their image, was she serious?'

'Sure she was, Winnie, but they won't manage it until they get rid of that fossilised waiter fellow.'

Lois was concerned for the waitress. For all her sauciness she maybe needed the job.

The meal could not be faulted and they enjoyed it. Both Lois and Winnie had taken a glass of wine and a refill and this had put them in a happy mood. No one could have accused them of being outrageous and their laughter did not disturb anyone. Rather it had the old dears smiling over and perhaps it reminded them of a time when they too had been young and carefree.

Tim looked at his watch. 'Sorry, girls, but I think we should be making a move.' He signalled for the bill.

'All good things must come to an end,' Winnie said wistfully, then turned her eyes to Tim. 'Thank you, Tim, that was really great and this has been a treat for me.'

'We'll do it again some time, Winnie, and let me say that I feel honoured to be the escort for the two most attractive women in the room.'

'Bit of a left-handed compliment,' Lois smiled. 'Not a lot of competition.'

Tim paid the bill and made a point of seeking out the head waiter.

'I do hope everything was to your satisfaction, sir?'

'Indeed it was, a most enjoyable meal.'

'Thank you.' He smiled a self-congratulatory smile.

'Perhaps I should mention that the waitress was most helpful and very efficient.'

The man looked very surprised. 'I am pleased to hear it. The young lady in question came to us from the agency. An emergency, I'm afraid, with one of our waitresses falling and breaking her wrist.'

'Lucky for you to get someone so efficient at such short notice.'

'As you say very fortunate.'

'First stop Laurelbank to drop you off, Winnie.'

'But that's daft going back on yourself. You can drop Lois first.'

'Dearest child you really have a lot to learn.'

Winnie was on the point of objecting to being called a child when the penny dropped. She coloured. 'Sorry, wasn't thinking,' she mumbled.

Tim was having a quiet laugh and if he hadn't been driving Lois would have given him a sharp kick on the ankle. Winnie was very embarrassed she could tell.

'Did you leave a note for Mum, Winnie?'

'No, I was out of the house before I thought of it.'

'She'll worry.' Lois was quite sure she would get the blame.

Tim was just the least bit irritated. 'We haven't kept Winnie out half the night. I'll have her home by eleven or shortly after and it is a Saturday. I bet you've been out a lot later, Winnie.'

'Of course. Heavens I'm not worried,' Winnie answered and yawned. The wine was making her sleepy. She didn't keep late hours but she wasn't going to admit that to Tim. When she was with her friends they had to keep to a ten thirty curfew but that would all change. 'Mum can be mad at me if she wants, I don't care it has been worth it. And another thing, Tim, if Mum had been nicer to Lois, Lois wouldn't be going away.'

Tim looked across at Lois and raised his eyebrows. That remark of Winnie's had made him think.

Little was said until Tim drew up at Laurelbank. The light was on in the front room, Harriet was waiting up. Probably she had been watching the clock for the last hour and wondering where on earth Winnie had got to. She never worried about Marie. If she was with Stephen she would be all right. And if they decided to go dancing it could be near midnight before Harriet heard the key in the door. Once she did hear that welcome sound Harriet could turn on her side and go to sleep. She wouldn't admit to being concerned but it was fine to know that her eldest was safely indoors.

Tim didn't drive off until Winnie was inside the house. Lois felt strange not to be getting out herself. Tonight she would sleep in a different bed if she managed to sleep. The thought of leaving Laurelbank had always been there but thinking about it as a possibility was very different from the reality. She was realising that now. The speed of events had taken her by surprise and she had just been swept along.

In the cloakroom of the Beveridge Hotel Winnie and she had made their plans to meet. Lois would not change her mind, she was adamant that she would never set foot in Laurelbank. Winnie would have to come and see her.

'How about making it Tuesday?' Lois suggested.

'Every Tuesday?'

'If that would suit you, but that could be changed to another day if that wasn't suitable.'

Winnie nodded vigorously. 'That's a date, every Tuesday and Mum and Marie can do the dishes that night. You always helped and I am not going to be left to do everything myself.'

'You won't be, Mum will help.'

'She's not all that keen and you know Marie.'

'Always an excuse.'

'You know something, Lois – you saying that about getting a job.'

'Got you thinking about it, have I?'

'It has.'

'Don't just think about it, do something.'

'I mean to,' she said, but Lois wasn't convinced she would.

Chapter Twelve

Lois spent most of that Sunday hanging her clothes in the wardrobe and arranging her shoes neatly at the bottom of it. The rest of her things went into the drawers which had been lined with fresh paper. One held a lavender bag and that went in beside her underwear. Her brush and comb and make-up went on the dressing-table along with a few glass ornaments and a framed photograph of her father taken with the three of them. Harriet had taken it and it had been one of her better efforts. Lois had removed it without asking permission but since it had been stuck on a cupboard shelf along with a box of snapshots it was unlikely it would be missed. There were books and other bits and pieces to go somewhere but until she decided where, they would go in one of the unused drawers.

Thanks to Tim, and what a lot she had to thank him for, Saturday night had been hugely enjoyable and unexpectedly funny. Winnie had loved it and Lois rather suspected that her young sister was a little in love with Tim.

Surprisingly, for she hadn't expected to, Lois had slept well that first night. The extra space in the bed allowed her to move about freely and she thought the three-quarter bed an excellent idea. How strange that it hadn't proved popular but that could have been because it hadn't been well enough advertised. She hadn't heard of if and how many were like her?

On wakening Lois had been puzzled as to where she was. Splinters of light were coming from the window where the curtains hadn't been properly closed and were picking out pieces of furniture that were strange to her. Was she dreaming? Then it came to her in a sudden flash that this big, old-fashioned bedroom was hers. This was where she would be sleeping from now on.

Was Winnie looking at the empty bed and feeling the loss of her company? Lois knew she was and was glad. It was important to her to be missed by someone. Marie might spare her a fleeting thought but it would be no more than that. Just of late Marie had seemed preoccupied, often unaware of being addressed or there again that could have been deliberate if she didn't feel inclined to answer. One could never tell with Marie. And the cause of it, the one to blame was her mother, and now the final estrangement. They were apart and that should suit them both.

The clock on the bedside table showed the time to be twenty minutes past eight. Not desperately late for a Sunday morning but it wouldn't do during the week. Winnie had suggested Lois take the little alarm clock since there was another, a spare. But she hadn't – the less she gave her mother to complain about the better. A clock was essential and it was to be her first buy but it hadn't been necessary. There was one in a cupboard that Lois felt sure must be broken but she had found it to be in perfect working order.

Settling in at Glenburn went smoothly, there were no problems. Winnie came on Tuesdays around 6 o'clock and kept her up-to-date with the news. Not that there was a great deal to tell but Winnie made the most of what there was. Most evenings were spent in Tim's company and once in a while she was invited to take tea with Miss Watt in her sitting-room.

Miss Watt, Lois discovered, was an interesting woman and very well read. She liked to talk about serious matters and encouraged Lois to express her own views and when she did they were carefully considered. Where they disagreed Miss Watt argued her case and sometimes, but not always, Lois was won over. In some ways Lois missed her home but not enough to regret leaving it. There would be some who would say that she had landed on her feet and Lois would agree. She was treated extremely well and did far less than she had at home. Mrs Barlow was kindness itself but she did like her own way. She was responsible for the smooth running of the house and looking after her mistress and she didn't welcome assistance with either. Lois made her own breakfast, tidied her bedroom and cooked herself a meal when that was necessary. The kitchen was always as neat as a pin and Lois was careful to leave it that way.

A day was arranged when Tim was to take her to meet his parents. Lois had wondered what to wear on such an occasion then decided on the same dress with its bolero she had worn for dinner at the Beveridge Hotel. Tim had said she looked terrific in it. She was nervous about meeting Mr and Mrs Napier but she needn't have been, they were a lovely, friendly couple who immediately put her at ease. It was easy to see they were devoted to each other but there was no embarrassing show of affection. It was shown in little ways, the way Mr Napier saw to his wife's comfort and the warm smile he received in return. Lois noticed because her parents had never been like that, there had been no warmth.

What should she take to Mrs Napier? That was proving to be a problem and Tim had been no help. She thought about a bunch of freesias if it were possible to get them at this time of year. She didn't know, she wasn't in the habit of buying flowers. Perhaps not a good idea – according to Tim the house was always filled with flowers. Most came from their own gardens but occasionally an order went to the florist. In the end Lois bought a box of Fry's chocolate creams and hoped they would be well received.

The Napiers had always been comfortably off but with the expansion of their business they had moved up to the wealthy class. No one would have guessed it from their style of living. The house was large and comfortable with nothing ostentatious about it either inside or outside. Wherever they would be sitting there would be an endearing disorder such as a cushion thrown to the floor because the chair was more comfortable without it, the book laid aside face down and open at the page to be picked up another time. The pipe and tobacco pouch on the table with an open box of matches and some spilled out. Lois knew that her mother couldn't have left it that way. She would have had to pick up the cushion or get someone else to do it, tidy the matches and pick up the book. Lois knew she was a tidy person herself but promised to watch out lest she was turning out to be like her mother in that respect.

Mr and Mrs Napier made no secret of the fact that they longed for grandchildren and wondered about this girl Tim was bringing home. He wouldn't be doing it unless he was very attracted. Was she to be the one? Or did he still think of Catherine, his one-time love? Had he got over her? It was hard to tell with Tim, he didn't give much away.

*   *   *

Lois put her box of chocolate creams on the hall table and the maid took away her coat. Then Tim was ushering her into the drawing-room, a large high-ceilinged room whose main feature seemed to be the handsome Adam fireplace. The carpet was in a pattern of fawns and browns and the curtains at the wide window were velvet in a shade of old gold and a matching pelmet with a fringe. In one corner there was a large vase of bronze chrysanthemums and a floral arrangement on top of the china cabinet. The furniture was dark mahogany. There was one large painting of Highland cattle and several small watercolours.

'Mother, this is Lois.'

Mrs Napier was already on her feet. She was quite tall and very thin with a pale skin and a bluish tinge just below the eyes. Lois thought she looked delicate.

'How do you do, my dear, we are so delighted to meet you.' She had a sweet smile and a low pleasant voice.

They shook hands. The woman's hand was very cold.

'I'm very pleased to meet you, too, Mrs Napier, and I do apologise for being unable to accept your previous invitation.'

'I do understand.'

'You were moving house, I hear,' Mr Napier said when it was his turn to shake hands.

'Yes, and I have your son to thank for helping me,' Lois smiled. This would be how Tim would look in the years to come, she thought. Father and son were about the same height with the same light grey eyes but the older man had a fringe of white hair that gave him a very distinguished look.

They were seated. Alex and Mary Napier in armchairs and Tim and Lois together on the sofa.

'Lois, you'll take a sherry?'

'Yes, please, Mr Napier.'

'What about you, dear?'

'I'll take a small sherry, Alex.' And to Lois. 'I have to be careful what I eat and drink. Such a bore but I suffer for it if I don't obey the rules.'

Lois nodded sympathetically.

Tim got up. 'I'll see to the drinks, Dad.'

'You do that, son, and you'll remember won't you, that your mother said small but I didn't.' He winked at Lois.

Tim smiled and poured the drinks. 'Two sherries, one small. Two whiskies, one good measure and taken neat and the other half whisky and half water,' he said to nobody in particular.

'A good drink ruined that is what that is, lad.'

'Tim is quite right, better to go easy when he is driving.' Mrs Napier looked over to Lois. 'Leaving home must be a very big change for you, Lois?'

'It is a big change, Mrs Napier, but I am happy where I am and quite settled,' she said firmly. She sensed disapproval and wondered what Tim had said. Probably the truth.

Everything had gone well but even so there was the very slight awkwardness so often present at first meetings and they were all doing their best to avoid gaps in the conversation. Tim, she noticed, had less to say in his own house than he had when he was elsewhere. Then when she thought about it it was perfectly natural. At home the family only spoke when there was something to say.

Lois hadn't imagined the disapproval although disapproval was perhaps too strong a word. Tim's parents were uneasy. They thought Lois a lovely girl with a charming manner but what kind of girl was it who left a good home? Tim had said it was a good home where he had always been made welcome. What could the real reason be? Girls only left home to be married or if their work or profession took them to another town. None of these applied to Lois. Tim had been reluctant to say why she was leaving home but felt he had to when they more or less demanded to know. The explanation that she didn't get on with her mother did nothing to allay their fears.

'Found this on the hall table, Mary,' Alex Napier said handing Lois's gift to his wife.

'Lois, is this from you?'

Lois nodded and prayed that she had made a good choice and Mrs Napier didn't have to pretend to like them.

'How very kind of you,' she said unwrapping them. 'Oh, how did you guess, these are my favourites. Aren't they Alex?'

He nodded. 'Partial to them myself.'

The talk was general until they were called to dinner.

'Come along you two, you'll be hungry, all you young people are.'

The dining-room was long and not as broad as the drawing-room but it boasted two windows that looked out on the back lawn and a terrace. The rose garden was looking tired as though it had given pleasure all these months and was due a rest. The furnishings in the room were simple but in good taste. There was a sideboard with mirrors and a long serving table where the food was placed before being brought to the table. Tim and his father wore dark suits and Mary Napier had on a fine-knitted suit in a pale apricot with a triple string of pearls at her neck. The maid brought the first course – oxtail soup – and handed round warmed rolls. Roast lamb with boiled and roast potatoes and a selection of vegetables followed.

'Lois, you must excuse us – in this house we tend to go in for plain fare.'

'This is just lovely, Mrs Napier, I very often choose roast lamb when we are dining out.'

'Sensible girl. My wife keeps out of the kitchen but she used to be very keen on—'

'I tried to be an imaginative cook, dear, and it was all a complete waste with you.' She smiled to Lois. 'My husband gave me no encouragement whatsoever.'

'Shame on you, Dad.'

Mrs Napier put down her fork and knife. She had been served a very small helping but even at that it did not look as though she would finish it. 'When we were first married I wanted to impress our friends with something different and went to no end of trouble but I'm afraid our friends were like Alex, they were polite, but let me just say that no one asked for the recipe.' She put a small piece of meat on her fork and ate it. 'Do you cook, Lois?'

'Yes, but I was only taught how to cook plain dishes. It was all we ever had at home. My father was a bit like you, Mr Napier. He used to say he liked the tried and trusted.'

Tim glanced at the clock then caught Lois's eye. She thought, too that this was the right time to leave and was relieved when Tim made a move to go and said they would stay longer the next time.

'Leave the garage door open, Dad.'

'I won't be venturing over the door, lad, so if you leave it open that is the way you'll find it.'

They were all smiling and moving to the door. The evening had been a success but the strain of a first meeting was there. There had been no pressure put on them to linger a while. Next time they would all be more at ease.

'Your parents are delightful, Tim,' Lois said when they were in the car.

'Thank you, find them quite likeable myself,' he smiled. Lois smiled too. It was so obvious to her that he adored his parents. 'You were a success: they loved you, sweetheart.'

'They aren't too happy about me leaving home,' Lois said quietly as the car swung out of the gate and turned sharp left.

When he had straightened he looked at her swiftly. 'Neither of them said anything about that in my hearing.'

'No, nothing was actually said, Tim, but I got that impression all the same.'

'Your imagination.'

'Probably.' The voice sounded heavy and sad. The evening had gone well but she had felt their unease and could understand it. Their own marriage was such a happy one and they would be anxious that their son made an equally happy union. She was a risk.

'Would you like to go for a drive?'

'Yes, that would be lovely.'

Tim kept to the country lanes instead of following the coast road. It was a lovely evening with a gusty breeze that kept the branches of the trees in perpetual motion and the long grasses moved with them. Neither of them felt like talking but it was a comfortable silence. After about forty minutes Tim saw an opening large enough to take the car off the road. He manoeuvred in and switched off the engine.

'More comfortable in the back,' he said turning to her and making it a question.

'More room anyway,' Lois smiled and prepared to get out. They had done this before. The first time Lois hadn't been too happy about it, feeling embarrassed and a little apprehensive. She shouldn't have been. Tim was to be trusted and she ought to have known that.

Once they were settled in the back seat, Tim put his arm around her and Lois laid her head on his shoulder. He heard the sigh.

'Why the sigh?'

'Nothing, no reason.'

'Must be, one doesn't sigh for nothing.'

'Does life ever frighten you, Tim?'

'No, it doesn't frighten me.'

'Puzzle you then?'

'Frequently.'

'Is that because you don't understand it?'

'None of us do, I don't think we are meant to.'

'But it is so unfair. If it was fair we would all get the same chance but we don't. Some people, through no fault of their own, have it very hard.'

'True, no one could deny that, but I think we are judged on how we cope with what we are given.'

'I'm not complaining about my own life, well maybe I am a little. Compared with many I am very fortunate.'

'You don't think that at all or we wouldn't be having this conversation. You feel very hard done by.'

She pulled away from him, angered at his words. 'Why shouldn't I feel hard done by? Even your parents had prejudged me – you must have told them—'

'Just a minute, Lois, I recall you saying that you didn't mind them knowing and when I was asked point blank why you were leaving home what else could I say but the truth?'

'I know, you couldn't do any other.'

'It doesn't matter, they have met you and are very satisfied—'

'No, they aren't,' Lois said sadly, 'and in their place I would feel the same. Even though I know I'm not to blame I can't help feeling that in some way I must be.'

'Stop worrying about it and maybe the day will come when it will be made clear to you.'

'Then you think there is a reason?'

'I don't know what to think, Lois, other than that there is a reason for everything.'

'Why won't she tell me then? I've asked and got no satisfaction so what more can I do?'

'You can't do anything but remember life is full of surprises.'

'And shocks.'

'A few of those too. It isn't like you to be so down in the dumps. What brought it on?'

'I don't know, I just feel confused.'

'Confused about what?'

'I wouldn't be confused if I knew.'

'Regrets?'

'About leaving home? No, none. That isn't to say I don't miss being there. It was home if you know what I mean, but, that said, I know I did the right thing.'

'You have me, so stop worrying,' he said softly and bringing her to him hugged her close.

A silver birch, a huge tree, was just behind the car and a branch kept knocking against the roof, a sad mournful sound that seemed to suit her mood.

'In a little while all the leaves will be gone and the countryside will look so bare. Autumn is the saddest time of the year.'

'Not for everyone, some see it as the loveliest with the leaves changing colour,' Tim said.

'I prefer the spring when everything is fresh and new.'

'Not the summer?'

'When it remembers it is summer,' she laughed. 'For me summer is second best.'

'You could never be second best, darling. You are a very special person and you do know I am serious about you?'

'Yes,' she said quietly.

It was his turn to sigh. 'You're not ready to settle down yet?'

'Not just yet, I need a little longer.'

'One upheaval enough for the moment?' He laughed but she could hear the hurt and it made her feel ashamed.

'Tim, dear Tim, I'm very honoured you should ask me—'

'Don't keep me waiting too long.'

'I won't do that.' She paused. 'I wish I didn't feel so unsettled, it's more than just being unsettled, it's the strangest feeling and I can't explain it.'

'Just reaction, you'll be back to yourself in a week or so.'

'What a very understanding person you are.'

'I try to be.' He kissed her gently then with more passion and she tried to respond. Perhaps she succeeded; he was smiling so she must have.

He was such a darling and she wasn't being fair to him. She would never meet a nicer or kinder man and yet she was holding back. Was it because marriage was so final, such a big step and she wasn't sure enough of her own feelings? A happy marriage was perhaps the greatest gift of all. Tim's parents had it. After all the years together they were still in love and that was what Lois wanted. Love that lasted through all life's ups and downs. Her own parents had missed out, there had been no magic in their union. Had they ever been in love? she wondered, or just imagined it. Whatever had kept them together it hadn't been love.

Chapter Thirteen

'Don't you like animals, Lois? Or are you a little afraid of them?' Miss Watt asked as they drank tea in her sitting-room.

'I like them, of course I do, but I'm not at ease because I'm not used to animals. My mother would never allow us to have a pet. She said they made work and she had enough with the three of us.'

Miss Watt smiled at that. 'What about your father, did he have any say in the matter?'

'I don't think he was too bothered. He liked a quiet life so he usually agreed.'

The woman put down her cup and the Siamese arched itself then began circling her legs. 'Silly pussy.' Rebecca got up, took the animal in her arms and before Lois was aware of her intention, the cat was on her lap. Lois was startled and Rebecca smiled encouragingly.

'She won't scratch you but if you want to make friends, Lois, you will have to be prepared to go halfway.'

'How far is halfway?' Lois asked faintly, afraid to move.

'Stroke the beastie, make a fuss of it. All females like to be made a fuss of and Her Nibs is no exception.'

'Is that really what you call her?' Lois giggled.

'I'm afraid so. Can you think of a better?'

Lois shook her head and began stroking the soft fur. The cat, believing it wasn't going to get the attention it deserved, was on the point of jumping down but changed its mind and settled on Lois's lap.

'Sophie called her that and like all silly names it stuck. Mr Sutherland, he's our clever vet, thought it a shame. He said a handsome Siamese deserved better.'

'What would he have called it?'

'The Duchess was one of his suggestions.'

'That would have been nicer.'

The cat slithered down from Lois's lap thinking she had been long enough there and wasn't getting too much attention. Arching her back again she jumped up on her mistress's knee to bestow a whiskery kiss on the lined face. Rebecca laughed delightedly obviously pleased.

'Knows on which side her bread is buttered does this one.'

'I'm sure she does,' Lois laughed. She got up and collected the cups and put them on the tray. 'If you'll excuse me I'll take these through to the kitchen.'

'Thank you, dear, that is kind of you and it will get them out of the way. But before you go there was something I was going to ask. A favour really.'

'I'll be only too happy to oblige if I can.'

'Mrs Barlow usually does this but none too willingly and of course the vet would come and collect her if I asked.'

Something to do with the cat obviously, Lois wondered what it could be and was less confident now if she could oblige.

'Would you carry her to the veterinary practice round in Oakfield Road?'

'Carry her?' Lois said faintly.

'Not in your arms, silly girl, she'll be in a basket.'

'That's all right then, I should manage that.'

'Thank you, I'll make an appointment for Saturday morning if that suits you?'

'Yes, no problem.'

Lois had it from the gardener that it was going to be a good weekend and it looked as though he was right when she looked out of the window to see a clear, cloudless sky. She had this animal to take to the vet and perhaps she would discover if he was Tim's friend. She was having breakfast in the kitchen when Mrs Barlow came in looking cold.

'Good morning, Lois, there is quite a nip in the air this morning.'

'Good morning, Mrs Barlow, the tea is fresh, want a cup?'

'I wouldn't refuse that,' she said taking off her coat.

Lois got another cup and saucer from the cupboard and poured out a cup of tea.

'Thanks, lass, that'll get me off to a good start. Have you plans for the morning?'

'Yes, I do, I'm taking that precious animal to the vet.'

Mrs Barlow smiled. 'She's got you roped in. Well, that is one job I'll gladly relinquish. I didn't mind going, that didn't bother me.'

'What did then?'

'A miaow coming from the basket, I felt all kinds of a fool trying to keep it quiet and folk thinking I was talking to myself.'

Lois grinned. 'Oh, great, I'm going to love this.'

Miss Watt had just succeeded in getting the cat into the basket when Lois appeared. She looked in the opening and met a pair of indignant yellow eyes.

'She'll settle quite happily,' Miss Watt said, 'she always does.'

'Incidentally what is the matter with your cat?'

Miss Watt looked blank. 'Nothing I hope.'

'Then why?'

'A six monthly check-up, just to make sure. Like her mistress she is getting on a bit.'

'You both look very well if I may say so,' Lois said smiling.

The basket was quite heavy or so it seemed to Lois and she kept changing hands. Fortunately she didn't have far to go and Her Nibs had either gone to sleep or had decided to be on her best behaviour.

Lois had passed this way a number of times and had seen the practice and various people coming and going. The long, low building had been erected on a large area of waste ground which had been cleaned up and the ruins of a cottage removed. Inside was divided into a large clinic, a reception area together with a waiting-room, a kitchen-cum-rest-room and a cloakroom with a washhand basin. If it proved necessary an extension could be built on.

David Sutherland allowed himself only the minimum for living expenses and ploughed as much back into the business as possible. He was building up a reputation and doing well but he was a canny Scot with a horror of debt. He bought only when he could afford to.

The woman behind the reception desk smiled to Lois and looked at the basket. She had just put down the phone when Lois approached.

'I believe Miss Watt made an appointment?'

'Yes, she did and this will be Her Nibs for her usual check-up.' She dropped her voice. 'I find it sad that some folk are so careful with their pets yet neglect their own health.'

'I'm sure that's true.'

'Siamese are quite beautiful, don't you agree?'

'To be honest I don't know much about them or any other animal for that matter.'

'Ah, here comes Mr Sutherland himself. I was just about to bring your next patient,' she said to him.

Lois looked at the young man in the white coat and felt her heart quicken. 'Did she make a fuss or was she well behaved?' he asked with a smile.

'Very well behaved.' Lois knew that she sounded breathless and only hoped he didn't notice.

He took the basket. 'Would you like to come this way,' David said, 'or would you prefer to stay in the waiting-room?' He had a very pleasant deep voice.

'I think I would like to come,' she croaked and followed the tall, loose-limbed figure as he led the way to the surgery. This was a clinically clean room with a table and shelves with various pieces of equipment. There was also a sink beside which was a bundle of clean towels. A boy who looked about eighteen or nineteen, wearing a short white coat, was cradling a puppy in his arms.

'Do sit down,' Mr Sutherland said to Lois. She sat in one of the white-painted chairs.

'Better have another look at that in a couple of days, Kenneth, I want to make sure there is no infection.'

'I'll tell them but I'm sure they won't come back.'

He frowned and shook his head. 'Make sure they know that it is absolutely necessary and say there will be no extra charge.'

The young man nodded happily. His boss was all right, he always put the well-being of the animal before profit, not like some. Carrying the puppy, Kenneth went through to the waiting-room where puppy and its young master were reunited. He had a word with the shabbily dressed woman who promised to return in two days.

'What happened?' Lois asked.

'A needle in its paw that had worked its way in, very nasty. For a whole week that animal must have been in agony and that makes me so angry.' He pushed his fingers through his thick, untidy dark brown hair. 'It all comes back to money and many have a more urgent need for theirs.'

'Was it painful to come out?'

He smiled at her concern. 'Didn't feel a thing!' A loud miaow came from the basket. David opened it and out jumped Her Nibs. 'Now this beautiful creature is spoilt rotten, wants for nothing. This, by the way, is just a routine examination, nothing to be squeamish about, but then I don't imagine you are the squeamish type.'

'I wouldn't know. As I told your receptionist I know very little about animals. Totally ignorant about them in fact.'

'Dear me, that is a terrible confession.' He shook his head and smiled. 'We must do something about it.'

Lois had wanted to ask Miss Watt about the vet but she hadn't liked to. In any case it would have been awkward since she didn't know the surname of Tim's friend. Come to think about it she couldn't recall his first name either. She had a vague idea that it might begin with the letter D. She tried Donald but that didn't sound right. David? Could be, yes it could be David.

The young man had been looking at her. 'Actually I'm wondering if you could be my friend Tim Napier's fiancée. He did say she was living in Miss Watt's house.'

Under his scrutiny Lois felt her face go warm. 'Yes, I do live there. I'm Lois Pringle and Tim and I are very good friends but we are not engaged.' Suddenly she wanted to make that quite clear.

'Sorry, my mistake.' He smiled apologetically. There would be an engagement before long, David was sure of that. And no wonder, this girl was an absolute knock-out. No, that didn't describe her, she was beautiful and anyone but Tim and he would have chanced his luck. Not with Tim though, not with his best friend. Trust the lad he had just about everything going for him. Looks, charm, money, a secure future and best of all he was one great fellow. What did he, himself, have to offer a girl? A promising future but a struggle beforehand.

'When I agreed to bring Miss Watt's cat I wondered if I might be meeting Tim's friend. I must tell him.' She smiled. 'He talks a lot about you.'

'Does he now? Nothing bad I hope.'

'He concentrated on your good points.'

'That wouldn't take him long.' They were both laughing and David loved the sound of her laughter. Spontaneous, neither forced nor affected. He hated to hear girls giving silly little laughs.

Has he a girlfriend? Lois was asking herself and getting the answer that he must. He was too attractive to escape. With something like horror she found herself getting upset at the thought of David with someone. How pathetic. She had known David Sutherland for ten minutes if even that.

David had forgotten her, all his attention was on the animal. Lois was greatly impressed and thought it wonderful to see such a big man with the gentlest of touches. Even the most panic-stricken beast would grow calm under his gentle probing and the soothing reassurance that was in his voice. Lois felt like weeping it was so lovely.

When it was over the cat purred, jumped off the table and padded over to where Lois was sitting as though to say 'Haven't I been a clever girl?'

'In you go,' David said taking her firmly and putting her in the basket. He stroked the fur then closed the lid. There was a miaow then silence.

'What shall I tell Miss Watt?'

'Tell her all is well, nothing to worry about.'

'That will be a relief to her.'

He nodded slowly. 'It saddens me, Lois, to see people become too attached to their animal. There has to be a parting one day and the loss to the animal can be as great as the loss to the human. We tend to forget that.'

'You love your work, don't you?' Lois said softly.

'Can't imagine myself doing anything else. And now it is back to work.' He held out his hand and when she gave him hers it was like a current of electricity. Her wide-eyed look met his and in that moment she could have sworn that he, too, had experienced those shock waves.

They walked together to the waiting-room where the noise had increased and quite a few people were waiting. One little boy in a woollen jersey out at the elbows was holding a cardboard box. Lois wondered what was inside. Something precious to the boy for sure.

'Give Tim my best and one of these days we must try and arrange something.'

'We would both like that,' Lois said politely and knew it to be untrue. How could she hide from Tim the attraction she felt for his friend?

'Fine, that's a promise.' His voice had turned casual and she forced hers to be the same. Just wishful thinking to believe that David had felt anything special for her.

Lois smiled at the receptionist and went out. David had followed her with his eyes. He loved her long-legged grace, the straight back and the proud tilt to her head. Seeing her go out of his life made him curiously depressed.

The days went by and Lois was kept busy. John Latimer was a tireless worker, an energetic man who never said no to a challenge or a plea for help. Lois was finding that working for the under-privileged was demanding and very often thankless. Sometimes his good intentions were misunderstood and resented. She knew he had to suffer verbal abuse. Once she asked him how he put up with it.

'Why do I put up with it, Lois? There are times I wonder that myself, then I think – there, but for the grace of God go I.'

'No, Mr Latimer, you would never sink to the level some have.'

'How can you tell? One can never be sure. With food in my stomach and a place to sleep it would be easy. Those are the essentials, without those it is very different. A hungry man is an angry man, particularly when he sees his wife and family suffering. He doesn't want to, but he takes it out on them because he feels himself to be a failure.'

That gave Lois something to think about then it was forgotten when Winnie arrived with her news.

'Stephen and Marie are engaged.'

Lois beamed. 'That's wonderful. I'm so happy for them and as for Mum I bet she is over the moon.'

'She's more excited than Marie if you ask me.'

'Oh, come on, Marie is bound to be excited. This is what she has wanted.'

'I suppose so.'

'Give them my love and I must buy an engagement gift for Marie.'

'Why don't you come over and give your good wishes in person?'

'You know I can't.'

'I know nothing of the kind. I know you are stubborn that's all.'

Lois ignored that. 'What is her ring like?'

'Sapphire and diamonds, very pretty.' She paused. 'Folk are talking and wondering why you've left home.'

'Let them wonder.'

'Don't you care?'

'Not particularly. It's my business not theirs. Who is asking?' She was mildly curious.

'The Simmers next door. Joan thought you must have taken a job out of town.'

'So I have in a way.'

'Muirford is practically on the doorstep,' Winnie scoffed.

'Anyone else?'

'Yes, quite a few including Mrs Henderson.'

Lois grinned. Mrs Henderson was the village gossip and what she didn't know she made up. Lois wondered what stories were circulating about her. 'That won't have done my reputation any good.'

They were comfortably settled in Lois's sitting-room. 'How did Marie get on with Stephen's parents?'

'Hasn't met them yet.'

'What?'

'Going there tomorrow evening.' Winnie made a face. 'Drinks at seven thirty and dinner at eight. All very posh.'

'That'll suit Marie.'

'Maybe. Marie has changed, that's all I'm going to say,' and Lois had to be content with that.

'How did it go with Tim's parents?'

'Lovely. Mr and Mrs Napier are really, really nice.'

'Thought they would be. Nobody seems to know much about Stephen's parents and he doesn't say a lot about them. I bet they are real snobs and Marie won't be good enough for them.'

'Of course she is. Marie is as good as any of them,' Lois said stoutly.

'Marie would agree with you there.'

'She's marrying Stephen not his family.'

'The two could go together.'

'Stephen isn't a weakling.'

'No, he is anything but that,' Winnie said, 'but remember he works with his father and he won't want any unpleasantness.'

'Marie will handle whatever comes her way.'

'I hope so.'

'You don't sound too sure.'

'I'm not. You haven't seen Marie for a while or you would see the difference.'

'Mum must notice, what is she saying?'

'Nothing. She's too busy planning a wedding.'

'Have they got the length of fixing a date?'

'No, but that isn't holding Mum back. She's thinking about Marie's dress and believe me that will have to be something very special.'

'And what will the bridesmaid be wearing?'

'Bridesmaids,' Winnie said quietly.

Lois grew very still. 'You mean Marie is having more than one?'

'She is having two. Stephen's sister is the other.'

Lois didn't know which was uppermost – relief or hurt.

'That should please the other side as well as Mum.'

'I think it is just dreadful,' Winnie burst out, 'and I told them both to their face. It should have been you and I told Mum that Dad would have been horrified.'

'What did she have to say to that?'

'That he wasn't here so it didn't arise.'

'She's right there, of course.'

'Mum has her own worries. She can't think whom to ask to give Marie away.'

'A problem with no close relative.'

'She's going over all the possibles like Dad's former colleagues and his golfing friends but she hasn't kept up with any of them.'

'Did she get the chance?'

'Just after Dad died a few of the wives issued invitations but she

decided they were a bit lukewarm and didn't feel like accepting.
Bet she's wishing she had now.'

'Time I heard about you. What is happening in your life?'

'Precious little. Annie's got herself a boyfriend,' she said gloomily
'so if I see her once a week I'm lucky. How about you and Tim?
Mum was desperately hoping that Marie would get engaged first
and she's got her wish.'

'Tim and I are happy the way things are. We are in no hurry
to get engaged.'

'That's what you say, but I'm not so sure about Tim. And it
isn't fair of you, Lois,'

'What isn't fair?'

'Keeping him hanging on because I am sure that is what you
are doing.'

'Then you are wrong. Subject closed.'

Chapter Fourteen

'I can't believe this, Mr Bryden, there has to be some mistake.'

The tall young man in the tweed jacket with leather patches at the elbow, shook his head and looked stunned. The recent death of his mother had been a dreadful blow and on top of that there was this!

With no qualified vet to take over, getting away, even for a half day, had not been easy but this appointment with the solicitor had to be kept. His receptionist had been instructed to keep that afternoon clear and being calm and efficient she was well able to deal with any emergency that might arise. Kenneth, his young assistant, was keen, willing and learning fast, but he could only be trusted with minor cases. Anything else would have to wait until David returned from Dundee.

'No, mistake, Mr Sutherland, I assure you.' The gravelly voice held a hint of reproach. The firm of Bryden & Edmondson, the prestigious family solicitors of Murraygate Dundee, was not in the habit of making mistakes. Matthew Bryden, the senior partner, was of the old school and he believed in checking and rechecking to ensure complete accuracy in all matters.

David apologised quickly. 'Forgive me, I didn't mean to give offence – it's just . . .' He shook his head in bewilderment.

'It has come as a shock, I do understand.' The solicitor nodded gravely.

David had been saddened by the loss of his father three years ago but the death of his mother had been for him so much worse. There had been a very strong bond between them.

Shocked clients were nothing new to the solicitor, it was all part of the day's work. They did, however, need a little time to recover and he kept silent. Matthew Bryden was sixty-two and looked every day of it. His once luxuriant hair had thinned until only a few carefully placed strands of grey hair kept him from being completely bald. A pair of steel-framed spectacles sat halfway down his nose and he peered above them to see his client.

David was glad of the older man's silence, he needed a few minutes to regain his composure. With half of his mind he was looking around the office and watching the dust motes dancing in the shaft of sunlight above the clutter on the desk. How long, he wondered, did it take the solicitor to find what he wanted. Why was it that their offices were so often dull and depressing? Was it something to do with their image? Piles of reference books and ledgers sat on the linoleum floor and it occurred to David that these could be responsible for the musty smell. Had they run out of cabinet or cupboard space and was this their permanent home?

Everything looked dusty and made him think he wanted to sneeze yet it couldn't be. A cleaner must come in the mornings or evenings but then again the poor woman may have been warned not to disturb anything and made do with a flick of a feather duster over the surfaces.

'Please don't think it is the money, Mr Bryden, although I would be lying if I said it didn't matter.' David fingered the case in his pocket and would have given a lot for a cigarette at that moment but better not. There was no ashtray which was a polite way of saying that smoking was not to be encouraged.

'Sadly in our world money is always important.'

'Everything was straightforward when my father died and I suppose I just expected it to be the same.'

'Your late father had very little to leave.'

'I know that,' David said a little impatiently. 'It was my mother who had the money, I've always known that.'

'Your stepmother,' Matthew Bryden corrected him gently.

'Very well, my stepmother, though I never thought of her as that. My own mother died when I was born . . .'

'When, may I ask, were you informed that Grace Sutherland wasn't your natural mother?'

'Not until I was in my teens, sixteen I think.'

'How did you take it?'

'That she was my stepmother?' David shrugged. 'She made so little of it, said it was of no importance, but the law would require me to know of it at some time. It made not the slightest difference to our relationship and being a pretty active teenager—'

'You could quickly forget about it,' the solicitor smiled.

'I don't imagine I forgot about it, but I didn't let it become important.' He paused. 'I had a very happy childhood and don't recall the matter ever being mentioned again.' He raised his hands helplessly. 'How could she have kept something like that from me?' His eyes were anguished.

'Circumstances.'

David continued as though there had been no interruption. 'I'm wondering now if my father knew, if she told him. Do you think it possible to keep that kind of secret from your life partner?'

'For a strong-willed person I would say yes, that it was perfectly possible. Your stepmother may have decided it was in everyone's best interests to keep silent.'

'Then why bring it all out now?'

'A need to make amends, perhaps.'

'I worshipped my mother, there was no one like her.'

'And now you feel let down?'

'Apart from shocked, I don't know what I feel.' He stopped and looked at the solicitor who was fiddling with a letter opener. 'What I cannot understand is why, if she didn't want it acknowledged, she didn't just leave things as they were. Why acknowledge a previous marriage at this late stage?'

Mr Bryden looked startled. 'There was no previous marriage,' he said quietly.

'Oh?' There was a long silence broken only by the ticking of the wall clock. Eventually David dragged the words out. 'This girl – this child my mother had. How old would she be now?'

'Nineteen or thereabouts.'

'You've known all along of her existence, haven't you?' David said accusingly.

'Of her existence, yes. The information, as you must know, was given to me in confidence.'

'Yes, of course, I see that. Does the secrecy still apply?'

'I don't follow.'

'Are you at liberty to tell me the facts since they do concern me?'

'I don't agree that they do concern you or if they do only insofar as you are a beneficiary under your stepmother's Will as is her natural daughter.'

'Without breaking confidentiality is there anything you can tell me?'

There was a tap at the door, then it opened and a middle-aged woman stood in the doorway with a ledger in her hand. In her clerical grey skirt and matching twinset she looked very much a part of the establishment, blending in with her surroundings.

'Excuse me, Mr Bryden, but I should remind you of your next appointment in a few minutes.'

'Thank you, Miss Ingram, I hadn't forgotten. You could see if Mr Turnbull or Mr Erskine is free, if not ask the gentleman if he would be good enough to wait.'

'I'll do that.' She withdrew and Mr Bryden put his elbows on the desk with his fingers pressed together. Before he could continue there was another interruption but this one was greeted with a smile. A harassed looking junior had arrived with a tray. The tea was already in the cups and there was a bowl of sugar and jug of milk. Four Rich Tea biscuits were on a plate. A little of the tea had spilt into each saucer.

'Put it down here, Ruby,' the solicitor said making a space on the desk.

She put down the tray and hurried out of the door without once having raised her eyes.

'Our newest recruit hasn't acquired a steady hand as yet but one lives in hope.' He smiled as he handed David his cup and indicated he should help himself to milk and sugar. David accepted the cup but he didn't want it. A little of the stronger stuff would have been very acceptable but like the cigarette it would have to wait.

He declined a biscuit and watched Mr Bryden sip his tea and nibble at a Rich Tea.

The solicitor reached for another biscuit but before starting on it he said, 'Now where were we? Ah, yes. Grace Melville, as she then was, would have been nineteen years of age when she discovered that she was with child.'

David felt irritated at the outdated language. Why couldn't he say she was expecting a baby or was pregnant?

'This was a well brought-up young lady, an only child of well-respected and deeply religious parents. To say they were shocked was to put it mildly. Their whole life was shattered and they would never be able to hold up their heads. Their daughter had brought disgrace and shame on their family name.'

'Not a lot of sympathy for their daughter?'

'You forget, Mr Sutherland, that this all happened about twenty years ago. Mr and Mrs Melville only reacted as many another would. They did not want to lose their daughter but found themselves quite unable to accept an illegitimate grandchild.'

'What about the father of the child, did he come into it at all?'

'He was a married man and already the father of a young child.' He said it with a measure of disgust in his voice.

'Which must mean the child was to be put up for adoption?'

'It wasn't as simple as that. The young woman proved to be very stubborn and no matter the threats from her parents to disown her, she refused to give up her baby to strangers.'

David smiled. That sounded more like the woman he had known.

'How did it work out?'

'Your stepmother said there was only one way she would part with her baby and that was if it went to its natural father.'

'Was he prepared to take on the responsibility?'

'Yes.'

'How about his wife? She would be the one chiefly concerned.'

'Apparently she agreed.'

'Very noble, in fact quite remarkable,' David said.

'I agree. Not many women would have been so forgiving.'

'Thank you for telling me.' David pushed back the half empty cup, he didn't want any more. 'To return to the Will for a moment . . .'

Mr Bryden nodded.

'Wrong of me I know, but I can't help feeling hurt, even cheated. It wouldn't have been so bad if it had been divided equally between us. But for this unknown girl to get two thirds while I only get one third and the house, it takes a bit of swallowing.'

The solicitor frowned. 'If you want my personal opinion although there again perhaps I shouldn't be giving it—'

'I assure you I would value it.'

'I do have some sympathy for you. The deceased was a mother to you and since she treated you like a son, an only child of her husband, you expected to be the sole heir to her estate.'

'Yes, I suppose I did.'

'As I said I have sympathy for you but I have a great deal more for this child of your stepmother. You were the privileged one to have had a happy home life.'

'Don't forget the girl was under the care of her natural father.'

'I hadn't.' He paused. 'How often is a father at home with his children? My own saw little of me when they were growing up. We don't know how the child fared. We can't tell if this woman was capable of giving the same loving care to this girl as she would to her own. In time she may have regretted taking on the responsibility. The facts are, Mr Sutherland, that we just do not know.'

'Would my stepmother have been in a position to find out?'

'Highly unlikely I would say. In these cases the natural mother is usually required to give up all rights to the child which would include having no contact in any form.'

'If she was brought up as one of the family won't it be hurtful for her to find out that she is illegitimate?'

'Very probably but at some stage she would have had to know.'

'The birth certificate?'

'Yes, there is no hiding the truth.'

'You've managed to make me feel ashamed,' David said wryly.

'No need for that. All perfectly understandable.'

'Poor Mother, all those years with her guilt feelings. She must have felt that this was the one way left to her to make up for abandoning her child.' He got up. 'Have you been in touch with the girl?'

'Not as yet, but we hope to be shortly.'

David held out his hand. 'I've taken up a lot of your time.'

'Which you are paying for,' the solicitor said with a chuckle and David had to smile at that. Mr Bryden had a sense of humour after all.

David was glad to be out of the office and into the fresh air. The shock feelings were going and he was coming to terms with it or he hoped so. Most unsettling of all was finding out that the person one loved should have been able to keep that secret from him. None of us, he thought, truly knows another, we all hold something back and perhaps that was as it should be.

Reaching into his jacket pocket he took out his silver case and brought out a much needed cigarette. He stopped to light it then joined the shoppers hurrying along the Murraygate to where his car was parked. Only when he had started up the car did David realise that he hadn't asked the girl's name. Still, did that really matter? There was no reason why they should meet and he was relieved about that. He wasn't curious about his stepmother's daughter. It was more than that, he had no wish to see her.

Chapter Fifteen

Marie was loving every minute of it and so was Harriet. The news of Marie's engagement to Stephen Hammond had spread like wildfire and everybody wanted to see her ring and congratulate her. Quickly forgotten was the talk that had been going around that Marie Pringle was wasting her time and if Stephen Hammond had been serious he wouldn't have taken so long to propose. Others who considered themselves more in the know whispered that Mr and Mrs Hammond did not approve of their son's choice of girlfriend and that was the reason Marie had not been invited to Silverknowe.

They had been proved wrong, Marie was on her way to Silverknowe.

'Terence arrived with his fiancée so you'll meet them as well as the parents.'

'Oh!' Marie was dismayed. This would mean she would have to share the limelight. 'What is she like?'

'Veronica? I saw her only briefly but she seems all right.'

'I meant what does she look like?' Stephen could be exasperating when he wanted.

'Not as pretty as you, if you are fishing for a compliment.'

'I'm not.' Marie tossed her head and smiled. It had been exactly what she had wanted to hear and it made her feel better.

'How long have they been engaged?'

'Not long.' He paused. 'Veronica is the daughter of Terence's colonel-in-chief.'

'Really!' She watched the passing scenery then thought she had better mention Stephen's sister. 'Will Flora be there as well?'

'No.'

Flora was in Switzerland at Finishing School and would not be coming home until Christmas.

Marie had spent a long time over her appearance. She wanted

to look her best and had used her lunch hour to have her hair done. It was a slack time and both hairdressers had fussed over her. The more experienced waved her blond hair and arranged it in the most becoming style. When the three of them were satisfied, Marie carefully covered her locks with a chiffon square. There was a dampness in the air and even the short journey from hairdresser to Madame Yvette's could make it go limp. A tighter curl and it would have stayed in longer but wouldn't have looked so natural.

Buying a new dress for the occasion was out of the question. Marie was accepting that the extravagances taken for granted before were no longer possible. Harriet had been at pains to make that clear. Under no circumstances, Marie was told, was the money set aside for the wedding to be touched.

Marie didn't argue with that, she didn't want any expense spared on her big day. Her time would come when she was Mrs Stephen Hammond. Then she would insist on a generous dress allowance but didn't foresee difficulties. Stephen wasn't mean and he would want to keep his wife happy.

In the car Marie kept telling herself that she wasn't nervous and that made her worse. Stephen seemed lost in his own thoughts and was not doing anything to help her. When he had come for her she had thought he looked well in his dark well-tailored suit and crisp white shirt worn with a quiet tie. No one could call him handsome but – presentable was the word that came to mind.

'You're quiet, not nervous are you? No need to be.'

'You know I'm not the nervous type, but I have to confess to being a bit . . .' She searched for a word to describe her feelings.

'Apprehensive?' he suggested helpfully.

'Yes. I wish it had been just your parents.' Her hands were damp and Marie wiped them on her handkerchief. It would be terrible to have sweaty hands when she was being introduced.

'Just the way it has worked out, I'm afraid, but at least you'll get it over at one time.' He gave a mild oath as a wobbly cyclist came in their path. 'Shouldn't be allowed on the road until they have proper control.'

'If you'd knocked him over it would have been your fault.'

'The motorist always gets the blame. Oh, should mention that we have my Great-Aunt Kitty staying with us.'

Marie's heart sank further.

'The poor old soul is unable to look after herself and unfortunately she isn't the easiest person to get on with. She can't keep a companion or a live-in housekeeper more than a few months.'

'She is that difficult?'

'When you get to understand her Aunt Kitty is all right, but now that she has given up her own house she is dividing her time between her relatives. We've had her for more than six months.' He turned to Marie and grinned. 'Hints, quite broad ones have been dropped but I don't think she has any intention of moving.'

'The others should take their turn.'

'None of them are gasping to have her. I like the old dear but mother could see her far enough at times. Be warned she is very outspoken and tactless with it. Her excuse is that it is one of the few privileges of old age.'

Marie thought that was enough about an ancient great-aunt.

'I should have had something new to wear,' Marie pouted.

'Nonsense, you might have bought something I didn't like.' Stephen could sense that for all her denials she was keyed-up. 'Darling, just be your natural self and everyone will love you.'

'I want them to like me.'

'They will, never fear.'

Marie knew she was lucky to have Stephen and everyone else did so too. He was kind and he was thoughtful and at first it had been wonderful to be taken to the best restaurants and driven everywhere instead of having to hang about waiting for a bus or a tram. If only he was more exciting – but he wasn't, he was dull, staid and predictable. And when it came to entertainment they had nothing in common. If only she hadn't been so stupid as to pretend she was enjoying a show when she was nearly bored out of her mind. At the time it had been sensible, she hadn't wanted to risk not being asked out again. To confess now would be humiliating.

The plain truth was that she would never have given him another look if he hadn't been a Hammond. Marie came abruptly out of her daydream when Stephen braked sharply and she was thrown forward, though not to her injury.

'Sorry, are you all right?'

'Yes.'

'My mind must have wandered and I had almost gone beyond the gate.'

'I'm not hurt but that wasn't like you.' Then she added in a rush. 'I wish we were just going somewhere on our own.'

'Me too, as it happens.'

'Why?' she asked, genuinely surprised. 'It shouldn't bother you.'

'It doesn't exactly bother me,' he answered as he drove through the entrance. 'Terence gives me the pip, he's such a pompous ass.' He gave a snort. 'Proud as a peacock because he has been promoted to captain.'

'Captain? I think that's marvellous!'

Marie thought it most definitely something to be proud about. Her future brother-in-law an army captain – very, very nice.

'Not so marvellous when the promotion comes because you happen to be engaged to the colonel-in-chief's daughter.'

'That's unkind. Perhaps he got it on merit and he could be in love with the girl.'

'No, Marie, she is just not his type.'

The elegant iron gates were always open and the drive had been swept clear of leaves apart from a few fluttering to the ground. Very soon now the branches would be completely bare. The drive curved gently and then evened out and Marie had her first view of Silverknowe since it had undergone extensive alterations. She couldn't but be impressed both with the house and the thought of how much money had been spent on it.

Seeing it now it was hard to imagine how the house had been when the previous owners had been there. Perhaps they didn't have the means or just liked the house as it was. Only one old man had been engaged to keep the grass short and weed the rose-beds in the front, the rest was left to nature. For the children of Greenacre it had been a paradise. A perfect place where they could play, make as much noise as they liked and be fairly certain that no one would come out to chase them away.

Looking at the shrubs, neat lawns and well-tended gardens Marie thought a straying child would get short shrift.

'You have a lovely home, Stephen,' Marie said as she got out of the car.

'You knew it before I did.'

'It wasn't like this then. Believe it or not we played in the back gardens and no one objected.'

'Wouldn't advise it now.' He smiled as he took her arm.

'Did you really mean that about not liking your brother?'

'Not much love lost but then we were at boarding school and didn't see a great deal of each other.'

'During the holidays?'

'I was two years younger and we had different interests. Nothing unusual about brothers not getting on, it happens with sisters too. Look at Lois, she got out because she wasn't happy.'

'Lois got out because she didn't have Dad. He always took her part.'

'And I'll always take yours,' he said giving her a squeeze.

Stone steps led up to a heavily carved wooden door with a huge black knocker that was never used but left as an ornament. It would have taken a lot of strength to move it and on the side panel of the door was a bell-pull that looked new and rather spoilt the effect. The large windows to the front of the house had imitation green shutters and ivy had been trained to grow up the wall. There were turrets but before Marie could get a really good look Stephen was urging her to move.

'Come on, Marie, they'll be waiting for us.'

Marie touched her ring, there was something comforting about its feel. A reminder if she needed one that she was engaged to Stephen and one day soon they would be man and wife. She was Stephen's choice and they would see that he had chosen well. What more could they ask? She was pretty, had nice manners, knew how to dress and how to charm.

Her head held high and a smile on her lips, Marie followed Stephen into the vestibule. This was a large area with a stone floor. It could have looked cold but was brightened by the colourful rugs brought back from the East. A huge Indian vase stood on a beautifully carved wooden stand and filled one corner. Another vase held long grasses. Marie would have liked to linger but, before she could and store it away to share with her mother, a maid appeared and stood waiting.

'Give her your coat, Marie.'

'Oh.'

Stephen helped her off with it then handed the coat to the girl. The maid was very young and looked no more than fourteen years of age. She wore a plain black dress with a small white apron tied at the back in a big bow.

'Where is everybody, Cissy, in the drawing-room?'

'Think so, Mr Stephen,' she whispered.

'Come on, darling.' He took her arm and she walked with him along the carpeted passage. A narrow passage that was made to look wider by the clever use of cream paint on the walls. The light colour seemed to push them out. A murmur of voices came from the drawing-room and Stephen opened the door.

'At last. Just about giving you up.' The booming voice came from the vicinity of the drinks table.

'Sorry, Dad, and we aren't that late.' Stephen led Marie over to a plump-faced woman. 'This is my mother, Marie.'

Marie smiled nervously.

'So you are Marie.' The woman held out a hand and Marie had hers shaken. The rings of the fat fingers dug into her flesh. Marie just stopped herself wincing. 'Simon,' she called to her husband, 'come and meet Marie then she can be introduced to the others.'

Her husband left the drinks table and came over. Simon Hammond was a head taller than his younger son and heavily built. Seeing them together it was hard to imagine that they were father and son. The older man had grey hair with a patch of baldness on the crown. He was high coloured, perhaps he drank too much, Marie thought. As a young man she thought he might have been quite good looking.

'How do you do, my dear. What would you like to drink?'

'A sherry, please.'

'Stephen, see to that and I'll do the introductions.' He took Marie's arm. A uniformed figure got up and Marie's heart missed a beat. She could never resist a uniform, an officer's uniform that is, and Terence Hammond looked splendid in his. He knew it too. Pompous he undoubtedly was but Marie would have forgiven him for that. She would have forgiven him for a lot.

'Marie, my son, Terence.'

'Charmed.' Terence gave a slight bow and Marie dimpled prettily. They shook hands. A girl joined them. 'This is my fiancée,' he smiled. She was tall and sporty-looking with long well-shaped legs and her long thin feet were in flat shoes. Marie wore black patent court shoes with a tiny buckle and two-inch heels. Marie envied her the long legs but smiled happily. There was no competition here, the girl was plain. She had white skin liberally sprinkled with freckles. A few might have been attractive and a dusting of powder might have toned down the rest but Veronica wore no make-up. She had wide nostrils and a too large mouth but when she smiled and that was often it was to show perfect teeth.

'How lovely to meet you, Marie,' she said in a pleasantly husky voice, 'and may I offer my congratulations to you and Stephen.'

'Thank you, and let me do the same and congratulate you and—'

'Terence in case you had forgotten.'

'I hadn't.'

'Let me see your ring, Marie.'

Marie held out her hand, proud of her ring and her beautifully manicured nails.

'Lovely and you have such pretty hands.' She held hers out for inspection. Veronica's ring was simple, three small diamonds. She had nice hands with long fingers and the nails cut very short.

'If you two have finished admiring each other's rings,' Stephen began as he lifted the tray of drinks to bring over, but he was interrupted. The disturbance came from the old woman who had nodded off in her chair and wakened in some confusion. Her eyes were on the uniform.

'Mercy me! What is going on? Has war been declared?' she quavered.

'No, Aunt Kitty,' Simon said quickly. 'That's Terence, he's home on leave and you spoke to him and his fiancée earlier on.'

'Did I? Can't say I remember. So the war hasn't started. The Lord be praised for that but it won't be long, mark my words and before we are ready. Such idiots of leaders we have,' she said disgustedly.

Stephen's mother raised her eyes to the ceiling.

'Aunt Kitty—'

'Yes, yes, Terence, this is you on leave and dressed to kill and this is the lass you have chosen. Well, I'll say this she has a bonny face but—'

'No, Aunt Kitty, you've got it wrong. That's Marie, Stephen's fiancée.'

'Mercy me is he getting married too?'

There was a titter. 'This is Veronica,' Terence said leading his fiancée over to the old lady, 'you've already been introduced.'

The woman's rheumy eyes looked at the girl then she nodded slowly. Her skin hung in folds under her eyes and chin but there was a sharpness about the old woman. Not much would go by her.

'No chance of you winning a beauty contest but you're none the worse for that. There's character and determination in your face, you remind me of myself at your age. We are the kind who stand no nonsense.' Her finger pointed at Terence. 'You had better look out. There will be no straying for you, my lad, this lass will see to that.' She chuckled. 'I'd say you've met your match and more.'

'Really, Aunt Kitty, that was unforgivable,' Mrs Hammond said. 'Veronica, I do apologise.'

'No need,' Veronica burst out laughing. 'Aunt Kitty, if I may call you that, you are just like a relative of mine. Everybody is scared of what she will come out with next. The family understand her but she can be embarrassing in company.'

'Have I embarrassed or offended you?'

'Not in the least. My brother got the looks in our family but since the poor lad is as thick as two planks perhaps I came off better.'

'Just a minute, Veronica,' Terence protested, 'your brother Harry is an officer in the army.'

She grinned. 'Enough said, wouldn't you say?'

They all laughed and Marie was a little disconcerted to see Stephen look over at Veronica with open admiration.

'When do we eat?' the querulous voice demanded to know.

'Very shortly,' Phemie Hammond answered. Simon's elderly relative was beginning to get on her nerves but it would be unwise to cross her. No one knew how the wretched woman was to dispose of her money once she departed this world and she was making it very clear that her Will was with the solicitor, but if she had a mind to change it she would.

Marie was feeling decidedly chagrined. It wasn't that she was being ignored exactly but she certainly wasn't the centre of attention. Terence's fiancée was that, yet Marie knew it wasn't deliberate. She hadn't bothered about her appearance. The navy dress with buttons down the front may well have been expensive but it was crushed as though it had been badly folded in the case and she hadn't troubled to have it ironed. Marie knew that Mrs Hammond would have ordered one of the maids to do it.

The secret of Veronica's success was because she was completely natural. Probably she regretted her plainness, most girls would, but since she could do little about it she accepted her shortcomings and minimised their effect on others by drawing attention to them herself. Marie had just about worked that out and to amuse herself she began to study the furnishings in the drawing-room since her mother would want it in detail. Everything was in good taste from the heavy brocade curtains to the thick pile of the carpet in shades of cream and brown that didn't clash with the rich design of the wallpaper. Marie thought her mother would be impressed, but she was less so. She saw the room as cluttered, too many little spindly-legged tables and embroidered footstools. The bookcase would have pleased her father. It was very handsome and, neatly arranged on shelves behind the glass doors, were leatherbound volumes with gold lettering. To be read or just for show? Just for show, she thought.

Sipping her sherry and smiling when it was called for, Marie turned her attention to what her future mother-in-law was wearing. Euphemia Hammond was of medium height and plump; Marie with her knowledge of fashion agreed with her choice of black. It was slimming but the effect was ruined by wearing far too much jewellery. It was as though she couldn't make up her mind what would be best and wore the lot. Marie wanted to giggle. Perhaps one day she should take Mrs Hammond in hand and educate her as to what should be worn by the older woman with a weight problem.

Great-Aunt Kitty did rather better. Her cerise dress was quite long and very plain with a high neckline which helped to hide the folds of flesh. The shawl draped round her shoulders was very fine and very beautiful. Marie imagined it came from abroad and just wished it could be hers. She could have worn it in so many ways.

A new dress hadn't been at all necessary and she was rather pleased with what she wore. The pale blue or hyacinth blue as she preferred to call it was perfect with her fair colouring and the white piping round the collar and imitation pockets set it off.

A welcome diversion was the appearance of the maid come

to announce to the hostess that dinner was ready to be served. Marie, like Veronica, made to rise but Stephen gave a slight shake of his head and looked to his great-aunt. Veronica understood immediately and Marie followed her example and kept sitting as Stephen went over to help the old lady. Once on her feet she waved him away. Her two walking sticks were beside the chair and she gripped one in each blue-veined hand. For a moment she remained still, then began the slow journey to the dining-room. The others gave her time to be settled in her chair before leaving theirs.

Aunt Kitty gave her walking sticks to the maid who put them in a corner until they would be required.

The dining-room had subdued lighting that gave a warm pinkish glow. There was a very large sideboard down one wall and a serving table beside it. The long dining-table was covered with a stiffly starched damask tablecloth and set with heavy silver cutlery. The side plates were of egg-shell china with an oriental design that looked Japanese but was probably Indian. There was a folded linen embroidered napkin at each place and the light caught the crystal glasses and made them sparkle. It was all very grand just as Marie had expected and she was beginning to think she might manage to enjoy herself after all.

The host and hostess took their places. Simon Hammond at the head of the table and his wife at the foot. Marie was sitting beside Stephen with Aunt Kitty on his other side. Terence and Veronica were opposite. It was a small company at a large table which gave plenty of space between each high-backed chair.

One maid began handing round dainty warmed rolls.

'This is terribly greedy of me but I am going to have two,' Veronica said smiling.

'Darling, I'm sure there will be more in the kitchen,' Terence drawled.

'You tuck in. I like to see a lass with a good appetite,' Simon said while putting two rolls on his own plate.

Marie thought it was bad manners, was surprised at Veronica whom she thought should have known better. She was after all an officer's daughter. When it came to her turn Marie just took one.

Veronica took a curl of butter and began spreading it on her roll then she lifted her head and looked across the table.

'Marie, do you play tennis?'

'No, I don't.'

Veronica looked surprised.

'You don't play at all?' This was from Simon Hammond and his voice held surprise too.

'That's right I don't play at all. I have no interest in the game.'

'Such a pity. We are all keen players. My wife and I were good in our time and we have always encouraged the family. Flora is our best hope – she shows a lot of promise and both boys are above average players.'

'Stephen, dear, you'll have to take Marie in hand otherwise she is going to feel out of it.' Phemie Hammond turned from her son to Marie. 'What game do you play, my dear?'

'I have no interest in sport of any kind.' Marie was feeling desperate. Why couldn't they talk of something else and as for Stephen he wasn't being much help. That fact must suddenly have occurred to him.

'Marie has a very busy life, she is a working girl.'

'A working girl! Are you really? How marvellous! I should just love that but the parents are such stick-in-the-muds they would never agree. No more, thank you,' she said as the maid went round the table helping them to vegetables. 'What kind of work do you do, Marie?'

'I work as an assistant in a small exclusive dress shop.' Veronica might be impressed or pretend to be but not the others.

Mrs Hammond shook her head. 'Veronica, of course you wouldn't be allowed to go out to work. Your parents would be shocked just as we would be if the suggestion came from Flora. That said I have nothing against charity work. A few hours a week given to that would be quite acceptable.'

'My mother does a lot of charity work,' Marie said quickly.

'Does she?' Phemie Hammond sounded completely disinterested. 'Tell me about Flora, Mrs Hammond, how is she getting on?'

'Very well, Veronica, and loving Switzerland. Such a pity she isn't with us but we will have her home for Christmas. Home for good,' she added.

'And aren't you glad?'

'Yes, it will be lovely to have her home.'

Aunt Kitty had been quiet just concentrating on what was on her plate.

'A waste,' she said.

'What is?' Phemie frowned down the table.

'Sending the girl to that school in Switzerland.'

'We don't happen to think so,' she said in a clipped voice.

'Speak for yourself, Phemie, I agree with Aunt Kitty. Finishing School – finishing what? Glorified holiday is what I would call it and good money down the drain.'

Veronica burst out laughing. 'Honestly it's not money down the drain. I was there and believe me it is no holiday, no picnic. We jolly well had to work though admittedly there were good times and why not? All work and no play, you know the rest of that.'

'Did you feel you benefited, Veronica?' Phemie asked.

'I did without a doubt. I was an awkward, gauche individual, the despair of my mother and totally lacking in self-confidence.'

'I've heard everything now,' Terence said.

'Absolutely true, darling. It was an ordeal for me to enter a room full of strangers.'

'That wouldn't worry me,' Marie said boldly.

'Why should it? You are pretty and making an entrance is probably something you enjoy.'

'How did the school work this miracle?' Aunt Kitty said sarcastically. The first course had been soup and she had spilt some of it on the tablecloth.

'Face up to difficulties, don't hide from them, that was rule one. I won't go through them all and bore you but as I say it worked for me. Yes, please,' she said as the glasses were being topped up.

'No more for me, thank you,' Marie said covering her glass with her hand then drawing it away quickly. She had done that in restaurants when she didn't want the waiter filling up her glass but wondered if it was acceptable behaviour. No one else had done that but then everyone else had their glass refilled.

'My mother has something against Terence,' Veronica said putting a portion of meat on her fork.

Everyone looked startled especially Terence.

'Nothing personal, darling, just that you are army and she would have preferred a more settled life for me.'

'How about you, Veronica?' Stephen smiled.

She shrugged. 'I understand the life, I was brought up with it. Sometimes my father's posting meant we could go with him as a family and my mother became very good at making a home anywhere. I thought she didn't mind but now I'm not so sure. She never complained but in time I think she wearied of it.'

'Well, of course my dear, there are advantages and disadvantages of being abroad. The family have to come home to be educated and the mother is torn two ways – whether she should be with her family or her husband. That problem goes away when they are old enough to be at boarding school.'

'You were in India and that was a sort of permanency. My mother never knew where the next posting would be.'

Marie thought it was about time she had her say. 'Stephen, will you have to go to India at some stage?'

'More than likely.'

'Does that put you off?' Simon Hammond smiled.

'Not at all,' she dimpled, 'I'm sure I would get to love the life.'

'You wouldn't have to lift a finger. That right Phemie?'

'Of course not, there are others paid to do that.'

'Paid?' Aunt Kitty said. She had seemed to be lost in her own thoughts but must have been listening. 'Precious little from what I've heard.'

'We treated our servants well,' Phemie said, the angry colour flooding her face.

'Glad to hear it.'

'Shall we adjourn to the drawing-room?' Simon suggested since his wife was neglecting her duties. 'And ladies, think yourselves lucky that the men are not removing themselves for port and cigars.'

'You underestimate us, Mr Hammond,' Veronica smiled. 'For all you know we could be having a quiet tipple on our own.'

Phemie had recovered. 'Veronica! Veronica! Veronica! What a girl you are.'

In the drawing-room Marie was quiet but no one seemed to notice. She felt herself to be the odd one out and it was an humiliating experience. She wished she could get up and walk away and if she did she wondered if anyone would notice. This was a new Stephen and one she couldn't take for granted. All evening he had paid more attention to Veronica than to his fiancée. Terence looked bored and had actually yawned on two occasions.

At last, at long last, the evening was over and they were on their feet and ready to go. Marie was determined to be gracious and show she had been well brought-up. She thanked her future in-laws for a very enjoyable evening, said that she loved meeting them all. They had replied that it had been a pleasure to meet her and Marie thought they sounded sincere. Terence had shaken her hand and Veronica gave her a peck on the cheek. Aunt Kitty snored on with an occasional unladylike snort. No need to waken her, Stephen and Marie would just slip out.

'The evening went off well wouldn't you say?' Stephen was slightly flushed as he opened the car door for Marie to get in then went round to the driver's side. He started up the car and the wheels spun on the gravel before taking a hold.

As far as she was concerned the evening had been anything but a success but she swallowed the words she longed to say. It wouldn't do to speak her mind, she might say too much and she didn't know how Stephen would react. An engagement could always be broken. Marie gave a little shiver. If that happened she would never live it down.

Stephen noticed the shiver. 'Cold?'

'No, just the change from the warm room. Your parents are quite charming. I liked them.'

'Thought you would.'

'Terence and Veronica make a nice couple.' They didn't but she wanted to talk about them.

'Think so?'

'Yes, don't you?'

'Not really.'

'Your brother is very handsome.' She paused. 'Veronica is nice but very plain.'

'Now there is a girl I like. I thought or rather I think she is terrific. To put herself down the way she does—'

'That is clever, Stephen. She knows she is plain and saying it herself makes it less obvious I suppose.'

'How wrong you are, Marie. Veronica has more than looks.

She has a sparkling personality and without her there the evening would have been pretty dull.'

'Thank you very much. That doesn't say much for me.'

'You looked very pretty.'

'But I didn't sparkle,' she said sarcastically.

'We are all different, Marie.' He yawned. 'I'm tired. Are you?'

'Yes,' she said shortly.

Stephen parked at the gate and Marie sighed. Her mother was waiting for her. The lights were on in the sitting-room. The curtains moved. Harriet must have heard the car.

'No need for me to get out, Marie,' Stephen said leaning over to give her a light kiss on the mouth. 'I'll wait until you are inside.'

'Yes. Good night, Stephen.'

'It's after midnight, should be good morning.'

Shutting the car door and just managing to avoid banging it, Marie ran lightly down the path. Before going in she turned to give him a wave of her hand.

Harriet wasn't in her dressing-gown, she was still fully dressed but white-faced the way she got when she was tired.

'There was no need to stay up,' Marie snapped as she threw her coat over the chair and eased her feet out of her shoes. Next time she would have to take a broader fitting.

'I know but I wanted to hear how you got on.'

'In the morning would have done, surely.'

'For the details, yes, but I had to know that everything went well.'

'Everything went off well and I'm tired.'

'Of course you are,' she said soothingly, 'I am too, I've been dozing for the last two hours. Winnie went to bed about half past ten. Do you want a cup of tea?'

'No.'

'Who was there?'

Marie told her. 'Terence was with his fiancée,' she added.

'The brother in the army?'

'Yes, he's a captain and very handsome.'

Harriet was more interested in Veronica. She didn't want anyone outshining Marie, not that there was much chance of that but she wanted to be reassured.

'This Veronica—'

'Nice enough girl but plain and no dress sense.'

'How on earth did she manage to attract Terence?'

'Stephen told me about that. He didn't fall for her looks.' Marie gave a giggle. 'Veronica's father is something high up – a colonel-in-chief or something like that and it was through him that Terence got his latest promotion.'

'These things happen.' She smiled. 'You had no competition then?'

'None at all and please, no more now, I want to go to bed.'

'Of course, dear. You go up first.' Harriet would sleep well, the all-important evening had been a success.

The letterbox clattered, the postman had been. Harriet bent down to get the letters that had landed on the mat. Two were for her and one was addressed to Miss Lois Pringle. Harriet studied it. The envelope was typed and there was no sender's name which was a pity. Harriet would have liked to know from whom it came. The postmark was smudged but Dundee could be made out with some difficulty. Probably something to do with that job of hers and the sender didn't know she had moved. Harriet sniffed. She never mentioned Lois's name if it could be avoided. Winnie saw her every week, she could take it over.

The envelope went on the mantelpiece where Winnie would see it. No call for her to mention it. Unfortunately the letter slipped behind the clock. The clock was quite heavy and did not take kindly to being moved. If it was it usually stopped and required a shake to get it moving again. Failing that the hands had to be moved to the correct time and the pendulum set going. Since it was such a trouble a flick of the duster was all it got and only once in two or three weeks was it moved to dust beneath it.

Chapter Sixteen

John Latimer wasn't a noisy person and he came in quietly. Lois looked up, smiled and completed the letter, she only had the 'Yours sincerely' to type.

'Hard at it, I see.' He brought over a chair and sat down near her.

'I wouldn't say that, Mr Latimer, I couldn't describe myself as overworked.'

'Good! I'm not a slave-driver then?'

'Anything but.' Lois wondered what it was he wanted. It wasn't like him to sit down, usually he just brought in work, greeted her in his friendly fashion and disappeared for most of the day.

'You do a good day's work, Lois, and my life has never been so well organised.'

She looked at him expectantly.

'This is nothing special, my dear, just a chat. It is a long time since we had one. Tell me first how you are settling down?'

'With Miss Watt? Very well. She is a very nice lady.'

'I would go along with that but she is hardly company for a young girl like yourself.'

'Company doesn't really come into it. The arrangement suits us both. I was looking for accommodation and Miss Watt liked to think that there was someone else in the house overnight.'

'There you are then, the old lady is lonely and she wants your company.'

'No, she doesn't. Far from it. Had it been that she would have engaged a companion.' Lois smiled. 'Miss Watt is perfectly happy with her own company but we do socialise in a small way. I take tea with her once in a while.'

'Which I am sure she enjoys.'

'Which we both enjoy. Mr Latimer, it is not a case of trying to make conversation, we have lively discussions on just about everything and I don't make the mistake of pretending to agree when I don't.'

'No, Lois, I don't see you doing that.' He paused and seemed to be giving consideration to what he would say next. 'Seriously, and forgive me for asking, but don't you have regrets about leaving home?'

'None at all.'

The vehemence of her reply seemed to disconcert him. 'I find that very sad,' John Latimer said quietly.

'So do others, you aren't alone. What I did was right for me.'

'I hear that almost every day and I find it distressing and worrying. Heavens! Lois, I do know what I'm talking about. I'm involved with youngsters who have left home, troubled young people who don't know the pitfalls. They think leaving home will solve their problems only to discover greater ones facing them. Then there is the harsh reality of having to fend for themselves. A job isn't easy to find if you don't have a home and one can't afford a place to live unless one is in employment. It is a no-win situation.' He shook his head. 'Hunger and loneliness are poor companions and before long there is a desperate longing to be back with the family they had once despised.'

Lois smiled. Mr Latimer off on his hobby horse as Mrs Wilson would say. He was so kind and such a good person but he did get carried away. 'They can always return,' she said lightly.

'Do you think so, Lois? Not so easy I would say. The young have their pride as you very well know and like the rest of us they don't find it easy to admit to being wrong. In many cases it is only pride that is holding them back.'

'I don't consider myself in that category. You mean well, Mr Latimer, and I appreciate your concern.'

'I didn't put you in that category apart from the bit about pride.'

'Pride isn't holding me back.'

'Are you sure?'

'Positive. I had a good home and I left it because I didn't feel welcome in it. My mother never wanted me and that isn't my imagination. That state of affairs was just tolerable when my father was there but it became impossible after he died. Mr Latimer, it is as simple as this. I was miserable.'

'I don't seem to have done anything to help and I apologise for interfering in what is none of my business other than that I feel some responsibility for you.'

'You don't have to apologise. Believe me, removing myself was the only way for me. Even so don't think it was easy because it wasn't. Leaving my sisters was difficult. I never see Marie but Winnie is a regular visitor and she keeps me up-to-date with the news. I miss the house, I don't deny it. It was after all the only home I've known.' Her face lit up. 'Winnie had good news. Marie is engaged to be married and that is quite exciting.'

'Doesn't that make you want to be back and be part of the celebrations?'

'No, it doesn't. I wrote a letter to Marie and sent her a gift. I know Stephen, he is a very nice boy.'

'Well, no rest for the wicked,' John Latimer said pulling a gold watch from his waistcoat pocket and glancing at it. He got to his feet. 'The last thing I wanted to do was upset you. I haven't have I?'

'No, you haven't and it is nice to have someone interested in my welfare.'

'Then promise me that if you are worried or find yourself in a difficult situation you will come to me.'

'I promise, but really there is no need to worry. I am old enough to stand on my own two feet.'

'And how often have I heard that! Oh, I meant to ask. Do you still see young Tim Napier?'

'Yes, from time to time.'

'Glad to hear it, he's a good dependable lad.'

He left and Lois pushed back the typewriter, put her hands under her chin, her elbows on the table and gazed ahead at the wall. What had made her say from time to time? She saw Tim two or three times a week. Why had she wanted to make it sound so casual? She was practically engaged, that last evening Tim had been on the point of asking her, she knew it. It was floating about in the air yet for some reason the words hadn't been said. Practically engaged – surely that said something? She was holding back, she knew that. Perhaps Tim was doing the same. They had a wonderful relationship, they were so comfortable with each other. A marriage could work, many survived on a lot less but Lois knew that it wasn't enough. Love was missing, the all-important magic just wasn't there. Unbidden a picture of David Sutherland came before her. Together for such a very short time yet it had been long enough for her to know that David Sutherland could have a special place in her heart. Even just thinking about him and she could see the long, loose figure, his careless disregard for clothes, the thick, untidy, dark chestnut-coloured hair and especially the soft brown eyes. Soft like a spaniel's.

How easy it would be to love David. Perhaps she already did but what was the use? Where would that get her? What hope had she? David saw her as Tim's girl and that was why he had been so friendly. If she read anything more into that moment when their eyes met, she was mistaken. Wishful thinking was all it had been.

Perhaps it was just as well she wasn't seeing Tim this evening. Pretending something she didn't feel was becoming a strain. The time was very near when she would have to be honest. But would she? Without Tim her life would be so empty.

After her meal Lois washed her hair and while it was drying did a few chores. This wasn't Winnie's evening for coming but that was her distinctive ring. Lois shut the dressing-table drawer and went quickly to the door.

'Winnie! Nothing wrong is there?'

'Why should there be? Thought I'd give you the pleasure of my company two evenings this week and let me in before asking questions.'

Lois stood aside then shut the door.

'I'm in the bedroom, I'd just washed my hair but we can go into the sitting-room if you like.'

'All one to me. Make it the bedroom, more like old times.'

The bedroom had two comfortable easy chairs. Winnie immediately made herself at home, flung her coat over the bed, kicked off her shoes and sat in one of the chairs with her feet under her.

There was a gas fire which Lois seldom made use of but she used a match to light it. Then she sat on the floor in front of it to dry her hair.

'Dead lucky you are to have naturally curly hair.'

'I don't agree. Curly hair goes its own way whereas you can have different styles with straight hair.'

'Rubbish, but never mind that.'

'All right what are you dying to tell me?'

'Nothing, but I need your advice.'

'That's risky, I might give the wrong kind.'

'I'd like to hear it, then I can decide if I want to take it or not. Your advice means more to me than anyone else's.'

'I'm flattered. Come on what is this all about?'

'It'll keep until after, I'll give you the other news first. You knew that Marie was going to Silverknowe to meet the Hammond family?'

'You told me, but I thought it was just Mr and Mrs Hammond.'

'So did Marie. She was a bit put out. May I have one?'

'Help yourself.' Lois got up and pushed the biscuit tin nearer. She always kept some for the occasions when she brought a cup of tea up to her bedroom.

'Plain ones, is that the best you can do?'

'All the corner shop had left. Said she was waiting for her new stock. Who was there?'

'Stephen's brother Terence and his fiancée. Just newly engaged.'

'A double celebration?'

'Not really. Marie said they weren't expected. Just arrived. Terence had a few days unexpected leave and took the chance to bring what's-her-name – Veronica – with him.'

'Anyone else?'

'An ancient great-aunt of Stephen's who is staying with them.'

'How did Marie hit it off with her future in-laws?'

'All right. Terence is a dream-boat. He's an army captain and looks gorgeous in uniform. You know Marie.'

'Hope she hasn't got designs on him?'

'Not a chance. She had just better behave herself and hang on to Stephen.'

'This Veronica is quite something then?'

'Dead plain according to Marie.'

'She must have something?'

'The right connections. Veronica's daddy is Terence's colonel-in-chief.'

'I begin to see daylight.'

'According to Marie, Stephen was terribly proud of her and I gather they were all paying her compliments. Mr and Mrs Hammond couldn't have been nicer to her and said Stephen was a lucky boy to have found such a sweet and charming girl.'

'Now you are making it up, the last bit anyway.'

'Maybe, but that was the impression she was trying to give and Mum, needless to say, was lapping it up.'

'What had she to say about the house?'

'Silverknowe? Wonderful, everything was wonderful. She used the word all the time. You know this, Lois?'

'What?'

'Half the time I didn't believe her.'

'Why not?'

'Think about it. They took their time about inviting Marie and then suddenly they are all gushing.'

'Could be Marie made quite an impression or, if not that, they are making the best of it. She is Stephen's choice and they do happen to be engaged.'

'Fair enough.'

'Marie is pretty and if the other prospective daughter-in-law is nothing to look at—'

'Could be. Whatever, Marie will do all right, trust her.'

'That's enough about Marie, what is this news of yours?'

'No one knows, I haven't said anything to anyone. You are the first and before I did anything about it I wanted your advice.'

'Come on, Winnie, this is killing me.'

'It is what I want to do but I'm still scared.' She moistened her lips. 'You know I still go to the manse?'

Lois nodded.

'Mrs Hutchison says I'm good with the children.'

'You are and I'm sure she is grateful for your help.'

'She doesn't need me so much now. There was a while when she was on the verge of a breakdown.'

'So I heard.'

'She's fine now. Honestly that husband of hers, a minister too, and he couldn't see what was happening under his nose. Helping everybody else and neglecting his own. Anyway, Lois, Mrs Hutchison forced a showdown – she told me all this – and she let him know that she couldn't do everything and she wasn't prepared to go on trying. Either she got adequate help in the manse and that didn't mean a simple girl who was willing but unable to do anything without supervision or she was leaving him and taking the children.'

'Good for her. He got the message then?'

'He did indeed. Almost floored him, said he had no idea and that of course, she must have help. He would see to it right away and why hadn't she told him this before instead of bottling it all up and making herself ill.'

They were both laughing.

'Your services are no longer needed.'

'I go just as usual, we are friends. The kiddies are nice I like them and, another thing, it gets me out of the house.'

'What has happened to your own friends?'

'Most of them have a steady boyfriend. I suppose I could have one as well but it's just my luck that the wrong ones ask me out.'

'I'm still waiting . . .'

'Friends of the Hutchisons are looking for someone to take charge of their two children. The little girl is three and the boy about eighteen months.'

'Mrs Hutchison suggested you?'

'Yes, but the job wouldn't be here. It would mean going to London.'

'London?' Lois said incredulously.

'That shocked you, it did me too.' Her voice was shaking. 'Timpson, that's the name of the people. Mr Timpson is being sent to London for a minimum of two years, it could go into three. Lois, he must have a very high-powered job because they take possession of a large furnished apartment in a posh area. Don't ask me where, I couldn't take in all I was told. Mrs Timpson is expected to do a lot of entertaining and be available to accompany her husband at other times.'

'Winnie, it all sounds marvellous.'

'I know, the more I think about it the more excited I'm getting.'

'Then you are giving it serious thought?'

'I am, Lois,' Winnie said quietly.

'What about Mr and Mrs Timpson, have you met them?'

'Yes.'

'You have?' Lois was more than amazed. 'You are a dark horse.'

'Mrs Hutchison took me to meet them. They don't live very far from the manse.'

'Pleasant?'

'Very. Couldn't have been nicer. They were going to engage someone when they got there but Mrs Timpson wasn't too happy about that and her husband suggested they look for someone local who could accompany them. Hopefully that would let the children get to know her before they left for London.'

'I take it you've been offered the post?'

'Yes. They suggested I come to them for two days a week so that we get to know each other.'

'Winnie, I'm not putting a dampener on this, far from it, but be sure of where you stand before you accept.'

Winnie frowned. 'What do you mean by that?'

'A description of your job. Are you a nurse-maid or a maid of all work?'

Winnie's face cleared. 'My one and only job is to look after the children. There is domestic help and I won't even have to tidy my own room. Both Mr and Mrs Timpson were at pains to have me understand that I would be treated as one of the family and when they go on holiday I go with them.'

'How about time off?'

'Yes, I get that. I also get a good salary – not wages, they called it salary. All found money.' Winnie was grinning.

'Seems you've landed on your feet.'

'I know.' She bit her lip. 'I'm still scared though.'

'What of?'

'What Mum is going to say.'

'Winnie, you are no longer a child and you'll have to learn to stick up for yourself.'

'Easy for you to say that. If you were at home it would be different.'

'I'm not though. This is something you have to do on your own.'

Winnie shrugged.

'When are you supposed to leave for London?'

'Beginning of January.'

'A while yet but it will soon pass. The Timpsons will want an answer quickly or they will look elsewhere.'

Winnie looked startled. 'I suppose they might.' She hadn't thought of that.

'I'll ask Mum.'

'No, you don't ask. You have already made up your mind and you tell her you are going with or without her consent.'

'You are much harder than you used to be.'

'I used to be a doormat,' Lois said tartly. Then she smiled and hugged Winnie. 'Why am I encouraging you? What am I going to do without my little sister. You are just about my only visitor.'

'You have Tim.'

'He doesn't come here.'

Winnie got up slowly. 'I'd better go.'

'Yes, you should and when you get back don't put it off any longer. It isn't as though Mum can say anything against Mr and Mrs Timpson since they are friends of the minister and his wife. She can't put forward any objections, Winnie.'

'Want to bet?' But she was smiling.

Lois had one more go before Winnie left.

'If you throw this away, Winnie Pringle, I'll never speak to you again. It is the chance of a lifetime. You are to be treated as one of the family which means you will meet new people, make friends and have a wonderful time.'

'Thanks, Lois, I'm glad I told you before Mum.'

'Don't tell her you did for goodness sake.'

'Give me credit for some sense.'

From the downstairs window Lois watched Winnie's departing figure and was it imagination or was there a new determination in the way she was striding out.

'Shall we try one of the restaurants out of town?'

'That would be nice, Tim.' The nights were cold and Lois had bought herself a warm tweed suit in soft shades of blue and with it she wore a blouse in a deep blue that buttoned up to the neck.

'Haven't seen you in that before. Very nice,' Tim said admiringly.

'Thank you, thought I'd treat myself.'

Eating out had become much more popular in the last year

211

and new restaurants were opening up not only in the towns but out in the country. They were staying open longer too. The one they chose had been open for about nine months but only now was it becoming popular. More attention given to advertising its existence would have helped but the proprietor had depended on word being passed on.

The lighting was subdued but was not too dim. One could still make out the faces at the other tables. Each table had in its centre a candle in a heavy glass container which was lit as soon as the table was occupied.

They took their time before making their choice and once the order was in began to discuss their day. Tim was good company and always seemed to have an amusing tale to tell. Lois was laughing at something he had said when someone approached their table.

'Hello, Tim.'

They both looked up and Tim got to his feet. Lois saw a very attractive young woman with gorgeous auburn hair. It was thick, wavy and shaped to her head. With her tall, slim figure Lois thought she could have been a model. Perhaps she was.

'Catherine! Where did you spring from?' Tim was slightly flushed.

'Over there. I'm with Mike and Liz.' A couple waved across to them and Tim lifted his hand in acknowledgement.

'Are you staying with them?'

'Yes, for a few weeks.' Her voice dropped. 'Mother died.'

'I'm sorry.'

'Don't be. It was a happy release. There was no quality of life left. For the last few months she didn't know any of us.' Catherine touched his arm. 'Do sit down, Tim.' She smiled to Lois.

Tim looked embarrassed and Lois was sure he had forgotten her existence. She had never seen him like this before. Tim never got in a flap.

'Lois, my humble apologies.'

'It's quite all right.' She smiled to show she wasn't in the least offended.

'I'm just trying to get over the surprise of seeing Catherine but let me introduce you. Catherine this is Lois Pringle and Lois this is a very old friend of mine, Catherine—' He hesitated.

'Catherine Allardyce, I'm still single.' She lifted her ringless left hand as though to prove it, then held out her other hand to Lois. 'Hello, Lois, I'm so pleased to meet you. Forgive me barging in but I just had to come over. Tim and I go back a long way. At one time our families lived quite close and do you know this wretched boy used to pull my pigtails and say the most dreadful things.'

'Lois wouldn't believe that of me.'

'I'm not so sure,' said Lois smiling. She liked this young woman. 'Tell me about the dreadful things.'

'All quite true, Lois, I'm not making it up. I used to go into floods of tears when Tim told me that I belonged with the Red Indians because I had red hair and I was young enough and stupid enough to believe him. My mother used to say that she would have a word with that Tim and all the time she was trying not to laugh. Happy times, Tim?'

'Yes, they were.'

Catherine turned round. 'I had better go, this looks like your meal coming. Lovely to have met you, Lois. Tim is a darling but I expect you know that. Goodbye, Tim.' There was something in the way they looked at each other, a wistful longing, that convinced Lois that they had been in love. She wondered what had gone wrong.

They both watched her walk back to her table. A striking-looking young woman in a fine-knit green suit that was perfect with her bright auburn hair.

The waitress served them, poured the wine and departed. They ate in silence for a few minutes. 'I can't get over it. What a surprise.' He was shaking his head as though even yet he couldn't believe it.

'I can see you were surprised.'

'We were great pals, Catherine and I.'

'Perhaps you were to begin with,' Lois said smiling, 'but you became a lot more than pals. That was delicious,' she said putting down her fish fork and knife.

'Enjoyed it too. Don't know what was rolled up in the sole but it was good. Why did you say that Catherine and I were more than pals?'

'Because I am not blind. Neither of you could hide your delight. You were in love once, weren't you?' Lois said softly.

'That was a very long time ago.'

'What went wrong?'

He raised his eyebrows.

'I mean she isn't married and for that matter neither are you.'

'Catherine's mother thought we were too young to become engaged. She pointed out and rightly, that neither of us had had the chance to meet anyone else and that marriage was a serious step etc., etc.'

'And you didn't agree with that?'

'No, I didn't. I was young and arrogant and all for getting engaged but Catherine was reluctant to go against her mother's wishes. I was hurt and angry and we had a blazing row. Catherine didn't get that colour of hair for nothing.' He grinned. 'Proper little spitfire she was.'

'And that was the end?'

'It might not have been but about that time Catherine's father died and Mrs Allardyce wanted to move to Perth where she had relatives.'

'Look, Tim, your friends are leaving.'

A tall man, his petite wife and Catherine had risen. Their table was nearer the door and the three of them waved before leaving.

Lois waited until they were having coffee then she said quietly, 'Tim, this makes it much easier for me. I was wondering how to break it to you—'

'Break what?' he said sharply.

'We must stop seeing each other, Tim.'

'But why? What has gone wrong. There's nothing – if you mean Catherine, that was over a long time ago as I said.'

'It has nothing to do with Catherine except that it makes it easier for me.'

'You've fallen out of love with me?'

'Tim, we were never in love. At first I did think I loved you and in a way I do, but it isn't real love.'

He was looking bewildered. 'We've had wonderful times together.'

'I know and I'll always remember them but it isn't enough, Tim. Catherine is for you and don't let her get away this time.'

'What about you, Lois? Does this mean that you have met someone?'

Lois thought about David but that was her secret. 'No, Tim, I've met no one but one day who knows.'

'I don't know what to say.'

She smiled warmly perhaps to hold back the tears. Her life seemed to be full of endings.

'You are a wonderful girl,' he said huskily, 'and I don't want to let you go.'

'We won't lose touch. I hope we will always remain friends.'

'Nothing surer.'

'Winnie, I was hoping you would come, I've been watching from the window.'

'Missed the bus. Not my fault I was in plenty of time but it must have been very early. There should be a better service on this route. That was fifteen minutes I had to wait,' she said indignantly.

They went into the sitting-room. Lois had set the coffee table. 'Want something now or shall we wait?'

'Wait I think.'

'You look cheerful so I take it all went well?'

'That would be expecting too much but I took your advice, Lois, and stuck to my guns and you know what?'

'No, tell me.'

'Sticking up for myself wasn't nearly as difficult as I thought it would be. Even so, Mum had plenty of obstacles to put in the way.'

'Like what?'

'Like I was a home-bird and I'd be lonely and miserable in London. Didn't I know that London was the loneliest city in the world.'

'Heavens! What does she know about London, she's never been there.'

'That's what I said and she said it was common knowledge.'

Lois smiled. 'What else?'

'I wouldn't know a soul apart from my employer and looking after children for an hour or two was very different from being with them all day.'

'She has a point there I suppose.'

'I'm not going for a holiday, I don't expect to enjoy myself all the time,' Winnie said sounding very mature. 'What else? Ah, yes, that was when she started on about losing Marie before long and how was she going to manage on her own, she had always depended on me. That I was too young to be away from home and that she would never have a moment's peace worrying about me.' Winnie grinned. 'I just let her rave on and when I could get a word in I said she had always been a busy person with plenty of interests. Actually, Lois, that doesn't apply so much these days, she has cut down and isn't on so many committees.'

'A chance to get back on them.'

'Just what I said.'

Lois was looking at her admiringly, this was a new Winnie. 'You really did say all that?'

'More or less. May I have some tea now? The rest will keep till then.'

Lois got up and went into the kitchen to make the tea. She put some rock buns on a plate and brought the lot through on a tray. Once the tea was poured Winnie went on with her story.

'Lois, I *am* going to London and nothing is going to hold me back. I'm spending two days a week with the Timpson kiddies and getting paid for it. It isn't so much the money, Mum isn't mean with me, but it is a nice feeling to be handed money you have earned.'

'Winnie, I'm terribly impressed with all this but it is time I asked about Marie. Have they got the length of setting a date for the wedding?'

'Not finally.'

'That's another thing, you are to be bridesmaid and you'll be in London.'

'I'll be home for the big day, Mum made sure about that. Mrs Timpson was told all about Marie being engaged to Stephen Hammond.'

'She must have known that?'

'Of course, but you know Mum, she just loves talking about it. Anyway Mum was to cease worrying and she was told that arrangements would be made to have me home for the wedding.'

'Very obliging of her.'

'I thought so too and I thanked her but she said being bridesmaid to my sister was very important and it was a bit of excitement for me to look forward to.'

'Are you excited at the thought or is your departure for London enough to be going on with?'

'Definitely enough to be going on with. Marie is amazing, Mum keeps asking her this, that, the next thing and she answers vaguely or not at all. To be honest she is taking no interest in the preparations for her own wedding.'

'She must be, this is Marie we are talking about.'

'I know, I expected her to be going crazy with excitement but half the time she is going about in a dream and gives a start if you ask her something.'

'Feeling the strain maybe. Marrying into the Hammond family is quite something.'

'Poor Mum she is the one who is excited and this wedding is going to be as big a splash as she can afford.'

'Yes, I expect so.'

'Another bit of news. Harry Lindsay came over to say goodbye to Marie. The bank have given him a transfer to Edinburgh.'

'That was nice of Harry.'

'I thought that too. Mum didn't, she was quite rude. It was she who answered the door and she didn't even ask him in. Said Marie was busy and she would tell her, but Harry said surely she could spare a minute and he wanted to tell her himself.'

'Poor Harry, he really was terribly keen on Marie.'

Winnie nodded. 'Marie must have heard the voices and I was all ears in the sitting-room. I heard Harry say in quite a commanding voice to get her coat and Mum saying he could come in for a few minutes. I didn't hear what Marie said but she went out with him and it was a good hour later before she came back.'

'Poor Marie.'

'Poor Marie, my foot, I bet she was loving all the drama. All the same she said she was sorry that Harry was going away especially as it was all her fault.'

'How did she arrive at that?'

'Apparently he couldn't bear to be in the area when she was married to Stephen but she told him to forget her and in time he would meet someone else.'

Lois giggled, she couldn't help it. 'She really has a tremendous opinion of herself.'

'Always had and always will and now, Lois, I'd better get going.' She got up and looked about her. 'You really are very comfy here. Tim fine?'

'Yes, and I might as well tell you now—'

'Knew it was on the cards, you're getting engaged?'

'No, it is all off. Tim and I won't be seeing each other again.'

Winnie had been about to put on her coat but she sat down instead.

'This I do not want to believe. Why, Lois? What went wrong?'

'Nothing. Tim and I are not in love and we both discovered it in time. Strange how things work out, Winnie. I had been wanting to break it off, I felt it wasn't fair to either of us to pretend something I didn't feel but I kept putting it off. Then the opportunity arose.' Lois told Winnie about Catherine.

'A pity,' Winnie said showing her disappointment. 'I would have adored Tim as a brother-in-law.'

'Sorry,' Lois smiled.

'Will you miss him?'

'Terribly.'

'You amaze me at times,' she said putting on her coat and buttoning it up to the neck. 'Good folk are scarce so I had better look after myself,' she said wrapping a scarf round her neck.

'Is it that cold?'

'I don't know but I came prepared.' She put her hand in her pocket then closed her eyes. She opened them and handed Lois a letter. 'Sorry! Sorry! Sorry! I meant to give you this the moment I was in the house. Mum put it on the mantelpiece for me to bring over, I don't know when that was, but it must have slipped behind the clock – remember that happened once before?'

'Don't worry it won't be anything of importance.'

'Probably too late whatever it is. Mum thinks it must have been there for a couple of weeks. Look if I don't get a move on I'm going to miss my bus. Cheerio.'

'Cheerio, Winnie and thanks for coming.'

Lois saw her sister off then returned to clear the tea things, take them to the kitchen, wash them and put the china away. She wasn't too bothered about the letter since it was typed. More than likely it was a reply to a business course she had seen advertised and at the time thought would be of interest.

Once upstairs and in her bedroom Lois opened the letter. The heading on the page was Bryden & Edmondson, Solicitors,

Murraygate, Dundee. The letter was very short. 'Dear Miss Pringle,' Lois read, 'Please contact this office at your earliest convenience to arrange an appointment with Mr Matthew Bryden.'

Lois frowned and read the brief letter again, then again. She had never heard of Bryden & Edmondson and knew that it hadn't been her father's solicitor. What would this solicitor want with Lois Pringle? There had to be a mistake. Just to make sure she checked the envelope but the envelope was correctly addressed. The feeling she had was of apprehension mixed with excitement and suddenly she wished it was morning and she could phone. Mr Latimer wouldn't mind her making use of the telephone.

Promptly at nine o'clock she was at her desk but forced herself to wait until half past before phoning. That would give them time to settle in. By twenty past she couldn't wait any longer. Her mouth was dry as she phoned.

'Good morning, Bryden & Edmondson, can I help you?'

'Yes, please, I'm Lois Pringle and I have a letter here asking me to make an appointment with Mr Matthew Bryden.'

'Mr Bryden just stepped out of the office a few moments ago but hold on and I'll get his appointments book.'

'Before you go I should tell you that the letter to me was delayed and I have only just received it.'

'Thank you. Hold the line.'

'Thursday at two o'clock, Mr Bryden should be able to see you then.' The person at the other end sounded very efficient but busy with little time to spare for enquiries.

'Yes, I should manage that but—'

'Was there something else?'

'I have no idea what this is about and I wondered if you could perhaps—' her voice trailed away. What had made her ask that? She could almost feel the shocked silence.

'No, Miss Pringle, I can't help you.'

'I'm sorry I shouldn't have asked that.'

'Not at all. Good morning.' The phone clicked.

Three more days to wait and wonder.

'I'm passing the post box, Miss Watt, if you would like those letters posted.'

'Would you, my dear, that would be helpful. I was about to

stamp them but I haven't my glasses and I don't want to put the stamps on upside down.'

'Let me.' Lois licked the stamps and was about to stick one on a letter when she saw that it was addressed to David Sutherland, the vet. She used the stamp on another envelope. 'No need to post this one, Miss Watt, I'll be going round by the vet and I can hand it in.'

'Just as you like, Lois. Will it be open?'

'If it isn't I'll pop it in the letterbox.'

Lois put the ones for posting in one pocket and David's in the other. Would he still be there? It had gone six but he was never in a hurry to shut shop as she knew. She posted the letters first then walked to the veterinary surgery and saw that the lights were still on. There was no reason to ring the bell, all she had to do was put the letter in the box. She was still swithering when the door opened and there was David.

'Sorry! So sorry!' he said taking her arm. 'Did I almost send you flying?'

'No, you didn't. I thought I would hand-deliver this instead of posting it since I was going this way. From Miss Watt,' she said giving him the letter.

'Thanks, Lois, that was very obliging of you. I wish there were a few more like Miss Watt.'

'She's that way with everyone, says she likes to pay her bills promptly.'

'Want a receipt now or shall I send it?'

'Send it, but no hurry.'

David used the main switch inside the door to switch off all the lights. 'Where are you heading if I may ask?'

'Back home. Glenburn.'

'This isn't one of the nights you meet Tim?'

'No.' Then she added. 'Tim and I won't be seeing each other again.'

'Why ever not?'

'It's all off, we discovered we weren't right for each other.'

'This I don't believe. I thought it was wedding bells.'

'Then you were wrong.'

'I have to say you don't sound broken-hearted.'

'I'm not and neither is Tim. There were no tears shed, David.

We had some lovely times but those have come to an end. Tim has been reunited with his one-time love.'

'You must mean Catherine?'

'Yes, I do. Do you know her?'

'At one time but they parted company ages ago.'

'Met up again.' And she told him how it happened.

'I'm just amazed.'

'You shouldn't be, I think they are perfect for one another.'

'I could agree with that, but then I would have said Tim and you were a perfect match. Won't you miss him?'

'I am going to miss Tim terribly and I don't mind admitting that.'

'You won't be lonely for long, not a girl like you.'

'I'm not sure how to take that.'

'Yes, you do, you are very lovely and you won't want for admirers, myself among them.' He paused and looked at her. 'I wonder if I dare ask you to have dinner with me.'

'You could risk it,' she laughed.

'That sounds hopeful. How about tomorrow evening if you are free?'

'I am.'

He liked that. There was no pretence with this girl. She had no other plans and didn't mind admitting to it.

'Great! Say seven thirty or as near to that as I can make it. I hope to be ready by then but one never knows for sure . . .

'David, I understand that. Why don't I just come round and wait for you?'

'You wouldn't mind?'

'Not in the least. Why should I?'

'Not many have been so understanding.'

'So there have been a few?' She grinned.

'Very few.' And none that meant very much to me, he could have added.

Marie would have said where was her pride but she didn't care. She was gloriously happy, her heart was singing and she couldn't believe this was happening to her.

They were standing outside Glenburn and neither of them could stop smiling.

'The first time I saw you I was attracted and if it had been

221

anyone else but Tim I would have chanced my luck and asked you out.'

'Would you?'

'Too true.' He bent down to kiss her cheek. 'Until tomorrow evening,' he whispered.

She nodded and walked up to the door like someone sleep-walking.

When Lois left Glenburn the wireless was on in Miss Watt's sitting-room and the voice of the announcer followed her until she was outside and the door closed. Miss Watt always had the volume turned up although she insisted that she was not deaf, just a little hard of hearing and that came with advancing years. Life, she grumbled, would be a great deal easier if people would take the trouble to speak clearly instead of mumbling. Lois had been pleased to learn that she spoke distinctly while Mrs Barlow made the mistake of shouting which was totally unnecessary. There was a wireless in Lois's sitting-room which she laughingly told Winnie was seldom switched on since all she had to do was open the door to hear Miss Watt's.

For her date with David, Lois decided to wear her most recent buy, her tweed costume since it was warm, casually smart and suitable for all occasions other than dressy affairs. David, she imagined, wouldn't be the type to worry over-much about clothes. He would go for comfort rather than appearance and always his main concern would be for his four-legged patients.

The vet didn't keep strictly to his hours and this everyone knew. He was always prepared to see a distressed animal either in its owner's home or at the surgery. Most pet owners were considerate people who accepted that Mr Sutherland was entitled to a life outside the surgery. Unfortunately there were others who did not.

Lois was happy and there was a song in her heart as she walked smartly to Oakfield Road. She rang the bell, heard hurrying footsteps and the door opened.

'Come in! Come in!' he said giving her his broad, welcoming smile. 'The other two have just gone so I am doorman as well as everything else.'

Lois stepped into the passage with its dull, serviceable linoleum.

There was a large coconut mat at the door and she cleaned her feet on it before venturing in. Judging by the footmarks on the linoleum not many bothered.

David had a cleaning lady who came in daily and she never ceased to complain to anyone who would listen that folk would clean their feet before entering their own house but didn't take the trouble to do so in other folk's premises.

'You're still busy,' she smiled.

'Afraid so, but another ten minutes should see me finished.'

'Don't rush on my behalf, I'm happy to wait.'

'You're an angel.'

'I'm not,' she laughed, 'but if there is something I can do to help, please say so.'

'There is, Lois.' His voice dropped as they reached the waiting-room. 'The old man in there, could you keep him company? He's a poor soul and if he doesn't want to talk just sit with him.'

'Of course, I can surely manage that.'

David left her and Lois pushed the half open door wider and went in. An elderly man with sunken cheeks and watery blue eyes looked up.

'Thought you were the vet.' He made it sound as though it was her fault that she wasn't. Dropping his head he returned his gaze to the floor.

Lois wondered if he was well enough. 'Are you all right?' she said timidly.

His head went up sharply. 'Of course I'm all right, nothing wrong with me and if there was I wouldn't be here, would I?'

'No, I'm sorry that was silly of me.'

They sat in silence apart from the occasional wheeze from the old man. Lois picked up a paper not to read but just for something to do. She heard the sigh and then he spoke. 'Getting old, that's the trouble with the pair of us.'

'No, it isn't, Mr Struthers,' David said leading in a labrador. 'This poor animal of yours is suffering from nothing more than over-eating. If you want to kill your dog you are going the right way about it.'

'Now see you here, young man, I'm not taking that. I'll have you know that I feed him good, recommended dog food,' the man said angrily.

'I'm sure he gets that, which would be enough, but what about all the extras?'

'A wee bit of what I am having myself.'

'Most of it I rather think. Mr Struthers, if you will forgive me saying so, you look as though you could do with a good meal yourself. I suggest you stop sharing it with the dog. It isn't a kindness you know.'

'All right! All right!' he said tetchily. 'I get the point. There's nothing wrong with him then?'

'Nothing.'

'And what will I be due you?' he said with dignity.

'Nothing.'

'Now that's real good of you lad,' he said getting up and shuffling out and taking the labrador with him.

Lois and David exchanged smiles.

'I can't see you ever making a fortune, David.'

'Nor can I.' He was unbuttoning his white coat. 'I'll have to change. Five minutes—'

'David, you don't have to.'

'Can't take a girl out looking like this.'

'Yes, you can.' She smiled feeling very motherly. 'Freshen up if you want but there is absolutely no need to change.'

'You mean I am acceptable in baggy flannels and an ancient tweed jacket?'

'Perfectly acceptable.' Lois decided she didn't like vain men and she thought that for much of the time David would be happy to go about in what he was wearing just now.

'This wasn't what I planned. We were to go to one of the new restaurants and since you would know about them I was leaving it to you to choose. Incidentally, I'm not always shabby I do have a couple of decent suits, one I keep here,' he grinned, 'and a kilt for dress occasions.'

'I never doubted that but for tonight I'd be perfectly happy to dine somewhere close by.'

'Walking distance you mean?'

'Yes that would do me.'

'Where do you suggest?'

'A fifteen-minute walk to the Stag's Head. I was there once with friends and the food was good.'

'I've been several times and I agree the food can't be faulted but I wouldn't say as much for the decor.'

'Which we can overlook.'

'If you say so although it isn't the place I'd take a young lady.'

'This young lady would be quite happy with the Stag's Head,' she laughed.

'And this young man would like to do something better.'

'I know you would, David, but it is a bit late when we aren't booked.'

'No doubt you have a point there. All right, if you are absolutely sure?'

'I am.'

A few people were in the Stag's Head, so named because there was a stag's head mounted on the wall above the door. The name would have been more appropriate for an inn. It was not an elaborate restaurant, in fact it was decidedly shabby, shabbier than she remembered. Clean it was, however, and there were freshly laundered cloths on the tables. All had seen better days and had fraying hems and small darns.

'I feel embarrassed about this,' David said as they chose a table near to the window.

'No need for you to be, I suggested it remember.'

'Tim wouldn't be seen dead here.'

Lois grinned knowing it to be true. 'You are right there but to be perfectly honest, David, one can get the teeniest bit tired of posh places.'

'No one in his sober mind could call this posh.'

'Sh – sh – someone might hear you.'

The waitress came over and David smiled to her.

'What delicacy is on offer?'

She giggled and looked at Lois. 'Steak and kidney pie with boiled potatoes, haddock and chips – you'll have to wait about ten minutes for that.' Her eyes went to the ceiling as though the menu was printed up there. 'Cold meat with chips and potatoes and peas of course. We had steak but it's off – I don't mean it's off, I mean we had a run on it and it's finished.' She giggled again and waited with her pencil and notepad at the ready.

'Lois?'

'Steak and kidney pie and boiled potatoes, please.'

'Make that two.'

'With bread and butter and a pot of tea?'

'Yes, please.'

She was a pert little thing and wiggled her hips as she went through the far door to the kitchen.

'Now there is a wee lass who makes me want to laugh,' David said playing with the salt and pepper. 'She's friendly and she's funny yet for all we know maybe she returns each night to a drab home and working here is the highlight of her day.'

'Or there again perhaps there is little money in the home but plenty of love and affection.'

David looked at her quickly but didn't say anything and at that moment the waitress returned to arrange the cutlery and bring to the table two thick white cups, saucers and side plates. Once she had it all to her satisfaction she departed only to return almost immediately with a tray and the food on it.

'That was smart.'

'You were lucky, the pie was just fresh out of the oven.'

'It looks lovely,' Lois said and it did. The puff pastry had risen beautifully and was golden brown. When Lois came to take her first taste of the meat it was so tender it required no chewing.

They forgot about the shabby surroundings, Lois did anyway and she thought David did too. She had never been so happy. Here was someone who would fit in anywhere, she thought, a young man with a passion for his work who would always put others before himself. It needed a special kind of person to be a good vet and David was that. For anyone who hurt an animal be it domestic or farmyard, he would have nothing but contempt.

They finished the steak pie and the waitress brought a fresh pot of tea. When she had gone David took Lois's hand in his.

'I can't believe my luck, having you here with me. Lois . . .'

She looked into his eyes and saw in them all she wanted to know.

'I'm in love with you,' he said softly, 'and it is far too early to tell you, isn't it?'

'No, it isn't too early,' she said breathlessly and her eyes were shining.

'Could I take that to mean—'

'That I feel the same way?' She nodded, shyness all of sudden coming over her and making her unable to speak.

'We should be celebrating this moment with champagne instead of strong tea in thick white cups. Is that the way you like your tea?'

'Not really.'

'Why didn't you say?'

Because it didn't matter, I could have been drinking anything, she thought. 'I thought you liked it that way.'

'I don't, but even if I did you should have said.' He caught the waitress's eye. 'May we have a jug of boiling water, please?'

'Be there in a minute.'

'There you are,' she said putting down a jug. 'Everything else all right?'

'Very nice, thank you. Better make out the bill when you are here.'

'No hurry, sir, sit as long as you like. No one is waiting for the table.'

They both smiled.

'Time to hear your life story, Lois. I want to know all about you.'

'And I would be interested to hear about yours. You start.'

'Ladies first.'

'Not this time.'

He leaned forward. 'Not a great deal to tell. I'm alone now, my father died about three years ago and my mother—' He stopped.

'You lost her quite recently?'

'Yes.'

'If you find it difficult to talk about it please don't, I do understand.'

'No, I can tell you.'

Lois had emptied the jug of boiling water into the teapot and filled the two cups.

'Thanks,' he said putting in two spoons of sugar. 'Dad had been ill for some time before he died so in a way we were prepared or as prepared as one can ever be. He was good to me and I missed him.' He paused. 'You know about that, you lost your father, Tim told me.'

'Dad's death was very sudden, we were very close and I still miss him dreadfully.'

He nodded sympathetically. 'I feel that way about my mother, I miss her terribly. I loved them both but I was closer to my mother.'

'My mother never had any time for me and I have never been able to find out why. She loved Marie and Winnie so it must have been something about me.'

'That I find impossible to believe. No one could not love you.'

Lois smiled sadly and shook her head. 'Sorry, I'm interrupting your story.'

'Strangely enough, Lois, it was my mother's death that devastated me. Her death upset me more than Dad's.'

'Why should that be strange? Children are often closer to their mother.'

'She was my stepmother, my own mother died when I was born.'

'That was sad.'

'For my father it must have been although he made a happy second marriage and I gained a mother.'

'Tell me about your stepmother.'

'I never called her that.' He glanced about him. 'Shouldn't we be making a move?'

'A few have been sitting longer than us.'

'You are more observant than I am.'

'No, I'm facing them, you aren't. Go on with what you were saying.'

'My mother wasn't a soft mark, don't let me give you that impression. I had to toe the line and if I went over the mark there would be a severe scolding and then it was forgotten. Best of all I think was that she always came to the school prize-giving and the end of term activities. Must have been dead boring but she always managed to look as though she were enjoying whatever was going on. On the sports field she used to cheer me on. Other mothers were there too but I was especially proud of mine. She knew better than to kiss or hug a schoolboy. God, Lois, I remember it yet, how embarrassing some fond mamas could be. And the hats, especially on prize-giving day.' He rolled his eyes. 'Such monstrosities.'

'Those monstrosities,' Lois laughed, 'were probably very fashionable and cost the earth.'

'Waste of money then.'

'Your mother was more conservative?'

'No, she was a very attractive woman but she dressed to please herself, not to cause a sensation. That's about it, your turn now.'

Lois thought of her own bleak childhood. 'If I had one advantage over you it was that I had two sisters whereas you were an only child.'

It was on the tip of his tongue to tell her about his stepmother's child. The daughter she had never acknowledged during her lifetime but the moment passed.

'Meaning an only child is a lonely child?'

'Weren't you?'

'No, I was encouraged to bring my friends to the house so I didn't feel deprived.' The waitress was making out a bill for the next table and David asked for his. When it came he paid it handing a good tip to the waitress.

'Thank you very much, sir, very kind of you.' She looked more than pleased, she looked delighted.

'That is for excellent service and not hurrying us out.'

'I would never do that,' she said shaking her head. 'Well, I might with someone awkward and we get a few of those.'

They left the Stag's Head and strolled hand-in-hand through the quiet streets. It was a moonlit night, lovely but bitterly cold. Lois and David didn't feel the cold and all too soon they were outside Glenburn.

'This is an evening I shall always remember, Lois,' David said softly.

'I shall always remember it too.' She raised her face to his and very gently he touched his lips to hers. Then his arms were around her holding her close. Lois was shaken. This was what had been missing with Tim. It was impossible to describe, even to herself, this wildly excited feeling. So wonderful, so soul-stirring that she could have wept with happiness. She could feel the thudding of his heart and knew that he was experiencing the same joy.

'When do I see you again?' he said unsteadily.

Lois was about to suggest Thursday and what was wrong with that? Her appointment with the solicitor in Dundee was for two o'clock which left the evening free. Why did she have this sudden misgiving? The chances were equal between it being good news or bad. Why should it be bad? Perhaps it was of little importance but if so why should it involve a solicitor?

'Would Friday be all right?' Lois found herself saying.

'Yes. Friday is fine and so is Saturday and Sunday and every day.' He laughed like a schoolboy. 'Lois, I want to see you all the time.'

'I'll do what I can to oblige,' she said demurely.

'And I'll try and be better organised.'

'No, David,' she said quietly and firmly, 'don't change your working routine, don't change anything. What I would like—' She stopped.

'Go on, what would you like?'

'To make myself useful.'

'I never turn down an offer like that. We'll find a job for you never fear.'

They kissed again then reluctantly drew apart. David opened the gate for her and she had her door key ready in her hand. Then she was walking quickly along the path and David, waiting under the street lamp, watched until she was inside then he walked away whistling quietly.

His rooms were in a rather bleak-looking house which had the advantage of being close to the practice and it would do very well until he put his plans into operation and had a house built for him on the spare ground around his place of work. There had been no urgency until now. Meeting Lois had changed all that and settling down with the girl of his dreams was suddenly very important.

David's one regret was that his mother hadn't been spared to meet Lois. He was sure they would have loved each other. Strange too, he hadn't thought about it until now, but there was that little chortle Lois gave before it became a laugh. His mother had done the same.

Chapter Seventeen

A busy solicitor wouldn't spend much time with her, certainly no more than half an hour she thought and by then she would know what this was all about. Strangely enough she was less excited now than she had been at the beginning. Thinking about it had dulled her curiosity rather than heightened it. Nevertheless she had taken the earlier bus into Dundee rather than risk a delay and being late for her appointment.

The day was dull but dry and the Murraygate was thronging with shoppers. Lois put off time glancing at the windows and occasionally stopped if the display was particularly inviting. She had timed herself to arrive at ten minutes before two and was outside the close then. Four highly polished brass plates were mounted on the wall at the entrance and one gave the name of the solicitors – Bryden & Edmondson. Lois walked into the well-maintained, half-tiled close and climbed the stone stairs to the first floor. Should she knock and go in if the door was unlocked? Then she noticed a bell, better to ring and wait. The ring was answered smartly by a young girl.

'You should have just knocked and walked in, that's what everyone does.'

'I'm sorry.' Lois stepped into the hallway, a large hallway with a number of doors leading from it.

An inky finger pointed to one of the doors. 'That's the waiting-room, first on your right. Who are you seeing?'

'Mr Matthew Bryden.'

A woman came out of one of the doors and tut-tutted. 'Ruby, how often have you to be told? You ask the lady's name, show her into the waiting-room, then advise Mr Bryden that his client has arrived. Off you go and carry on with whatever you were doing,' she said shaking her head and smiling to Lois. 'Some take longer to train than others.' And that is one of them, her tone implied.

'I'm Lois Pringle and my appointment with Mr Bryden is for two o'clock.'

'Please take a seat in the waiting-room. Mr Bryden should be ready to see you at two o'clock or shortly after.' She went away closing the door behind her and Lois was alone in the cheerless room that was in much need of a fresh coat of paint and fresh curtains at the window would help, preferably colourful ones. The thin, beige material looked as if it had been there for ever. Were the curtains ever washed, Lois thought not. They were unlikely to stand the strain. There were four chairs and a low table with a selection of magazines on it. A quick glance showed that none would be of interest.

The same woman in her dark grey skirt and light grey twinset arrived promptly at two o'clock to say that Mr Bryden was ready to see her now. Lois got up quickly and followed the woman. She had been congratulating herself on being so calm but that deserted her now and her heart began to beat violently.

Lois was shown into a room and a voice said, 'Thank you, Miss Ingram.' An elderly man got up from behind his desk to shake her hand. 'Do sit down, Miss Pringle.'

'Thank you,' she whispered and sat on the edge of the chair.

Matthew Bryden went back behind his desk with Lois sitting facing him. She saw the scraggy neck showing above the stiffly starched collar and saw, too, that he was almost bald. When he looked up from the papers on his desk the steel-framed spectacles were halfway down his nose.

He coughed to clear his throat. 'Miss Pringle, may I ask why it took you so long to get in touch with this office?'

'I'm very sorry about that, Mr Bryden, but I was in no way to blame.' She told him how it had happened.

'Quite so.' He paused. 'Your father—'

'My father is dead, Mr Bryden,' she said quickly.

'I am aware of that, Miss Pringle. A sad loss to you and if I may be permitted to say so his death came at a particularly awkward time in view of events.'

She stared at him. What events? What was he on about?

'Had he been spared it would have fallen on him – ahem – to acquaint you with the circumstances of your birth.'

This was getting more confusing by the minute, what had her birth to do with anything? 'I just don't understand what you are trying to tell me,' Lois said sounding as bewildered as she felt.

'I'll do my best to explain.'

Was that sympathy in his voice or was she just imagining it? For a minute or two he studied the papers on his desk then he looked up. 'Miss Pringle, it is my duty to inform you that under the Will of the late Grace Melville, I use her maiden name, you have been left two thirds of her estate.'

Lois smiled with relief. 'I thought there had to be some mistake and now I know there has been. Mr Bryden, I've never heard of a Grace Melville.'

'Perhaps not, but there is no mistake. You, Lois Pringle, are the person mentioned in the Will.'

'But why? Why should a stranger leave money to me?'

'Because, my dear, Grace Melville was your natural mother.'

Every vestige of colour left her face leaving the skin chalk white and both hands were gripping the desk. The room swam and surely if she had not been sitting she would have fallen down.

Mr Bryden had been prepared for shock but this girl looked on the point of fainting. Years in the profession had taught him to hide his feelings but just occasionally they showed. He wished now that he had handed this case to one of his colleagues. He felt anger too, anger at the stupidity of some people. Why couldn't they see ahead instead of putting off what had to come out at some stage? It was so selfish. He had always advocated and argued strongly that a child should be informed if brought up by foster parents and that knowledge not kept from him until he was older. Sensibly handled a young child would quickly come to terms with it. Leaving it so often caused heartbreak and resentment. Especially so when a birth certificate had to be produced before marriage could take place. Another case in point was the civil service. It was sad but true that those born out of wedlock were not usually considered for an appointment.

'I'm sorry it had to be broken to you this way. Shall I get you a glass of water?'

Lois shook her head, she had recovered slightly. 'No, thank you, it was the shock, I had no idea. I'm all right now,' she said through stiff lips.

'I think I'll get that glass of water just the same.' He got up and went out.

Lois didn't want the glass of water but she welcomed the few minutes on her own. She felt as though she were in the dark and fumbling to make sense of what she had been told. She began to see that it made sense in one way. It explained her treatment at the hands of the woman she had thought of as her mother. Lois didn't feel that was the least bit upsetting. What she couldn't come to terms with, what she couldn't accept, was her beloved father not being her real father.

Mr Bryden came in and put a glass of water on the desk in front of her, then went back to his own chair.

'Thank you, that was kind of you.' She drank a little and was surprised to find it did help. 'Mr Bryden?'

'Yes?'

'Grace Melville was my mother you tell me.' She stopped to moisten her lips. 'Who was my father or was his identity not known?'

He frowned. 'Let me make this clear, Miss Pringle, you were not adopted. You were brought up in the house belonging to your father, Andrew Pringle and his wife.'

Lois closed her eyes and sent up a silent prayer. Now that she knew that Andrew Pringle was her father, her natural father, she could cope with the rest.

'Are you in a position to tell me about my mother and how this happened?'

'There is the question of confidentiality, Miss Pringle.'

'I accept that but surely you can tell me so much. I would have thought I was entitled to that.'

He nodded. The girl looked a bit better now. There had obviously been a strong bond between father and daughter. 'We must go back about twenty years when the shame of an unmarried mother was greater than it is today. The stigma remains of course but we are more tolerant. Then it was the worst nightmare for parents and they would have done anything to hide their daughter's shame.'

'No sympathy for her plight at all.'

The solicitor continued as though she hadn't spoken. 'Your

mother was the only child of well-respected and deeply religious parents. They were in a terrible state and couldn't bear that others should hear of it.'

'They disowned her?'

'Many would have but they didn't. They did what they thought best.'

'Best for whom?'

'Best for everyone,' he said irritably, he didn't like to be interrupted. 'Your mother was sent away to have the baby and arrangements were to be made to have the child adopted.'

Lois was having great difficulty in realising that the child in question was herself.

'Was my mother willing to give me away?'

'No, she was proving to be a very stubborn young woman and no threat by her parents to disown her would make her change her mind.'

'She wanted to keep me?' Her voice trembled.

'Indeed she did.'

'What happened?'

'Perhaps she realised just how difficult it was going to be and she said she would be prepared to give up her baby if it went to the child's natural father.'

'Why didn't he offer to marry her?' She knew the answer but she had to ask.

The solicitor pursed his lips. 'He was a married man and there was a young child.'

'Marie. Marie had been a baby then. Did my father want me?'

'Apparently he did.' The solicitor sounded wearied as though he longed to be through with this client. Maybe Lois saw the tiredness but she hardened her heart. This would probably be the only opportunity she would get.

'I'm not an adopted child. That was my home as much mine as my sisters'.'

'Your half-sisters. Miss Pringle, in my view, and I think most people would agree with me, your stepmother comes out of this with the most honour. To forgive an unfaithful husband is one thing but to agree to bring up that other woman's child as her own was an act of great charity. A remarkable woman. You had no idea, no inkling?'

'That she wasn't my mother? No.'

The solicitor became brisk. 'I have another appointment shortly so it is time we returned to the matter of your legacy.'

Lois looked at him blankly, she had forgotten about the money.

'I don't need it, not just now. What do you advise?'

'Investing most of it, but one would have to be extremely careful.'

'I could leave it in your hands?'

'Very well, I shall make enquiries and acquaint you with the details.'

'No, don't do that. I trust you to look after my interests.'

'I hope you are not always so trusting.'

'No, I'm not, but you are a solicitor.'

He smiled at that. 'Even in our noble profession we get the odd rotten apple but have no fear your inheritance is in safe hands. What I would advise is transferring a sum of money into an account for your personal use, to draw on at any time. I am not one to encourage spending but I think in your case you deserve to treat yourself.' He got up and extended his hand.

'Goodbye and if I can be of further service don't hesitate to get in touch.'

'I won't and thank you for being so understanding.'

She stopped at the door and turned round. 'Forgive me, one more question. Would you know if my mother was happy?'

'She married a widower and I believe it was a successful union.'

'Thank you, I'm so glad.'

Out in the street Lois felt light-headed. She found herself outside D.M. Brown's store with no clear idea how she had got there. They had a restaurant and she was longing for a cup of tea. Normally she would have just gone in, but today she wanted somewhere smaller and quiet where she could sit undisturbed and think. So much to think about and her mind seemed unable to grasp the half of it. Thank goodness she hadn't made arrangements to go out this evening. And there was one benefit in being on one's own. No questions to answer except those she put to herself.

There was a small restaurant in Union Street not far from the railway station and she went there. Twice she had crossed the road without looking and it had earned her the wrath of the motorist. This wouldn't do, she must get a grip on herself and pay attention to what was going on around her. If she didn't she would land herself in hospital or worse.

She ordered a pot of tea and the waitress replenished the cake-stand. The rush was over and not many tables were taken. No danger of someone asking to share her table and perhaps try to engage her in conversation.

When the tea came she gave herself up to her thoughts. She was illegitimate. Lois said the word two or three times to herself. It was just a word and she wasn't the only one to find herself in this position. In many ways she had been lucky. No one knew. No, that wasn't true. One other person did know and why had she kept silent? Lois could understand it when her father was alive but, once he was dead, what had held her back? Not love that was for sure. What then?

Had Harriet Pringle ever forgiven her husband or had she made him suffer for all those years? Her thoughts shifted to Grace Melville. Had she known that Andrew Pringle was a married man? Had he told her or had he not bothered? Surely her father hadn't been capable of cheating on both women? No, he had been kind and good, quite incapable of hurting anyone. Blaming him was too painful, a raw hurt to add to the other hurts.

She preferred to think that Grace and her father had been deeply in love and that it had been too strong for them both. She was making excuses and what they had done was inexcusable. Mr Bryden had been right. Only Harriet had come out of this with honour. It was hard to accept but she should be grateful to Harriet. In the school playground she might have been called a bastard – such an ugly word – she shuddered and a woman sitting at the next table looked at her with concern.

Lois took a cake from the stand, she didn't want it but she had better eat something, she thought. Taking the knife she cut it in two and took a bite. It tasted to her like sawdust but she forced it down and then drank some of the tea. Time to go if she was to get that bus and catching the waitress's eye she asked for her bill. When she got up and made to pass the table the woman who had been watching her touched her arm.

'Excuse me asking but are you all right?'

'Yes, I'm all right.' But she was struggling to hold back the tears.

'I thought you looked distressed and I wondered if I could help.'

'Thank you, it was kind of you to be concerned. I was a little upset but I'm quite all right now.' She smiled and went to pay her bill at the desk.

Darkness was already falling, the gloaming, that romantic time between the dark and the light. A time for lovers. That reminded her of David and a cold hand touched her heart. Would it make any difference to David to know that she had been born out of wedlock? She didn't think so but could she be sure? Was it possible to really know another person, know into that person's heart? No, it wasn't. She had thought she knew her father yet she hadn't.

Only when she was on the bus did she give thought to her inheritance. Her mother, Grace Melville, must have been comfortably off and on her death she had wanted her daughter to benefit. What had she been like, the mother she would never know? Lois hugged the thought that she hadn't been forgotten. In the end she had reached out, perhaps to make amends for giving her baby into the care of another woman.

There was nothing she particularly wanted for herself but the money in the account would come in useful. She would buy a good wedding gift for Marie, spend more than she would have. And Winnie – Winnie must get a nice dress or coat for London. Her little sister must be smartly dressed for her job in London. Not her sister, her half-sister. She didn't want them to find out. They wouldn't be told if she had anything to do with it, but Harriet might decide in her own time to tell them.

Chapter Eighteen

After a restless night when sleep only came in fits and starts, Lois got up feeling washed-out and depressed. The same face looked back at her from the mirror yet inside herself she felt different. What she had always taken for granted was slipping away. Her sisters were only her half-sisters, they shared the same father but not the same mother. It should have pleased her to know that Harriet wasn't her real mother, only strangely it didn't. In spite of everything and deep down she had always hoped that the woman she thought of as her mother would come to love her. Moving away from home hadn't altered that. If the truth were known she was angry and confused, not sure about anything any more. In her heart she ought to be able to forgive Harriet, even to feel some gratitude, only she couldn't. If she even tried to say she was grateful the words would stick in her throat.

Coming to terms with what her father had done was going to be difficult. She knew now that he hadn't been as perfect as she had believed. He had cheated on two women and caused a lot of unhappiness. In one short afternoon her whole world had been turned upside down and somehow she had to learn to live with the knowledge that she wasn't the person she had believed herself to be. What would David think about it all? If they were going to have a life together he would have to be told now. Was being born out of wedlock so terrible? If it had been the other way round would she have held it against him? Of course not. But people held different views on these things. Easy enough to pretend it didn't matter when it concerned someone else. Her stomach churned with the fear of what she might see in David's face. If she watched carefully that first unguarded moment would tell her. She would know the truth even though he might try to deny it. It would be the end. There would be no marriage. Her pride wouldn't let her go through with it if there was the slightest chance of her being made to feel shame for something that was in no way her fault.

When Lois set out for the office, the morning was crisp and clear but with a hint of snow in the icy wind. A savage wind that was whipping the last of the dead leaves from the trees. Autumn was going to have its last fling before bowing out. A sudden sharp gust sent the dry leaves into a panic-stricken frenzy rudely stopped by a wall where they joined the others swept there by one of the householders.

She should have been looking forward to the evening instead of which she was searching for an excuse to get out of it. A phone call would do it. But why postpone what had to be said? She still had to confess. Then she stopped dead in her tracks and a woman behind her tut-tutted in annoyance. 'Sorry,' Lois muttered and began walking again. Confess – why had she used that word? What was there to confess? She had done nothing wrong.

Perhaps she was paler than usual, but if Mrs Wilson noticed she made no comment. Mr Latimer came into the office wearing his overcoat and his usual cheerful expression. She smiled at him.

'Good morning, Lois. Bitterly cold morning, cold enough for snow.'

'Good morning, Mr Latimer. Yes, it is and I thought I felt snow in the wind.'

He gave a mock shiver. 'Not far away then. Pity when it comes this early it makes for a long winter,' he said, taking out his fountain pen and putting his signature to the letters. 'As you would have gathered I didn't bother to come in last night. There was nothing all that urgent and you'll be posting these some time today.'

'I'll put them in the box before the collection at eleven.'

'Good girl.' He put the cap back on his pen and put it in the inside pocket of his coat. 'Get your business transacted to your satisfaction?'

'Yes, I did and thank you very much for giving me the afternoon off.'

'My pleasure. Dundee busy?'

Had it been? Lois couldn't remember. 'Much as usual,' she said.

Once he'd gone Lois tried to keep to routine as much as possible, it was the only way to get through the work, but there were times when her thoughts drifted and her hands fell idle. What had her real mother been like? Did her daughter resemble her? How had they met – her father and Grace Melville? Falling in love was no excuse for what they had done. It had been selfish and irresponsible and the tragic result of those stolen moments had cost dear. Six people had suffered and that included Grace who must have suffered most of all. Telling her parents must have been a dreadful ordeal and from all accounts they had been less than supportive. Their main concern had been for their good name and to protect that they had wanted their daughter out of their sight and banished with her secret shame.

Poor Grace, how awful to go through all that pain and suffering to bring an unwanted baby into the world. Some would say her father was the villain of the piece but she could never think of him as that. His own marriage hadn't been made in heaven, they were an ill-matched pair, Lois thought, or was she being unfair. Had he killed that love? Harriet was a proud woman and the humiliation must have been hard to bear, which made it all the more difficult to understand why she would have agreed to bring up her husband's and Grace Melville's child. It didn't make sense or had some kind of pressure been put on her? Perhaps a condition of her husband remaining with her? A possibility Lois thought. Harriet would be thinking of her own child. Marie's welfare would come first and if that meant bringing up this other child then so be it.

Lois had idolised her father and her faith in human nature had been given a bad jolt. It made her wary about trusting anyone and that had to include David. Loving a person didn't mean one could trust them. She loved David, but did she know him? Love could happen in a twinkling, a look across a crowded room and two hearts could begin to beat wildly. Getting to know someone took a lot longer.

By the time the working day was over and Lois had tidied up and gone she was feeling more like herself. Shock did that, made everything look blacker than it was. She was making too much of it. Far better that she should wait to tell David when she was less emotional.

* * *

David looked exhausted, it had been a hectic day, not helped by a misunderstanding about an appointment which had left the usually calm receptionist very angry. David had been called to soothe tempers and an irate woman, carrying a Pekinese in her arms had grudgingly agreed to take a seat in the waiting-room until David could see her little darling. Miss Douglas was not best pleased and showed her displeasure by a pursed mouth and stormy eyes. She stamped about making more noise than was necessary and on the dot of half past five put on her coat and hat and stormed out of the building without as much as saying she was going.

The phone rang just as Lois came in.

'Oh, God! Lois can you get that?' David raced back to the surgery.

Lois hurried to the phone and lifted it.

'Is that the vet?' the voice said urgently.

'This is the receptionist, can I help you?' Lois said in her best businesslike voice.

'I'm so sorry to be late but could you possibly make an appointment for . . .'

Lois dragged over the book: everything was neat and clear. She wrote in Mrs Carnegie's name in the first space, and felt rather pleased with herself as she put the phone down. Her own office training had come to her assistance and she was pleased David had asked her. Now she would just sit and wait for him.

She heard the hum of voices and then a well-dressed middle-aged woman carrying a large basket glanced over at Lois on her way out.

'Goodnight,' she said to Lois.

'Goodnight,' Lois answered.

'Thank you so much, Mr Sutherland, I don't know what we would do without you,' she said smilingly.

'There would be someone else, Mrs McKenzie.' Lois heard David's laugh. 'Any problems, there shouldn't be any, but don't delay . . .'

'I won't and thank you again.' The door shut and David came over.

'Sorry to have taken advantage of you like that but this, if you will pardon my French, has been one hell of a day. Incidentally, who was that on the phone?'

'A Mrs Carnegie, she wanted to make an appointment and

as there was a space on Thursday afternoon I pencilled her in for that.'

'Not only beautiful but efficient.'

'David, I do work in an office.'

He grinned. 'I know.'

'What was so awful about today?'

He rolled his eyes. 'I'm in the dog-house, a curiously apt expression come to think of it.'

'What did you do?'

'I let my receptionist down by taking the coward's way out and suggesting that she might, just might mind you, have made a mistake with the times.'

'And had she?'

'Of course not. Miss Douglas does not make mistakes, not that kind anyway.'

'Then why did you suggest she might have?'

'Because I thought it would save a lot of trouble.'

'That is no excuse, David, I'm surprised at you.'

'Circumstances, Lois. Circumstances. I was up to my eyes and I wasn't going to waste time in an argument. I only suggested that there might have been a misunderstanding . . .'

'Not necessarily making it out to be the fault of Miss Douglas?'

'Sort of making it either way,' he grinned.

'And how did it end?'

'With the customer looking as though she had scored a victory. Head high, little darling in arms, she agreed to wait in the waiting-room until I could manage to see them.'

'Stop it, David, it isn't funny. Miss Douglas was probably very hurt, she would have expected better from you.'

'I know and I think I have sunk very low in her estimation.'

'Did you apologise to her?'

'Didn't get a chance. She never leaves on the dot but tonight she did and without as much as a "good night, Mr Sutherland",' he said sadly.

'Be especially nice to her on Monday and I'm sure she'll find it in her heart to forgive you.'

He nodded. 'A large slice of humble pie should do it.'

She smiled. 'A storm in a teacup.'

'Exactly. We'll forget about it and just give me five minutes.'

'No rush, I'm quite comfortable.'

'We could go for a coffee somewhere and talk.'

'I'd like that.'

'And Lois?'

'Yes?'

'Saturday, I hope you're free so that we can have the whole of the afternoon and evening together.'

She nodded happily. 'I am.'

'Thank heaven for Saturdays,' was his parting shot as he hurried away to get ready.

It was a day like Friday but the wind had dropped making it more pleasant. After a short discussion they decided to drive to Carnoustie and have a snack, a walk along the beach and then go on to Arbroath for dinner.

Only a few hardy souls were braving the cold and Lois and David were among them. They had that holiday feeling and were walking hand-in-hand along the front just happy to be together. Lois had tried putting her worries to the back of her mind but they would keep surfacing.

'David?'

'Yes, sweetheart.'

She smiled at the endearment. 'Do you always manage to keep a secret?'

'You do ask the strangest questions. Let me see, at school I was quite good at keeping a secret and if told something in confidence it wouldn't go any further. Does that answer your question?'

'Not quite. If you feel you should tell but find it difficult, what do you do then?'

'If no one gets hurt I don't see that it matters. Short of murder that is, one would have to confess that.' He grinned. 'Hey! I'm getting interested, have you a dark secret?' His expression was mocking. 'Don't tell me there are skeletons in your cupboard?'

'You never know.'

'Intriguing. Is this leading up to something and am I going to hear what it is?'

'There isn't anything.' She tried to laugh but failed and it ended in a half sob.

He stopped there on the beach and turned her to face him.

'Something is wrong, something is worrying you and I want to hear what it is.'

'Nothing is wrong. Good grief it was just nonsense talk.'

She wasn't going to confide in him, that much was clear and it would be folly to try. Instead he said lightly, 'You wanted to know if I had any skeletons in my cupboard?'

'Have you?'

'Not as far as I know.'

'Meaning your life is an open book?'

'I wouldn't quite put it that way but I am not hiding anything or I don't think I am,' he added remembering the girl mentioned in his stepmother's Will. Was this the time to tell Lois? He thought not, it wasn't after all of much interest to Lois. Another time would do very well when she was less preoccupied.

Lucky David, she thought. A few short weeks ago and Lois would have said she had no secrets.

David was far from satisfied, clearly she was troubled and in time she would tell him or perhaps she wouldn't. Either way it would be her decision.

The wind had got up again blowing the sand and they walked on the grass then over to the road. The invigorating walk had put the colour into her cheeks and given them both an appetite. The little café was in the High Street between a shoe shop and a grocer's. They went in and a few housewives with shopping baskets were having a cup of tea and a gossip before returning to make the family tea. They looked up at the young couple who had entered and smiled. Just then the waitress arrived with a tray of china and told them where to sit. The afternoon tea was hugely enjoyable with everything baked on the premises. The china was in the Willow pattern and Lois began to tell David the story of the runaway lovers as she had been told it.

'Not the way I heard it.'

'What did you hear?'

'Can't remember but it certainly wasn't that. We had Willow pattern plates, a few had survived from the dinner service and I remember asking my mother about the bridge.'

'Her version was different from what I've told you? Doesn't matter, I suppose there were a lot of stories.'

They helped themselves to scones and pancakes still warm with the butter melting as it was spread. After paying the bill they had a leisurely walk down one side of the High Street then crossed over and looked at the shops on the other side. Lois bought a box of peppermint creams for Miss Watt as a small thank-you for the afternoon tea they occasionally enjoyed together.

Back in the car they drove to the Eastcliffe Hotel in Arbroath which commanded a wonderful view of the sea and passing ships. A popular hotel and at the height of the season it was busy with guests, many of them resident for a week or longer. Those staying a month tended to rent a house which was a lot cheaper and gave the children more freedom.

This was a quiet period and those arriving for a meal – lunch or dinner – were given a warm welcome. Before going in Lois and David stood for a while admiring the view. The screeching of seagulls was all around as they swooped low down, then flew away high into the sky until their cries were no longer heard.

'Shall we go in?'

'Yes.' She turned to smile at him. 'I love the sea, don't you?'

'I do, but then I love the country too.'

They were shown into the lounge, given menus to study and asked if they wished a drink.

The dining-room was beautiful, nothing gaudy or striking just in quiet good taste. The tables were well spaced and covered in pale pink tablecloths with a matching stiffly starched napkin at each place and two long-stemmed wine glasses in front of the heavy silver cutlery. They weren't alone, a few tables were occupied and a pianist played softly on a grand piano. The food and the service were excellent and Lois knew that she would have been completely happy if only she didn't have the nagging worry of her secret.

'David, where did you live before you settled in Muirford?'

'Dundee, the Downfield district. Our house – I suppose I should call it mine now—'

'You have a house of your own?' She looked at him in surprise.

'It was left to me but I'll have to be thinking about putting it on the market. Bit of a wrench parting with it but I have to live where my work is.' He paused while they were served coffee. 'The house is a bit far out but it does have a lovely view of the Sidlaw Hills.'

Lois smiled. 'My parents lived in Dundee. That's where they

were brought up, and I can remember my father saying that he and his friends used to take the tram to the Downfield terminus and go for a walk on the Sidlaws.'

'That's something we'll have to do and I'm glad you happen to be the outdoor type.' He smiled as though remembering something that had amused him. 'Lots of people like your father and his friends took to the hills at the weekend. A few would pass our way and my dad used to chat to them over the garden wall. Mum used to say it was any excuse to take a rest from gardening.'

After all that fresh air, Lois should have had no difficulty in sleeping but though her body was wearied her mind was busy searching for answers and knowing there weren't any. She got up feeling dull and unrefreshed.

Mrs Wilson was worried, the girl had become almost like family to her and she could see that Lois was having to make an effort to act as usual. When asked if she was well enough her only reply was that she had a touch of cold like so many others in this damp raw weather. They were all needing the summer and a bit of sunshine. Mrs Wilson knew that a slight cold didn't put blue shadows under the eyes, worry was more like it. Perhaps Lois was having regrets about leaving home but felt she had burnt her boats. Or maybe it was something quite different. The young had their problems too.

Lois was well ahead with her work which was a pity, she would have preferred to be busy with no time to think. Harriet was constantly in her thoughts and she wondered if she knew that Grace Melville was dead and if she did had it affected her in any way? Not very likely. Lois knew that her mother went through the columns of births, deaths and marriages but she may have missed it. After all it would be under Grace's married name and if the name meant nothing it was improbable that she would bother to read the rest of the announcement. She might not know that Grace had married. Come to think about it Lois didn't know her real mother's married name. Not that it mattered, it wasn't important.

Grace – Lois liked the name, so much nicer than Harriet. No wonder Harriet hadn't inflicted the name on either of her daughters. She thought if she had a daughter she would like to call her Grace. David might not agree, he might want his daughter named after his stepmother who had meant so much to him. Her thoughts switched to Marie and Winnie. How would they feel about her being only a half-sister? Marie might dismiss it with a raised eyebrow but Winnie would be sad just the same as Lois was. Was it too much to hope that they would never find out?

Chapter Nineteen

As the day of departure drew near Winnie was getting more and more excited. She couldn't settle to anything and whenever possible she took the bus over to Glenburn to be with Lois.

'Mum isn't being much help,' she grumbled as she accepted a cup of tea. 'I do need advice, I mean what do I take with me?'

'You can't take everything that's for sure. Select the clothes you are happiest in and forget the rest. Anything you find you especially want you can ask Mum to send on.'

'I suppose she would do that.'

'Remember it is London you are going to and once you have a bit of money in your pocket you'll be able to buy something really stylish. In fact you can go mad.' Lois smiled as she said it, knowing that Winnie was unlikely to venture into the West End stores on her own.

'Some hope, maybe if I had you with me it might be different.' Her eyes brightened. 'Lois, why not? You could come for a holiday, couldn't you?' she said eagerly.

Lois hadn't given it a thought until now. What was to hinder her? She was due holidays, she had the money and it would be lovely to see Winnie in her new surroundings. Her sister was no actress and she would know if she was happy or just pretending to be.

'I might just do that, Winnie.'

'No kidding?'

'No kidding, but I'll give you a chance to be settled first.'

'If I asked Mrs Timpson she might let you stay with me.'

'No, don't do that. Mrs Timpson is your employer and no matter how kind she is it would be a mistake to take advantage.'

'It was the expense I was thinking about. Won't accommodation be terribly expensive?'

'I told you I'm not short of money and, before I forget, have you got a suitcase? Sorry I can't be of help there, if you remember I got the use of Tim's.'

Winnie nodded. 'That reminds me of the time he took us out. Yon was a great night. Wish it was still Tim and you.'

'Well, it isn't and we were discussing suitcases not Tim.'

'I know we were and I suppose it will have to be that big heavy case, it weighs a ton even with nothing in it,' Winnie said gloomily.

Lois laughed at the exaggeration. It was heavy, but not as bad as Winnie was making out.

'Mrs Timpson will keep you right. If you are in doubt about anything ask her.'

'Ask her what?'

'The arrangements about your luggage for one thing. I imagine it will all go off together well in advance. You won't be expected to lug around a heavy case.'

'Thank heaven, that's a relief. Lois, you are brilliant.'

'What you will need is a small case for the train.'

'Haven't got one, I'll make do with one of Mum's shopping bags.'

'Winnie, for goodness sake.'

'It will have to do, Lois, I can't ask Mum for anything else. Haven't had a chance to tell you, but she bought me a new coat and a skirt. The coat is cherry red and it has a small beaver collar that if I want I can button it up to the neck.'

'Sounds nice and you'll suit the colour.'

'My choice. Not the skirt,' she made a face, 'Mum made me get the oatmeal coloured one, said it would go with everything.'

'Suppose it will, Winnie, and it was generous of her.'

'Do you think so? I don't. Remember I only get pocket money and she hasn't bought me anything big for ages.' She paused and seemed to be regretting what she had said. 'No, you're right it was generous, I mean she does have this wedding to pay for.'

Lois nodded. It would make a big dent in the savings, she thought and wondered how her mother was managing. She might be having to struggle. Lois felt guilty having all that money and in happier circumstances she would have been only too happy to help out financially. On the other hand when it came to the wedding the Hammonds knew that Marie's mother was a widow and they might offer to foot the bill though Lois thought it unlikely.

'More tea?'

'No, thanks.'

'Has Mum met Mrs Timpson?'

'Yes, we had afternoon tea with her, I told you that. She didn't meet Mr Timpson, he's never home in the afternoon, but she liked Mrs Timpson and she thought the children were cute.'

'Very encouraging. She's come round to you going to London?'

'No, just resigned which is the most I can expect. I wanted to ask have you any regrets about you and Tim splitting up?'

'None at all. It was lovely while it lasted but we weren't in love.'

'Lots of people aren't when they get married but it sort of develops.'

Lois was amused. 'Very profound and how come you know about that?'

'I do read you know.'

'Tim is in love with Catherine, Winnie, and I told you that before.'

'I know you did, you've told me a lot of things. How about this vet? What is so special about him?'

'David? What about him?'

'Is he the one?'

'Yes, I'm in love with him,' she said softly.

'How do you know?'

'I just do. It's something you can't explain, Winnie.'

'Just hits you and that is that.'

Lois smiled. 'More or less.'

'I wonder if it will ever happen to me?' she said wistfully.

'Nothing surer.'

'So you say. Will I get to meet David before I go?'

'I very much hope so, but if we can't fix up something beforehand I'm sure he'll come to the station with me.'

'You are coming to see me off then?'

'Try and stop me. I'm coming to make sure you get on that train. How about Mum? Will she be there with Marie and Stephen?'

'I wouldn't bet on Marie and Stephen showing up, it would be nice if they did.' She shrugged.

'Have they fixed a date for the wedding yet?'

'Toying with a few dates according to Marie, but to be honest she doesn't seem all that bothered. She worries Mum and infuriates me.'

Lois frowned. There was something wrong she was sure there was. 'That doesn't sound a bit like Marie. Try not to be too hard on her, Winnie, she could be suffering from pre-wedding nerves.'

Winnie looked scornful. 'Pre-wedding nerves my foot and a bit early for those with the date not even fixed. This shortbread is good,' she said taking another piece.

'Mrs Barlow made it. Winnie, are you doing anything special this Saturday?'

'No. Why?'

'Thought we could take the bus into Dundee and look at the shops.'

'I come here or do we meet in Dundee?'

'Whichever you prefer.'

'I'll come here then, but what about the boyfriend? Won't he expect you to spend it with him?'

'Not this Saturday and he'll understand. I want to buy you a present, something to take with you.'

'You don't have to buy me anything,' Winnie said in a rush.

'I know that, but I want to and don't worry, I'm not short of money.'

'If you're serious about this fellow shouldn't you be buying things for your bottom drawer?' She gave a giggle. 'What a stupid expression that is.'

'Forget the bottom drawer, that is old-fashioned.' Lois thought about the money in her account. It was peace of mind and she should never experience financial hardship, but it had come at a price.

'Something small then.'

'Like a handkerchief?'

'Or a box of hankies if you want to go mad.' They were both giggling as they had so often done, but now their laughter was tinged with sadness. Soon there would be many miles between them and of the three sisters Winnie was the least suited to branching out on her own.

'I thought about giving you one of those very neat little cases for the train for your odds and ends, and a handbag.'

'One or the other would be marvellous but certainly not both.'

'Just you be quiet and let your elders decide these things. And try to remember that I haven't spent anything on entertainment since I don't know when and Miss Watt hardly takes anything from me. Actually I'm incredibly lucky.'

'Maybe you are lucky, but you are also very generous. Thanks, Lois, I couldn't have a better sister,' she said and burst into tears.

Saturday was showery and cold, the showers being of sleet, but it didn't spoil the outing for the sisters. They had a lovely time going from shop to shop before eventually deciding on a purchase. Draffens had a good leather department and it was there that the case and the handbag were bought. Winnie would have been scandalised, might even have caused a scene, had she known how much money Lois was spending. Fortunately the assistant was quick on the uptake and made sure the price ticket was out of sight. The cash transaction took place when Winnie's attention was engaged elsewhere.

'Lois, I never expected all this and I just don't know what to say or how to thank you,' Winnie said as they left the store with their purchases.

'Just to know you are pleased is thanks enough and no, not that way, we aren't going for the bus yet, might as well make a day of it.'

'Where are we going?'

'For something to eat.'

'Thanks again and that will be welcome.'

'Thought it might and in return I'll expect to hear from you regularly,' Lois said severely.

'Of course I'll write to you and you'll have to reply.'

'As if I wouldn't. My letters will keep you up-to-date with what is going on at home.'

'How can you when you never go near Mum?'

'Does Mum ever mention my name?' Lois asked.

Winnie's silence answered it.

'Thought not. You'll get the local news from Mum and if I see anything of interest in the newspaper I'll cut it out and send it with my letter.'

'Bless you. That's what the manse children have started to say. It gave Mrs Hutchison quite a turn, she hadn't realised how often she said it herself until she heard them.'

'Could have been worse.'

'A lot worse. The workmen have been doing some modernising in the kitchen and the children have picked up a few choice words from them. Mrs Hutchison didn't want to make too much of a fuss in case they thought it was clever and came out with some in front of the church members.'

They had tea and cakes and left the restaurant carrying a parcel each. At the bus stop Winnie said abruptly. 'I wish I was in London or on my way. That isn't to say I'm desperate to leave Greenacre, I'm not.'

'You want to get the goodbyes over,' Lois said gently.

'No, I can cope with those.'

'What then?'

'Silly I know, but I have this awful feeling that something is going to happen to prevent me going to London.'

'What could happen?'

'Anything could happen.'

'Don't talk like that, Winnie. Even if we have to half carry you David and I will have you on that train.'

Winnie smiled and looked at the neatly wrapped purchases. 'Better keep these away from Marie, especially the handbag.'

'Think she might take a fancy to them?'

'Don't think it, I know it.'

'On no account are you going to let her borrow the handbag.'

'I won't, but she'll think it is wasted on me.'

'Winnie Pringle there are times I want to shake you. You must stop putting yourself down. You are a lovely, warm-hearted girl and someone is going to notice that very soon.'

'And someone meaning Mum is going to see what you've given me. The minute I get in the house she is going to see these.'

'Don't make too much of them, Winnie.'

'I am going to make a lot of them. I am sick and tired of the way you have been treated and I am going to have it out with Mum before I leave. She's got some explaining to do I'm telling you.'

'Winnie, it won't do any good. Better to leave things as they are.'

'No, I won't and that is the bus coming. Hope it isn't full.'

It wasn't and they both got a seat but not together.

'How did the shopping spree go?'

'It was hardly that, David, but Winnie was delighted with her little case and her handbag.'

'I missed you.'

'I'm glad,' she said softly. 'What did you do?'

'I put the time to good use and answered some long overdue letters.'

'That's something off your mind then and my sister, Winnie, wants to meet you before she goes.'

'Does she? That's nice and I would very much like to make her acquaintance and indeed the other members of your family.'

'Just Winnie, I think, but if you come to the station you may meet the others.'

'The others – does that include your mother?' David said quietly.

'I don't know. She may prefer to say goodbye in the house.'

'Understandable, I suppose, but I hope not. It would have been an opportunity for me to meet your mother.'

Lois's brow puckered into a frown. 'David, I did explain to you my reasons for leaving home.'

'I know you did—'

'Some people get on better apart and that is the case with us.'

'Pity.'

'Perhaps it is but that is the way things are.'

'Should be some sort of contact, Lois.'

'Why?' She was beginning to be annoyed.

'Mother and daughter – it isn't natural. All families or most of them, have disagreements from time to time but they just have to forgive and forget.'

'David, you mean well but forgive me if I say you don't know what you are talking about. This was no little tiff. This is something that has gone on for as long as I can remember.'

'I should shut up.' He smiled apologetically.

'Yes, you should, David.'

'Not another word on the subject I promise but one day you may feel like telling me all about it.'

'I can't tell you what I don't know myself.'

'Probably fascinating stuff, the story of your life. You started telling me about it but we didn't get very far.'

'Neither did you with yours,' she shot back.

'Is that so? Well, Lois, the reason I spend so much time here,' he said looking about him, 'is because I am in no hurry to return to my digs. The only thing in its favour is that it is close to the practice. What I am hoping to do is have my own house built on that waste ground at the back. A friend of mine is an architect and I mean to get in touch with him to have plans drawn up.' He was smiling into her face as he finished.

Lois felt a flutter of excitement. Was she included? Would she have a say in the plans? He answered her unspoken question.

'I hope you'll be very much involved with those plans.'

'I'd love to help,' she said colouring.

'You'll have to if it is to be our future home.'

'Are you serious?'

'Never been more serious in my life. Hey, you aren't backing out, we are going to be married?'

'Yes, but—'

'But nothing. I love you and I thought you felt the same?'

'I do.'

'Then where is the problem?'

'No problem.'

'Glad to hear it.'

'You are hopeless, do you know that?'

'A hopeless case without you. It's true, Lois, I waken each day and remember that I am unofficially engaged to the most beautiful girl in the world.'

'How about a cup of tea?' she said demurely.

'Excellent suggestion, I'll make it and you rake around and see if there is anything fit to eat.'

'I bought some buttered scones.'

'Good thinking.' David filled the kettle from the cold tap and the water roared out in a sudden gush that splashed over him. 'Blast and sink it.'

'You need a plumber, I told you that before.'

'Nonsense, simple job I'll see to it myself some time.'

'And how long have I been hearing that?'

'Not so very long. This Sunday without fail, not the best day I grant you but sometimes needs must.'

Lois set a corner of the table and David made the tea.

'A week on Sunday, could you keep that clear?'

'Yes. Why?' said Lois.

'I have the house to clear out and I'll have to get started soon. Not something I am looking forward to doing, but it won't be so bad if we do it together.'

'David, of course I'll help.'

'Most of the furniture will go to the saleroom.'

'Don't be too hasty or you might regret it.'

'Meaning we might be able to make use of some?'

'It's a thought.'

He looked thoughtful. 'Put it in store until we need it?'

'Worth thinking about.'

'It is. We can decide what we want to keep, but most of it will have to go. It is very old-fashioned, belonged to my grandparents or to be more correct my step-grandparents if there is such a relationship. All very good stuff but would be out of place in a modern house.'

'Not necessarily, it is possible to mix the old with the new without it looking ridiculous or in bad taste.'

She thought he looked pleased. 'Nothing has been touched, my mother's clothes are still in the wardrobe just as she left them. What should happen to those?'

'A charity would be glad of them.'

He nodded. 'Mother would have approved of that. How would you go about it?'

'Mr Latimer would know.'

'The very person. I can leave that with you then.'

Miss Watt was watching this romance and was happy at the way it was going. Not a romantic by nature, nevertheless she was taking an interest in Lois and Mr Sutherland. There had been no young men in her own life, there might have been if she had given them any encouragement but she hadn't and she had no regrets. Some women were born to be wives and mothers and others to be independent. Rebecca Watt was fiercely independent and she once declared to an amused company that the man wasn't born who would order her about.

Lois was different and it was a good thing. It would be a sad day for the world if there were too many like Rebecca Watt. Money and position, the old woman knew, wouldn't count very high with Lois. The girl would never go short of admirers and as for Mr Sutherland he was a fine lad. There couldn't be much wrong with a man who loved and understood animals the way he did. Lois had been a godsend coming the way she did and she would be sadly missed when she did go as she surely would. Still when one door closed another one opened and Rebecca had taught herself to look on the bright side.

The year was drawing to an end. In a little while they would be celebrating Christmas and shortly after that Winnie would be leaving for London. Lois felt like weeping and that was stupid since she had given her sister every encouragement to take up the challenge and make a new life for herself. If only it wasn't so far away, she thought and sighed. Winnie was going to be missed.

Marie came into her thoughts and she didn't feel too kindly disposed towards her older sister. Not once had she come to Glenburn and what annoyed Lois most was that Marie hadn't troubled to acknowledge the engagement gift. She had thought long and hard about a suitable gift and eventually decided on two good quality linen napkins and two very attractive napkin rings. Lois had been so sure that Marie would appreciate a present like that. They could have gone on the breakfast table or be used when she and Stephen were to be dining alone. Perhaps they were appreciated but surely she could have written to say so if she hadn't wanted to come to Glenburn.

Winnie had been a regular visitor to Glenburn. Rain or shine and there she would be with her own brand of humour. Occasionally she was down in the dumps but never for long. Winnie was a happy person but she was anything but at this moment when Mrs Wilson knocked and showed her into the office. That in itself gave Lois a shock because her sister had never been inside the office, it was something she wouldn't have encouraged. Only something very serious would bring her here. She was in a state that much was clear. She looked white and shaken but her eyes were stormy.

Lois had risen from her chair and she and the housekeeper exchanged glances.

'I'll make tea and bring it.' The words were more mouthed than spoken and Lois nodded gratefully. Then she was making Winnie sit down.

'Winnie, what is it? What's the matter?'

Winnie's eyes filled with tears and Lois went over to put her arms around her sister. She held her until the storm of weeping was over.

'Better now?'

'Yes, I'm sorry.'

'No need to be. Not the first time I've felt like that myself.'

Mrs Wilson arrived with a tray. 'The kettle was boiling and that is freshly made tea. Give it a minute or two to infuse.'

'Thank you very much, Mrs Wilson.'

'If there is anything else, you know where to find me.'

Winnie managed a watery smile.

'Don't say a word until you drink your tea.'

Winnie took a few sips then put down the cup. 'I'm all right really.'

'I'm not, I'm shaking. What's happened, Winnie?'

'Marie has run away.' She said it flatly without emotion.

'What do you mean run away? Where to for heaven's sake?'

Winnie shrugged. 'She's gone isn't that enough?'

'But why?'

There was a flash of temper. 'Because Marie is a selfish beast. She doesn't care about anyone but herself.' She paused, sniffed and dabbed at her eyes. 'She left a note for Stephen with her ring in the envelope. Something about not being able to go through with the marriage, that she had discovered that she didn't love him.'

'And that was all?'

'She added a bit about being sorry to hurt him and she wasn't brave enough to face them all.'

'She left a note for Mum as well?'

'No, she didn't get hers until later. I felt sorry for Mum having to hear it from Stephen. He thought she must have known.'

'What a rotten thing to do, but I'm not making sense of this. Why would Marie run away?' She clapped her hand to her mouth. 'You can't mean – not Stephen's brother?' Lois sounded horrified.

'No. Funny you should think that, I'm sure that went through Mum's mind and I think in time she would have come to accept that. I mean Marie would still be marrying into the Hammond family.'

'Then—'

'Just listen and I'll tell you all about it. You do remember Mary Beveridge?'

'Marie used to be friendly with her?'

'Yes. Marie made the excuse that she was to stay overnight with Mary, she has done it before and Mum thought nothing about it. As for me I should have noticed—'

'It's easy being wise after the event.'

'Even so when I saw her with that soft brown bag—'

'That little hold-all?'

'Whatever you like to call it,' Winnie said impatiently. 'She had been taking it to the shop and making the excuse that she was having a few of her clothes altered.' She paused to look at Lois. 'Marie must have been gradually getting her clothes away.'

'Then this wasn't a sudden decision?'

'Anything but, planned for months I'd say or weeks anyway.'

'I'm still waiting to hear whom she's run away with.'

'Harry Lindsay.'

'Harry Lindsay!' Lois almost squealed. 'You're having me on.'

'No, I'm not.'

'I can't believe this and what about Stephen, is he taking it badly?'

Winnie shrugged. 'Hadn't much to say about it at all.'

'Must have been shocked?'

'Suppose so. Look I'm sorry to burst in on you like this. I'd better go, what if your boss walks in?'

'It wouldn't matter.'

'Even so I think I should go. It was just I had to tell you, I couldn't wait.'

'I'm glad you came. And as for Mr Latimer, he is a very understanding man and a crisis is nothing to him. He deals with plenty of those.' Lois looked at her sister closely. 'I haven't heard it all, there's more isn't there?'

'The rest will keep until later.'

'No, it won't and let me ask the question. When did Mum get her note from Marie?'

'I have to tell you this first, then you'll understand. Marie was supposed to be staying with her friend and Mary's father was to give Marie a lift to work or that was what we thought.'

'A pack of lies. Fancy Marie doing that to Mum.'

'Selfish beast that is what she is. To begin with Mum thought Stephen was pulling her leg and I thought so too.'

'Did Marie tell Stephen it was Harry Lindsay?'

'No. She just said it was someone she had known a long time.'

'That should have told you it wasn't Stephen's brother.'

'I don't think we seriously thought it was.'

'Did Mum guess?'

'I saw her face drop so I think she must have. As for me I was scared to say his name.'

'Mum never liked Harry.'

'No, Lois, that isn't true. She didn't dislike him, she just didn't think he was good enough for Marie.'

'An opinion shared by Marie,' Lois said drily.

'Must be love then,' Winnie answered. 'Looking back I don't think Stephen was brokenhearted. A bit shocked but that was only to be expected. Probably feels he had a lucky escape. Coming back to the note, Mum got hers through the post this morning.'

'How cruel, that was unforgivable.' Lois felt sorry for her mother. All her hopes and dreams shattered.

Winnie finished her tea and Lois moved the tray to the top of the filing cabinet to be removed later.

'Mum was all for going to see Madame Yvette to hear if Marie had handed in her notice. She wouldn't be dissuaded and insisted I go along with her.'

'Had she given in her notice?'

'No, Madame was in high dudgeon. Her note was on her desk when she went in in the morning. She went on and on about this being a fine way to repay her for all she had done for Marie. Leaving her, too, at the busiest time of the year. Half the time, Lois, she forgot to put on her phoney French accent. Josie, the other assistant, was brought through and Madame had her in tears. Apparently Josie had known all about it and had thought it terribly romantic. She said that Marie had pleaded with her to help and she was really very sorry about forgetting to post the letter to Mrs Pringle but when she did remember she posted it straight away.'

'Marie would have needed someone,' Lois said thoughtfully, 'but fancy forgetting to post the letter to Mum.'

She did remember, but not until later. All I can say is Marie chose a right dumb cluck to confide in. Mum would have been better prepared for Stephen if she'd got the letter when she was supposed to.'

They both looked to the door when Mr Latimer came in and he smiled to them both. 'We have a visitor I see.'

'My sister, Winnie, Mr Latimer. A family crisis I'm afraid. My other sister, Marie, has run away.'

'Dear me.'

'Run away to be married,' Lois nodded.

'Run away with a scoundrel?'

'Oh, no, not at all. Harry is a very nice, respectable boy, but Marie was engaged to be married to someone else.'

'Very unfortunate but not exactly a tragedy. She is in no danger.'

'No, but she has caused a great deal of trouble.'

'That I don't doubt, but in time it will all be forgotten.'

'Not for a very long time,' Lois said shortly. Mr Latimer wasn't being especially helpful, she thought.

'You are thinking I am making light of your problem. Indeed I am not, my dear, but one shouldn't despair. An unhappy marriage could be a life sentence and this will be no more than a nine days' wonder.'

Lois knew it would be a lot more than that but she did recognise that Mr Latimer was trying to show them that perhaps in the long run it would work out all right. He didn't, however, know Marie, Lois thought grimly. There might come a day when she would regret giving up the chance of a life of plenty and should that day come poor Harry would get the blame.

'Lois?'

'Yes, Mr Latimer.'

'You and your sister will have a lot to talk about. Just you pack up and go. I see by the message pad that no one is screaming for my services and there are no urgent letters.'

Winnie came in hastily. 'No, really that isn't necessary, Lois and I have said all there is to say and I'll get off home now.'

He smiled thinking how miserable the girl looked. 'No, I insist and Winnie, I hope when next we meet it will be in happier circumstances.' He went out quietly and left them.

'What a nice man.'

'He is, isn't he?'

'Are you going to do what he said?'

'Have to or he'll be annoyed. Is Mum expecting you back?'

'I don't care if she is, we are hardly on speaking terms,' said Winnie.

'That is a bit uncomfortable for you both.'

'I can't talk about it not just yet.' Her voice broke.

'All right don't upset yourself. Just tell me when you are ready.' Lois wondered what else there could be. 'Where are Marie and Harry or don't you know?'

'We know. Josie let slip that they were going to Gretna Green.'

Lois's mouth fell open. 'I don't believe this – Gretna Green?' Then she burst out laughing.

'So glad someone is amused.'

'I can't help it but of course it is typical Marie.' She wouldn't be having a big splash, no white wedding, but she was going to make it a day to remember for all that. 'Gretna Green that is going to have the tongues wagging.'

'I've heard of it, of course, who hasn't, but whereabouts is it?'

'I think it is near Dumfries.'

'That's where eloping couples go?'

'Yes. Very often it is when the marriage is frowned upon or the girl is very young. One can be legally married there at sixteen.'

'Marie is well over that.'

'The romantic side of it would appeal to her.'

'Mum wouldn't tell me anything about it when I asked.'

'Want me to tell you?'

'I might as well know what goes on.'

'One of the girls in my class at school knew someone who was married there. She told us bits and I've read about it.'

'What is Gretna Green?'

'A small village, but it's the blacksmith's shop or the Old Smithy as it is known that is famous. Couples go there to get married over the anvil—'

'What's that?'

'Sort of block where the smith used to work the metal.'

'I wouldn't call that romantic,' Winnie said, sounding disappointed.

'There is more to it than that if you would let me get on with the story. Remember, Winnie, for years and years there had been no fires. The place wasn't used and there was no heating at all. Yet, and this is the important part, couples being married over the anvil swear they can feel a warm glow.'

'Really?'

'Yes and it was said that loving hearts were welded into one by the blacksmith.'

'Can't see Harry going for that,' Winnie scoffed.

'Amazing what love can do. Harry is in love with Marie and if that was what she wanted then he would go along with it.'

'Think the marriage will last?' Winnie asked.

'It is to be hoped so.'

'Could be she'll regret giving up a life of luxury and when she does I wouldn't like to be in Harry's shoes.'

'Don't underestimate Harry, he'll let Marie get away with so much then he'll put his foot down.'

'If Dad had been alive Marie wouldn't have done this.'

'Winnie, if Dad was alive I wouldn't be living in Miss Watt's house and Marie would have had second thoughts about incurring Dad's anger.'

'This way Mum has been saved one worry.'

'What's that?'

'She didn't know anyone to ask to take Dad's place and give Marie away.'

'One of Dad's colleagues would have obliged I'm sure.'

'She felt she didn't know any of them well enough.'

'Poor Mum.'

'Coming from you that's rich and not so much of the poor Mum. You can save your sympathy for me,' Winnie said furiously.

'Calm down! What have I said?'

'Didn't mean to snap, but I'm just so angry. Mum says I have to give up all thought of going to London. My place is here with her, she says.' Winnie's voice caught on a sob and she gave herself a moment to recover. 'She doesn't know I'm here, she thinks I am over at the Timpsons' explaining to them the reason why I can't go.'

'Why should you suffer for Marie's sins?'

'That's what I said but it would appear I am expected to. Indeed I should have enough sense to know that myself.'

'Didn't you tell her that you were entitled to a life of your own? She isn't an invalid, far from it.'

'I tried, Lois, I really did.' She shook her head helplessly. 'Mum has forbidden me to go to London and she says that's an end of it.'

'You can't just give in.' Lois was appalled.

'What can I do?'

'Take a leaf out of Marie's book and do what *you* want.'

'I wish I was brave but I'm not and I'm so angry, so very angry. Honestly, Lois, I felt like smashing everything in sight just to relieve my feelings.'

'Pity you hadn't. You could have spared the best china but it would have been worth a few plates.'

Winnie gave a small laugh, then her eyes filled.

This wasn't the time for sympathy and Lois hardened her heart.

'Winnie, listen and listen carefully. Mum is quite able to look after herself and you have the same rights as anyone else. Marie has chosen what she wants to do with her life and I left home because there was no other way for me. We found the courage and so must you. Don't go near Mr and Mrs Timpson. Tell Mum you didn't go, you came here instead and you can tell her what I said if you want.'

'I wish—'

'No use wasting your time wishing. You must find the courage and remember the Timpsons are depending on you. You will be letting them down badly and Mrs Hutchison too for that matter. She recommended you after all.'

'I know all that and I feel rotten about it.'

'So you should. You do have the strength, Winnie. Think back to the difficulties you had getting this far.'

'It wasn't easy.'

'Nothing worthwhile ever is. Come on, time we had something to eat. We'll go along to the kitchen and you can give me a hand.'

Winnie got up looking undecided. 'I should go.'

'Meaning if you don't it will be too late to call on the Timpsons?'

Winnie flushed but didn't answer and Lois knew she was right.

'All right, I'm a coward.'

'Yes, you are.'

'If you would come back with me I could face Mum then,' she pleaded.

'Winnie, there is an awful lot I would do for you but that is asking too much.'

'Meaning it is up to me,' Winnie said hopelessly.

'Yes, it is up to you and remember this is your future you are throwing away. Chances like this don't come very often.'

Winnie picked up her coat.

'You aren't staying?'

Winnie shook her head. She gave Lois an agonised look then quickly left the room. A minute later the front door closed.

Lois stood watching from the window and wondered if she had been too brutal. She hoped not, she had only done her best.

David had two evenings when the surgery remained open until seven p.m. and on one of those evenings Lois took the receptionist's place. Tonight she was five minutes late.

'So sorry David, I was held up.'

'It's all right, sweetheart.' They kissed with only the little Scotch terrier to see them. 'You look pensive,' he said as they drew away.

'Do I?' She would wait until they were closed for the night.

After David had hung up his white jacket, Lois said, 'Marie has eloped.'

'What did you say?'

'I said my sister, Marie, has eloped.'

'Took cold feet and couldn't face an elaborate show.'

'You couldn't be more wrong, about Marie that is. She would have adored a big splash. No, David, it is all off with Stephen. Marie has gone off with Harry an old boyfriend.'

'Gone off where?'

'Gretna Green, would you believe.'

'They may not be married, there are new rules now.'

'How do you know?' Lois was amused.

'You would be surprised what I know. Much of it trivia I must confess. Seriously, Lois, they could be brought back or maybe have second thoughts themselves. I think the couple have to be in residence in the village for twenty-one days before the marriage can take place.'

'No, David, I read that somewhere too, but it doesn't apply to people resident in Scotland.'

He nodded slowly. 'You could be right. The three weeks would be to give frantic parents the time to get there and stop the wedding from taking place.'

'Winnie is the one to suffer and I am so sorry for her. Mum has made this an excuse for stopping her going to London.'

'Why should she do that?'

'Says she needs Winnie at home.'

'And does she?'

'She does not. Mum is quite able to look after herself, more than able I'd say. I tried to talk sense into Winnie but I've a feeling she'll just give in and Mum will get her way.'

'Don't blame yourself, you did your best.'

'I tried and Winnie desperately wants to go to London.'

'Are you sure about that?'

'What do you mean?'

'I'm an outsider looking in, but I'd say if Winnie was all that desperate to go to London she wouldn't let this put her off. She would go with or without her mother's permission.'

'You don't know Winnie.'

'I know I don't, but I see it another way. Maybe she isn't as keen to go to London as you think and this could be a way of getting out of it.'

Lois stared at him.

'Of course I could be quite wrong.'

'You are.'

But was he? Could David have hit on the truth? Lois was no longer sure.

Chapter Twenty

The bell rang and Lois put down the dish towel beside the draining-board and dashed to the door to answer it. Winnie stood there in her raincoat and a matching rainhat covering her hair. Snowflakes were melting on her hat and shoulders and her fur-backed gloves looked like two small, bedraggled animals. She hadn't wanted to wear them or her woollen gloves and normally she would have asked her mother for the loan of a pair of her leather gloves with the warm lining. Unfortunately there was a coldness between mother and daughter and Winnie couldn't bring herself to ask a favour.

'Winnie, I didn't dare expect you in this weather,' Lois said pulling her sister inside as the swirling snowflakes found their way in.

'I was at the bus stop when the snow came on again and I nearly changed my mind and went home. Anyway here I am,' she said cleaning her feet on the mat.

'Better not stay too long,' Lois said worriedly. 'If the temperature takes a drop the roads could be very treacherous.'

'I'll be home before then.' Winnie took off her hat and raincoat and Lois took them from her and hung them up on the hallstand. The fur gloves went on the table.

'Look like a couple of dead rats.' Lois smiled.

'What about my wellingtons, do I take them off here? I've shoes with me, I came prepared.'

There was a chair in the corner of the hall. 'Sit down and I'll pull them off.'

Winnie sat down and held out first one leg and then the other. The boots came off along with a pair of woollen socks worn for the extra warmth.

'Thanks.' Winnie put on her shoes and took her socks with her to put in front of the gas fire.

'I've got the sitting-room lovely and cosy.'

'Good! Lead the way.' Once settled in a comfortable chair Winnie looked sideways at her sister. 'You can ask me, you know, or are you scared?'

'I suppose I know the answer. You aren't going to London, are you?'

'Now why would you think that?'

'Just a feeling and you sound a bit nervous.'

'That could be because I am.' She paused to put out her hands to the fire. 'I am going to London, Lois, I've made up my mind about that, but it doesn't stop me feeling funny inside.'

'That could be partly excitement.' She got up to give Winnie a hug. 'I'm proud of you, very, very proud. It wasn't going to be easy that I knew. In fact that last time you were here I wondered if I had perhaps said too much. I wanted you to go because I thought this was a wonderful chance to spread your wings and get away from home for a bit. Only I had no right, it isn't for me to tell you what to do. It is your life.'

'You didn't say too much, Lois. Like you said it was time I stood on my own two feet and that was more or less what I said to Mum.'

'How did she take it?'

'How did you expect she would?' She gave a small shrug of her shoulders. 'Said I was being very selfish with no thought for her and after all she had done for her family, all the sacrifices she had made—'

'What sacrifices?'

Winnie grinned. 'Didn't say and I knew better than ask. She went on and on like that and then played her trump card – after Marie had almost broken her heart how could I do this to her?' Winnie gulped.

'That was nearly your undoing?'

'I did feel horribly guilty, Lois, then I thought it was most unfair of her. Why should I be the one to be made to feel guilty? Why should I have to suffer for Marie or for—'

'Me for that matter?'

Winnie looked uncomfortable. 'Not the same as Marie, but you did leave home. It's very hot in here.'

'Yes, it is, I'll turn the gas down a bit.' She lowered the

flame. 'Tea now or do you want to finish what you were saying?'

'Better get it all off my chest then a quick cup and I'm off home.'

Lois nodded and leaned back in her chair.

'Actually I went along to the manse before I told Mum I was definitely going to London with or without her permission.'

'Did you go there to talk it over with Mrs Hutchison?'

'Yes. I know her really well by now and she is easy to talk to.'

'Helped you to make up your mind did she?'

'Sort of. She said pretty much what you did, but she drew the line at advising me what to do. She said it wasn't her place, but she did tell me to think about the many spinsters there are in our small parish.'

'What had that to do with it?'

'That's what I wondered too.'

'Thinking about it there are quite a number of unclaimed treasures, there is—'

'I've gone over them, but what Mrs Hutchison was getting at was the selfishness of some old people. They had their chance of happiness but in many cases denied that same chance to their daughter, usually the eldest she said was the one to suffer.'

'That is well known, Winnie.'

'Very unfair though.'

'Lots of things in this life are unfair.'

'She also said that not many of them complained, they just accepted it as their duty to look after their parents in their old age.'

Lois looked at Winnie. 'Do you think she was perhaps getting at Mum in a roundabout way?'

'Possible isn't it?' She grinned. 'Except that in this case it would be the youngest. Lois, do you think Mum is selfish?'

'Yes, I'm afraid I do. That said she does want your happiness, but not if it is going to interfere with hers. She doesn't want to be left alone.'

'Funny though. Marie is her favourite and she didn't want to hang on to her. She was dead keen to get her married.'

'Marrying into the Hammond family she would have been living close by and could you see Marie staying at home?'

'Absolutely not.'

'Mum knew that too.'

'Marie is most like Mum isn't she?'

'Yes.'

'We take after Dad?'

'I like to think so.'

'You are like Dad in colouring and everything, but Marie and I are fair-haired like Mum. Even so we still look a bit like Dad.' Winnie put her head to one side and looked intently at Lois. 'Try as I might I can't see anything of Mum in your face.'

'Not noticeably,' Lois said carefully. She would change the subject. 'Any news from Marie?'

'Yes, Mum had a letter but she wouldn't let me read it – just read bits out.'

'They are married?'

'Oh, yes, and blissfully happy from all accounts. Harry managed to get furnished accommodation not far from the bank and she said it would do until they get their own house. I think she said the bank give loans at low rates to assist their staff in buying their own home. One way to keep the staff happy Harry said.'

'What had she to say about Gretna Green?'

'Don't know. As I said, Mum only read out the bits she wanted me to hear. I wasn't too bothered I'll read it for myself when she isn't around. I mean, why not, it's family news?'

'How will she fill in her day with Harry working?'

'Looking at the shop windows,' Winnie grinned. 'Already she adores Edinburgh and especially the shops in Princes Street.'

'Will she start looking for a job or be a lady of leisure?'

'No, she intends working and says with her experience she should have no difficulty.'

'That's probably true. Did she apologise for all the trouble she caused?'

'Did you expect her to? She did say she was sorry to leave Madame Yvette the way she did, especially as she knew how difficult she would be to replace.'

'She didn't say that?'

'She did, but you haven't heard the best piece. Lois, you would hardly credit this but she has asked for her engagement gifts to be sent on.'

Lois was shocked. 'She can't do that, she has no right to them.'

'Marie disagrees. Stephen, she said wouldn't be interested and in any case engagement gifts were always intended for the bride.'

'Not if she exchanges bridegrooms,' Lois answered then they both took a fit of the giggles.

'Typical Marie wouldn't you say, Lois?'

'As you say typical Marie. Mum will send them on?'

'Of course. She may not approve but she'll send them on to Edinburgh to grace Harry's house.'

Lois went round to see David the following evening. Both the receptionist, Miss Douglas, and Kenneth the assistant vet considered her almost staff. Which in a way she was since she was prepared to help in any way she could.

'Hello, Lois,' Miss Douglas smiled, 'Has that sleety rain stopped?'

'Just about.'

'I'd much rather have snow.'

'So would I.' Lois hung up her coat on the hook next to the one used by Miss Douglas. Her heavy tweed coat was on a coat hanger and had been on the go for many a year but according to its owner there was still many years of wear in it. Her dark brown velour hat and hand-knitted scarf were on the peg and directly below on the floor was a pair of brown lace-up shoes. If she didn't change her shoes, she frequently declared, her feet would be killing her before the day was over. Miss Douglas was of the old school and there were certain words one did not use. Lavatory was one of them.

'Anything I can do, Miss Douglas?'

'Yes, Lois, there is.' Her voice dropped. 'Could I ask you to take over the desk for a few minutes while I go and powder my nose? So embarrassing when one is the only female.'

'Off you go then.' Lois went behind the desk and Miss Douglas walked quickly along the corridor to the door on the far left. Lois had a quiet smile to herself. Why couldn't the silly woman say she wanted to go to the toilet instead of making the excuse that it was to powder her nose? Particularly silly in her case since she wore no make-up. Nothing but soap and water touched her skin, she proudly said and that would be the way of it until her dying day.

David came along to look at the appointments book. 'Hello, darling, is this you holding the fort?'

'Only for a few minutes.' There was the faint but unmistakable noise of a lavatory being flushed and in a few moments the receptionist was on her way back.

'I'm off.' David winked and shot back into the surgery before the receptionist reached her desk.

The working day was at an end and the last four-legged patient, tail wagging, was seen off the premises with its owner. Then it was time to tidy up and for this it was all hands on deck. Kenneth McDonald raced through what he had to do since he now had a steady girlfriend and he liked to spend as much time as possible with her. Miss Douglas was tidy by nature and only a little clearing up was necessary. They said good night and departed.

It was the signal for Lois to make coffee for David and herself and to have ten minutes or so to catch up with each other's news.

'I was wrong, Winnie is going to London and I couldn't be more pleased.'

'People never cease to surprise, Lois. Anyway, good for her. Did you put sugar in this?'

'I did.'

'Not very much.'

'Too much sugar isn't good for you.'

'Nonsense it is a source of energy,' he said putting a heaped teaspoon in his coffee and stirring it.

'Trust Mum, she had to go and make Winnie feel guilty.'

'Don't be so hard on your mother, darling, she hasn't had her sorrows to seek. Losing her husband then three daughters can't be easy.'

'She is a very managing woman, David, with plenty of interests out of the home.'

'Even so, she's going back to an empty house once Winnie goes. I agree though that your young sister shouldn't be made to feel any more guilt than—'

'Than Marie and it is a roundabout way of you getting at me.'

'Not intended I assure you.'

'Yes, it was. You want me to feel guilty and just you try and remember this, David,' Lois said angrily, 'just because you had such a wonderful relationship with your mother doesn't mean it is the same for everyone.'

'I am well aware of that,' he said quietly. 'It could be that getting away from home when you did was a wise move. Distance makes it easier to see the other's point of view, and perhaps to get a better understanding of the difficulties.'

'Is that so?' Lois said sarcastically. 'Coming from somebody who knows nothing about it that is rich. In future, David, I would be obliged if you would refrain—'

He put up his hands. 'Sorry! Sorry! Sorry! Didn't mean to upset you but I have.'

She smiled apologetically. 'I'm sorry too, but my home life is something I am very sensitive about.'

The railway station was a dull place at the best of times, but worse this evening. It was cold and damp and wet beads clung to the wall then slowly began to drip. Those waiting for trains or seeing others depart stamped their feet to keep the circulation going. There was that forced cheerfulness so often seen at partings. No one voiced it, but all were secretly willing the time to pass so that they could board the train or leave the station and go home. Everything that could be said had been said and now there was the constant checking of the time and comparing of watches with the station clock.

Winnie, in a state of nervous excitement, had introduced Lois to Mr and Mrs Timpson who were surrounded by friends. They had taken charge of the children and Winnie's duties would only begin once they were on the train, a smiling Mr Timpson had told her.

'What a lovely couple,' Lois said when they were on their own.

'I know, they couldn't be nicer.'

Winnie looked cosy and attractive in her new cherry red coat and kept admiring her leather handbag. Mr Timpson had relieved her of the small case which joined the other hand luggage.

'You'll never guess who came to see me yesterday. It was to say goodbye and he brought me a box of chocolates for the train.'

'A boyfriend? You've been holding out on me.'

'No, I haven't, it was Tommy Roy,' she said smiling broadly.

'You've never mentioned him.'

'Nothing to mention. We only got talking last time I was at the farm for eggs. Usually he just smiles and that is all.'

'Perhaps he was going to ask you out.'

'I think he might have been, but before he got the chance I told him I was going to London.'

'Did he seem disappointed?'

'I hope so, but I don't honestly know.'

'Of course he was, otherwise he wouldn't have come to the door with the box of chocolates.'

'No, I suppose not. Mum says he must be coming out of his shell, he's always been such a shy boy.'

'You could drop him a line and let him know how you are getting on.'

'I thought I would. I mean he did make the first move.'

'He did and now it is up to you.' Lois was looking around her. 'David is going to do his best to be here, but emergencies keep cropping up.'

'Good thing you came, Lois, or I would have had nobody.'

'Thought some of your friends would have turned up.'

'No, they came to the house or two of them did anyway.'

'Here he is,' Lois said her face lighting up. She waved and David came striding over.

'My apologies, I had hoped to get away earlier.'

'Never mind, you are here now.' Lois made the introductions.

'Winnie, I'm delighted to meet you and I just wish it wasn't hello and goodbye.'

'Me too.'

'For the train,' he said handing her a large box of chocolates.

Winnie blushed. 'Oh, goodness you shouldn't have done that, I mean it is far too much. Thank you very, very much.'

'It isn't every day I see my best girl's sister leaving for the bright lights,' he teased.

The three of them were laughing and Winnie waited until David's back was turned for a moment then she gave the thumbs up. David had passed the test.

Someone shouted that the train had been signalled and there was a general move forward. The moment had come and Winnie's heart was in her mouth. She threw her arms round Lois and her cheeks were wet when she turned to David. He saw the swimming eyes and he gave her a reassuring brotherly hug.

'You'll be fine, Winnie,' he said kindly. 'You are the lucky one going off to London.'

Mrs Timpson was waving frantically.

'Winnie, on you go,' Lois said giving her a gentle push just as the train steamed in.

'Goodbye, Lois, goodbye, David.' She rushed away and Mrs Timpson took her arm and they both got in the train. Doors banged, the green flag was waved and slowly and majestically the London train steamed out of the station.

Lois was crying.

'Come on, darling, this won't do.'

'I know, I'm just being silly, but Winnie is such a b-baby and I'm going to miss her so much.'

'Not so much of the baby, she struck me as a very sensible girl.'

Chapter Twenty-One

Winnie had written two letters, one to her mother and the other to Lois, to say that they had arrived safely and the children had slept for most of the train journey. According to Mr and Mrs Timpson she hadn't done so badly herself though she couldn't recall dozing off for more than a few minutes between stations. The three-storey house they were occupying seemed very grand and there was every comfort. It was only a few minutes' walk from Hyde Park and she rather thought that she would be taking the children to play there. Certainly she wouldn't be expected to do any housework and that was a relief. This was taken care of by a pleasant young woman who spoke nineteen to the dozen and Winnie could only catch a word here and there. Mrs Timpson said not to worry, just to smile as if she understood. She was having difficulty herself following the flow, but was sure they would very soon get used to it. Londoners were always in such a hurry that it was only to be expected that their speech would be hurried too.

Her own bedroom was very nice with pale pink curtains and a matching bedspread and the furniture wasn't dark like at home it was all in lightwood. Finally she came to the weather and that was much warmer than in Greenacre though to hear the 'locals' it was perishing cold. Lois smiled as she folded the pages and put them back in the envelope. Winnie was going to be all right. No doubt there would be days when she would be homesick but it would pass. Most people experienced that on their first time away from home. Winnie was lucky to have such good employers. Mrs Timpson would keep an eye on her without restricting her freedom. As for Lois herself she could stop worrying about her young sister and instead turn her attention to helping David. On Sunday they would make a start on the family house in Downfield.

They left Muirford in chilly, damp weather but by the time they reached the outskirts of Dundee the sky had cleared and there was a blink of sunshine. The journey passed quickly and now they were in Strathmartine Road and driving towards the tram terminus. Then came a right turn bringing them to a row of houses with small front gardens and beyond that to a pretty little church. In the distance the hills sparkled where the sun had caught the snow.

'How lovely,' Lois said pointing ahead to the Sidlaws.

'Yes, I always think so. Mind you, Lois, that snow will take some shifting, I've seen it summer before it has all disappeared.'

'Far to go?'

'No, almost there, but be warned the road gets worse if you could call it a road.'

'I don't mind being bumped about, but it can't be good for the car springs.'

'It isn't and I had better slow down and show some respect for my elderly vehicle.'

This was farm country they were in, with miles and miles of fields. Most of it was green but here and there were patches of white. How peaceful it looked, Lois thought and how quiet. David negotiated a sharp bend and a moment later said with pride in his voice, 'That's it, Lois, that's the house.'

Lois looked at it – alone and aloof – and her first thought was that it wasn't a beautiful house, no one could call it that. Plain, almost austere, the grey stone blended into the landscape as though it belonged and had been there since time began. Families would come and go but this stone-built house looked as though it would stand for ever.

'Very impressive. Has the house been in your family for a long time, David?'

'My mother's grandparents had it built but I couldn't tell you the year.' He smiled. 'They were a grim-looking pair I can tell you. I've seen photographs of them. And my grandparents, they were a bit grim too. Not my real grandparents, my step-grandparents. I think my mother had a very strict upbringing and she said when I was very small and they were coming to visit I would go into hiding.'

Lois laughed picturing the little boy perhaps hiding under the table or behind the sofa.

'When they died the house became my mother's and we came to live here.'

'Has the house a name?'

'Of course. Viewfield House. Not very original I've always thought, then I tried to think up house names and discovered it wasn't so easy. I mean, Lois, just when you think up something it is only to find that someone was there before you.'

'Sidlaw View, how about that?' Lois said triumphantly.

'Sorry, darling. A few round about here are called Sidlaw something or other. Mind you many would be hard put to find a window with a view of the hills. Ah! here he comes, thought he'd be around. That's old Tam.'

David braked and stopped in front of the gate and a man came forward. He wore dark corduroy trousers, an ancient jacket patched at the elbows and a cloth cap. After raising his hand in greeting he opened the double gate and David leaned out of the car to speak to him.

'Thanks, Tam, that'll save me getting out.'

'So it will, Davie lad. I was on the look-out for you.' He peered into the car at Lois. 'You're not alone, I see you've brought a lass with you.'

'Yes, Tam, let me introduce Lois.'

Lois smiled into the bluest eyes she had ever seen. His face was weather-beaten and was a healthy reddish brown.

'The house is still there,' David grinned.

'And will be for many a year. See both of us away and maybe your bairnies too. They knew how to build in those days. We were up to put the fires on so it will have taken the cold air away, but you'll mind an empty house takes a lot of heating.' The man spoke slowly and clearly and Lois thought he would do his work slowly and methodically. He wouldn't rush, there was always tomorrow. 'There's milk in the pantry and I daresay the good lady has put in something to keep you going.'

'Very much obliged, Tam, and I'll be in to see you and Mrs McKenzie before we go.'

He nodded and walked away. An elderly countryman in heavy boots and with a slight stoop to his shoulders. David drove on and stopped at the front door and then they both got out of the car.

'I like the way he calls you Davie.'

'Only one who does. When I was a nipper, Lois, we were great pals and I used to follow Tam everywhere. He and his wife are the salt of the earth and quite frankly I don't know what I would have done without them.'

'Do they live nearby?'

'Look down there.' David pointed to a straggle of cottages. 'They have the end one. They live very simply, Tam does any job that comes his way and Mrs McKenzie keeps hens. She's a lovely woman but no one would dream of addressing her by her Christian name. I don't even know it.'

'Her husband must use it.'

'He doesn't or if he does I've never heard him. She is either the wife, the lady wife or Mistress McKenzie.'

'I like lady wife, it sounds really nice.'

'Must remember that.' David grinned as Lois looked about her. 'Tam is a good man to have around, he can turn his hand to just about anything. Come on, you can study the outside of the house another time.' David took a bundle of keys from his pocket and selected one. 'I usually go in by the back door.'

'Then we'll do that.'

'Not on your first visit.' David turned the key and opened the door into a vestibule. Just inside was a bristle mat and they both cleaned their feet although there was little need. Before shutting the outside door David opened the one into the hallway and Lois went ahead. It was quite large with two handwoven rugs covering most of the floor. Along one wall was a mahogany table with a brass candlestick at either end and in the centre and on a crocheted mat was a tall crystal vase. There was an umbrella stand in one corner with a selection of walking sticks and two umbrellas with bone handles.

'Mum loved flowers or bits of greenery and she had the vases filled for much of the year. At Christmas she went mad with holly, filling her own house and giving armfuls to those who didn't have any.'

'No wonder you loved her, she sounds wonderful.'

'She was and I wish you two could have met. I'm sure you would have loved each other.' He sniffed. 'Slightly musty smell don't you think?'

'Can't be avoided when the house has been closed up.'

'Had this been the summer we could have opened all the windows. Never mind I expect we'll be warm enough in the sitting-room, it was always the easiest place to heat, but to begin with keep on your coat.'

David didn't have a coat with him, he seldom wore one and never when he was in the car. What he wore was dark grey flannel trousers, a heavy tweed jacket and under it a shirt and long-sleeved pullover.

Lois didn't know what was the matter. She had just come into the living-room and was experiencing the strangest sensation. Not exactly scary, and strange was the only way to describe it. For a moment she thought about mentioning it to David but he would probably laugh and call her fanciful and she didn't want that.

The living-room was cluttered, the way so many family rooms are. Lois found it easy to picture a family happy together and following their own interests. It was so homely and inviting as though the lady of the house had just left the room for a few minutes and would be returning. That was a strange thing to think but Lois couldn't help it. She almost expected to hear a step.

She looked up at the high ceiling then at the walls covered in a cream embossed wallpaper and then at the splash of colour that came from the ruby red curtains hanging at the double window. They just cleared the floor and the leather sofa was big and looked as comfortable as a bed. The armchairs were shabby as though they had known years of wear and Lois pictured a small boy sprawled out on one. There would be no danger of a rebuke. A fire burned brightly in the grate and the logs spluttered and crackled. Beside the fireplace was a brass box piled high with more logs and there was a fender with a seat at either side. Lois thought it all delightfully old-fashioned and quite enchanting.

'David, I love it, what a wonderful house to be brought up in. Did you sit on the fender seat when you were small?' She smiled at him.

'Made a bee-line for it when I got home from school. Mother liked to bake and she always had something waiting. She knew I was too hungry to last out until Dad got home.'

'Then you discussed your day with your mother,' Lois said wistfully.

'Absolutely not. Good heavens! Boys would never discuss that sort of thing, football maybe and only if I was asked.'

'Shows how much I know about boys. Girls usually have plenty to say.'

'Did you?'

A shadow crossed her face. 'No one asked about my day.'

David let it go at that. Lois wasn't very forthcoming about her early life.

'You sit right where you are, my sweet, and I'll go and make tea.'

'Can't I do that?'

'You wouldn't know where to find anything. Next time maybe. Shan't be long.'

It was a good ten minutes before David returned with a battered tin tray and on it the tea things. With his foot he dragged a small table nearer to the fire and placed the tray on it.

'Sorry about the tray, there are others but I don't know where to find them.'

'This is just fine.'

'I've the teapot to bring.' He came back with a china teapot and began pouring the tea. Lois collected hers and went back to the fender seat and David brought forward a chair. There was a plate of sandwiches and he offered them to Lois. She took one and he did likewise. 'As you will have gathered Mrs McKenzie doesn't go in for dainty bites.'

'No, she doesn't,' Lois laughed as she held hers in both hands and took a bite. 'It's good though.'

The sandwiches with the crusts still on had been intended for a hungry young man. The bread was thickly cut and the meat between the slices was plentiful.

'Wondered about cutting off the crusts before bringing them through.'

'Glad you didn't, I don't mind crusts, quite like them in fact.'

'Mrs McKenzie would never dream of removing them, she would call that downright wasteful.'

'Which it would have been.'

'Not so, the birds would have had a feast.'

'Poor things, they don't get much to eat just now.'

'They have to look a bit harder that's all, nature always provides food.'

'Winnie and I used to feed the birds. My father bought us a

bird-house one Christmas and we were told never to forget water, that birds need a drink after eating dry bread or stale buns.'

'Speaking of crusts my mother always removed them. She said it made the sandwiches look more tempting and that crusts needed strong, young teeth.' He took a big bite then indicated the room with a sweep of his hand. 'What do you think of it?'

'I told you I love it. This is my idea of a family room,' she said looking about her with appreciation.

'Very old-fashioned.'

'Well, of course, it is.'

'Don't tell me you prefer it to modern furniture?'

'Not necessarily, it depends on the house. Modern pieces would be out of place here.'

He nodded in agreement and reached for another sandwich. 'Help yourself.'

Lois took another and decided that would do her. 'Your mother knew how to make a home,' she said and was glad she had when she saw how pleased he was.

'Remind me there are eggs to take back with us. She won't let me pay for those but I am due them money for other things. The McKenzies would never ask they have too much pride.'

'I know there are some people like that and unscrupulous folk take advantage of them. If you've finished I'll take these through to the kitchen.'

'Yes, that'll do me.'

Lois put the cups and saucers on the tray. 'You take the teapot, David, and lead the way.'

The kitchen had a stone floor with canvas matting on top. There was a well-scrubbed table, a rather ancient cooker and a large pantry. One wall had cupboards the length of it. David had refilled the kettle and put it on to boil and they used it to wash the cups and saucers. Lois found a dish towel and dried them and David showed her where they went. It was cosily domestic and Lois pretended to herself that they were married and this was their own home.

'David, we came to work and we've done precious little.'

'I know but there is no great rush. Since I've waited this long another week or two won't matter.'

'Why don't you just tell the truth? You are reluctant to put the house on the market, aren't you?'

'I'm not denying it will be a wrench to see it going to strangers but there is no alternative. I need the money if we are to build our own house.' They looked at each other and smiled.

'Our own home, doesn't it sound lovely,' Lois said softly.

'Perfect. I love you, Lois, you do know that don't you?'

'Yes, and I love you too.' Lois looked at him and shook her head. 'Why do you seem so uncertain of me?'

'If I do it is because I can't believe my luck and I keep wondering if you have any feelings left for Tim.' He looked anxious.

'No feelings other than as a friend. Tim is *our* friend.'

'And I'll be forever grateful because it was through him that I met you. You are looking very lovely.'

'In my old clothes? I put these on because I expected to be working.'

'I've gone off the notion but I'm all for a cuddle on the sofa.'

'It does look very comfortable,' she said blushing as he led her over and they sat down. They were very close, his arms around her and Lois's head resting on his shoulder.

'This is nice,' he whispered.

'Mmmmm.'

'Darling?'

'What?'

'Why wait? Why not announce our engagement now?'

She turned to look into his face. 'Am I being selfish?'

'You could never be selfish.'

'Then, please, dearest, let it be our secret for a little while before we share it with others. Don't you feel that way?'

'No, I want to shout it from the housetops that we are to be married but if this is the way you want it then your wish is my command.'

'An Easter engagement, David, I would really love that.'

'Then Easter it is.' He kissed her gently then with rising passion. Neither wanted to move but both were aware of the danger and as if by mutual consent they got up.

'A short engagement,' he said huskily.

'A very short engagement,' she readily agreed.

'We can get accommodation until our own home is ready,' David said eagerly. Then he began to laugh. 'You wouldn't like to do as your sister Marie did and get married at Gretna Green?'

'I would not,' she laughed.

'Seriously I have to get Viewfield on the market and get a rough idea of what it is likely to fetch—'

'I wouldn't mind living here.'

'Neither would I, but it is out of the question.'

'I know, dearest.' Was this the time to mention her inheritance? David wouldn't overstretch himself she knew that, he had a horror of debt. She wished now that she had mentioned it earlier and wondered why she hadn't. No, that was untrue the real reason was that if she had told David about the money he would have had to hear the rest. A chill went through her. How long could she keep her secret from him? So silly of her to worry about it. Surely she knew David well enough. If only there had been no inheritance and she had been the rightful daughter of Andrew and Harriet Pringle. If only – if only – life was full of if onlys. David was speaking and she thrust the worries to the back of her mind.

'I do have some money, Lois, but not as much as I had hoped.'

Was that bitterness or disappointment in his voice?

'It wasn't as I expected. I wasn't the sole benefactor in my mother or rather my stepmother's will. It came as a very big shock and just shows that one should never take anything for granted.'

'A relative of your stepmother you knew nothing about?'

'You could say that.' He paused, about to say more then stopped himself.

'The house came to you so that was something.'

'As I said it won't fetch much. People are wary about coming out this far especially with the winters we get. Blocked roads are almost a way of life. Not getting to school was no hardship, just an unexpected holiday, but for those with a job to go to it was worrying. Not all employers are sympathetic and many take the view that one has no business living this far out.'

'They have a point.'

'Put your coat on and I'll take you for a tour of the house before we go, if you would like that?'

'I would very much,' Lois said picking up her coat.

They started with the lounge once known as the drawing-room. Where the living-room had been shabbily comfortable this was bigger and grander and where the family would have done their entertaining. There was a baby grand piano with a sheet of music lying open on the stand.

'Do you play, David?' What a lot they had to learn about each other.

'No, no talent in that direction. Mother was the pianist.'

'Was she good?'

'She would have said no. I imagine she was average or a bit above. Do you play?'

'Never got the chance. Winnie took piano lessons and got her first certificate.'

'A good beginning.'

'My mother was so proud. Winnie was only three marks short of honours and Mum had such high hopes. A concert pianist it was to be at the beginning and then that was modified to music teacher.'

'Poor Winnie didn't live up to expectations?'

'No wonder. Anyway she lost heart and lost interest, but I'm sure if Mum had left her alone she might have made something of it.'

'Would you like piano lessons?'

'At one time but it is too late now.'

'It is never too late, my darling. Tell you what, we'll keep the piano and you can take lessons or failing that one of our offspring might be a budding musician.'

'You never know.'

'Come on, at this rate we'll never get round,' he said leading her to the dining-room. 'Take a quick look, it faces north and is the coldest room in the house.' He shut the door quickly and Lois followed him up the carpeted stairs with their brass rods keeping it in position. 'The bathroom is on the half-landing,' he said not bothering to open the door. 'Functional is about all one could say about that place. It needs to be ripped out and if the new owners have the wherewithal they may very well do that. I know I would.' A further flight of stairs brought them to the bedrooms, four of them and a boxroom. 'The boxroom is full of junk although my mother would turn in her grave if she heard me say that. You know the saying one man's treasure is another man's junk. Have I got that right?'

'It goes something like that.'

'Not likely to find any valuable stuff, but you are welcome to have a rake through it some time.' He went ahead. 'My room,

I've already taken what I want so we don't have to bother with it. Next to mine is a guest room and then my parents' bedroom.' He opened the door wide.

Lois saw a double bed with a quilt and bedcover in rose pink. The curtains had sprigs of blue flowers on a white background and must have been for the summer months. Two wardrobes stood side by side and on the opposite wall was a dressing-table. A quilted dressing-gown hung on the back of the bedroom door.

'All Dad's things have gone. We did it right after the funeral. Mum said it was easier to get it done then than have to face it later.'

Lois felt like weeping. She was remembering when her father's clothes had been removed from the house. It had seemed like the final act and it had upset her terribly.

'Next time we come I'll get some cases down from the boxroom to take back what we want. Mr Latimer can get the rest and give them to some deserving soul. And, Lois please, I want you to go through the drawers and take anything you want.'

'I couldn't do that.'

'Why not? You are going to be my wife.'

'I don't like—'

'Think of the future – our children – they have a right to them.'

'All right I'll put aside what I think should be kept.'

'No one enjoys disposing of the contents of a home but it has to be done. When there is no one close it has to be done by strangers and that is rather terrible.' He looked at his watch. 'Come on I've the McKenzies to see.'

'What about the fires?'

'The one in the lounge is almost out and I'll put the guard up in front of the one in the living-room but don't worry Tam and his wife will come up later and check that all is well.'

'Will they come in the dark?'

'The darkness doesn't trouble country people.'

Lois and David came out of the cinema and walked the few yards to the Golden Café where the owner greeted them like old friends.

'How are you both?' He was a fat man with a genial smile.

'In need of a good cup of coffee,' David said.

'Come to the right place then. Many in the first house?'

'It wasn't full,' Lois said, 'but then the film was nothing to write home about was it, David?'

'Didn't see much of it.' He grinned. 'Dozed off for a bit but I did see the end.'

'I'm not one for the pictures, the wife goes with her sister. Me now I'm all for the music hall. Nothing like a good laugh to make you feel better.'

Another couple walked in and Lois and David went to sit at a table. The girl came for their order.

'Two coffees, please.'

'Anything to eat?'

'Lois?'

'No thanks, just the coffee.'

'Two coffees that's all,' David smiled.

She came back with two brimming cups.

'Miss Watt recovered from her chill?' David asked as he added two spoonfuls of sugar.

'Yes, but she doesn't venture out often. She says that February is her least favourite month and she feels cheated when it is leap year and she has to suffer an extra day of winter.'

'That sounds like her. By the way, Tim was asking kindly for you?'

'Was he? Where did you see him?'

'In the street, we went for a drink. Just a quick one.'

'So you say. What did you talk about if I am allowed to ask?'

'This and the other, then we got on to our respective girlfriends. Did I tell you that he is tickled pink about us?'

'Yes.'

'And no to your unasked question, I didn't say we were unofficially engaged but I rather think he guessed.'

'I don't think I would mind Tim knowing, he can keep a secret. Are he and Catherine engaged?'

'I don't know about an engagement, but they are getting married in June.'

'That's lovely.'

'We'll be getting our invitation in due course but I'll need to find someone to look after you because Tim wants me as his best man.'

'That's an honour. Am I right in thinking Tim is to be yours?'

'Yes.'

'It's a nice feeling to know that you come first with someone,' Lois said shyly.

He covered her hand with his. 'You will always be first with me and I hope I'll always be first with you.'

'That I can promise.'

'Want more coffee?' It was the girl back again.

'Lois?'

'No, thank you.'

'No, but bring the bill when you are ready.'

They sat another ten minutes. Two of the tables had not been occupied so they didn't feel guilty about spending so long over one coffee.

'Lois, all right with you if we spend this Sunday at the house?'

'Of course. I was going to ask you about that.'

'This time we'll mark the pieces of furniture we want put in store and with those out of the way we can see about the rest going to the saleroom.'

'Don't be too hasty.'

'What do you mean?'

'The house is better to have some furniture in it, an empty house wouldn't sell so easily or so I imagine.'

'Good point.'

Chapter Twenty-Two

They were in the house and trying to decide what furniture they would want for themselves. The heavy sideboard and dining-room table would be out of place in a modern house and they were looking more to the smaller pieces. The piano was to be kept and David wanted his father's bureau. Lois had her eye on two tapestry chairs and an embroidered footstool that would grace any home. The crystal, cutlery, china and the contents of the linen cupboard would come in useful and would all go into the largest trunk. Lois had fallen in love with a little French clock she discovered on a shelf in a cupboard. David smiled when he saw it. He remembered his father overwinding it and breaking the spring and how annoyed his mother had been at the time. She had intended getting it mended so either she had forgotten or more likely it was beyond mending.

'I do like it, David.'

'What do you want with a clock that doesn't go?'

'I'll get it mended.'

'Might not be worth the expense or it can't be done. It is foreign.'

'Someone can surely do it.'

'It can't be valuable or it wouldn't have got stuck away in a cupboard.'

Lois looked stubborn. 'Please let me take it back with me.'

'Heavens! Take it, you don't have to ask. I told you to have anything you want.'

'Just this,' she smiled. 'I'll take it to the jeweller's in Dundee and it can stay in my bedroom until we need it. David?'

'What now?'

'Is it possible to be too happy?'

'I shouldn't think so. What a funny thing to say, but then you never cease to surprise me.'

'I'm a little afraid inside as though it couldn't last.'

David stopped what he was doing. 'Lois,' he said quietly, 'there is nothing absolutely sure in this world, but we have to believe in ourselves. Happiness is a gift and we have to treasure it. I will always treasure you and do what I can to keep you happy.'

'I know.' No wonder David thought her peculiar, she supposed she was. Her upbringing had ensured that. It would all be so different when she was married, she would feel secure with David beside her.

'Is that stool going with us?'

'Yes and the chairs.'

'Put stickers on them where they can be seen.'

'No they could damage the material. I'll put them on the bottom.' She collected the stickers. 'The kitchen china I'm taking some of it in the car.'

'Enough in the back seat without that.'

'Perhaps you haven't noticed, but there isn't a matching cup and saucer in your kitchen. All you have are odd cups and those are badly stained.'

'Stained! My china!' David made a show of indignation.

'Yes, stained,' Lois said severely. 'Cups should be rinsed out after use and not left with cold tea or coffee in them. No wonder Miss Douglas guards her cup. You might not know it, but she keeps hers in the top drawer of the filing cabinet.'

'Does she now? I have the greatest respect for my receptionist but there is no getting away from it, she is a fusspot. Darling, you aren't going to turn into one are you?'

'I may have to, to keep you in order. What about the carpets and the curtains are they to be left?'

'Hadn't given it a thought, what do you think?'

'Leave them – they suit the house and they wouldn't be much good elsewhere.'

'The new owners might want a clean sweep.'

'Not very likely.'

'Come to think about it the solicitor said it was better to leave the carpets and curtains and possibly some furniture. Make it less cold-looking and more important it wouldn't show up the faults.'

'Are there any?'

'Faults? No house as old as this could be fault-free but that said I think it is in a reasonably good state of repair. God, I hope so,' he added.

By late afternoon they were congratulating themselves on having done so much and Lois stood up and straightened her back.

'I would never have believed clearing a house was such exhausting work.'

'Comes from folk accumulating such a lot in their lifetime and so much of it useless. A bonfire would be a good way of getting rid of some.'

Lois looked shocked. 'Fancy thinking about setting fire to what might have been cherished possessions. What would your mother have thought?'

'She probably did the same when her parents passed on.'

'I feel filthy, I'm going to have a wash before I do another stroke of work.'

'You'll find hot water in the kettle and I don't know about towels, better check.'

'I've already done that. I put two clean ones on the towel rail.'

'Good girl, and remember I'm following so put the kettle back on for me.'

'Will do.'

After a freshen up they began again. David had discovered some *Boys' Own* Annuals and was happily turning over the pages.

She looked over his shoulder. 'Those can go to the Scouts for their fund-raising.'

'Not on your life. These could be worth a fortune one day, perfect condition every one. I looked after my books. Ah, look, he was my favourite character—'

'You are supposed to be working not enjoying yourself reading an old schoolboy annual.'

'Brings back memories,' he said closing the book and putting it beside the others. 'These go on the back seat along with your clock. Can't risk them going astray.'

'That reminds me, David, I was to ask you if there was anyone you wanted to give something to?'

He shook his head. 'Just the McKenzies, they can have their pick before the stuff goes to the saleroom.'

'How about that other person, the other benefactor in the Will?'

For a moment David was startled. Was the girl entitled to something? No, of course she wasn't or mention would have been made. It would only complicate matters and he had a strong reluctance to come face-to-face with his stepmother's illegitimate daughter. He didn't question why that should be.

Lois was waiting.

'No, darling, I don't think so. She got plenty.'

'Just the McKenzies then?'

'Yes and speaking of them I must mention to my solicitor, Mr Bryden, that Tam has always looked after the garden and hopefully the new owners whoever they might be will retain his services.'

Lois gave a start at the mention of Mr Bryden. Was it possible that she and David shared the same solicitor? Very possible she thought. Bryden wasn't a common name. She felt uneasy as if trouble was creeping up on her. Why hadn't she just unburdened herself to David? Had she done so everything would have been in the open. Instead of which she was carrying this weight around. Probably worrying herself over nothing. She could almost see David dismissing it as of no importance and being amazed that she had had any doubts. She would do it, not today but very soon. Harriet would have to be contacted and a request made for her birth certificate to be sent on. A stamped, addressed envelope would be best. Her mother would have to comply. How would she go about it? Why hadn't she been told before this, that was what was so perplexing? With her husband dead his widow could have chosen her own time. Had that time not yet come and were there more shocks in store?

'Mrs McKenzie would like to meet you, Lois.'

'I'd like to meet her too.'

'Very emphatic that we should call in at the cottage on our next visit. You will like her she is quite a character.'

'Like her husband?'

'Only in the sense that they are a lovely couple.'

David drove straight to the cottage, parked the car in the yard and sent the hens scattering in all directions. Mrs McKenzie stood at the open door, arms folded and smiling broadly.

'That'll put them off laying.'

'Sorry.'

'My little joke, a bicycle sends them into a panic. Come away in, you won't mind the kitchen? I've been doing a baking and it's fine and warm.' She went on hardly stopping for breath. 'You won't see the man himself, had a call from the Kilpatricks to give them a hand.'

They stepped into the narrow passageway. 'Mrs McKenzie,' David laughed, 'give me a chance, I haven't managed to introduce Lois yet.'

'Neither you have, where are your manners, lad? So this is your lass,' she said, taking a good look at Lois who was trying not to show her embarrassment.

'You've picked a bonny lass but then I expected you would. What was that name?'

'Lois.'

'Foreign is it?' she said suspiciously.

'No, I don't think so, Mrs McKenzie. My father liked the name and that is how I come to have it.'

She nodded as though satisfied with the explanation.

'There's many a lass with a bonny face, but I'm glad there is more to you. You've honest eyes and a firm line to your chin.'

'All that at a first glance,' David grinned.

'As impudent as ever.' She smiled, then she looked at him gravely. 'The eyes are the mirror of the soul, lad. I know by them if a person is trustworthy.'

'Do you ever make mistakes?'

'I have been known to be wrong.' She bustled about setting two places then pouring the tea. 'There you are, sit down the pair of you and mind it's all for eating.' A pudgy hand indicated that morning's baking.

'My goodness, this looks wonderful,' Lois said. Mrs McKenzie must have been up since early morning. There were scones fresh from the oven, sponges, shortbread and a sultana loaf with a knife beside it.

'Lois, you'll excuse me not taking you into the parlour. I could have been swanky like and taken you in there—'

'Why was I never invited into the parlour?' David asked with a wink to Lois.

'Because, lad, you were like one of the family. Only those and such as those are taken in there. The minister on his six monthly visit is one and a cousin of mine with a good opinion of herself is another. That's enough of my blethers I'll leave you to eat your fill and get on with the work. You know the saying no rest for the wicked.' She left them.

Lois and David exchanged smiles.

'You were right, David, she is lovely and fancy going to all this trouble for us.'

'She would call it a pleasure. Mrs McKenzie was like a second mother to me and when I couldn't be found my mother knew where to come.'

Mrs McKenzie must have heard and she came in. 'Yon were happy times, lad. I miss your mother sore, she was a fine lady. A gentle creature but she had an inner strength. No side with her, she treated everyone the same. Your father was a good soul too and he was good to your mother. Would have done anything for her.' She sighed. 'It is to be hoped the next family will look after the house. I always say a house has feelings.'

What a lovely thing to say, Lois thought.

'We were lucky with you and Tam, you gave wonderful service and I'm grateful to you. I'm to ask the solicitor to put a word in for Tam and hopefully they'll want him to carry on doing the garden as before.'

'That was thoughtful of you. With the house sold I hope you won't be making a stranger of yourself.'

'No chance. Lois and I will come and see you from time to time.'

'See that you do and Lois, lass, I've a few eggs for you. Nothing like a fresh boiled egg for breakfast and you won't get fresher than these,' she said putting a box on the table.

'How very kind of you, Mrs McKenzie, that will be a treat.'

'If you've had enough to eat I won't hinder you. You'll be anxious to get started then get yourselves home.'

Once they were in the car Lois asked David if the McKenzies had a family.

'A married son abroad, they don't hear from him very often. They lost Janey, she was the apple of Tam's eye.'

'What happened?'

'Died of scarlet fever.'

'How sad, how old was she?'

'Nine. They don't talk about her now but they have never got over it.'

'No, they wouldn't.' They were both silent.

This was her third visit to Viewfield House and Lois was finding it less upsetting now to go through a stranger's belongings. She hadn't as yet mentioned it to David but she wondered why there were no photographs. No family portraits on chests or drawers or china cabinets. One would have expected to see a few of a little boy at the various stages of his development but there were none on view.

When the opportunity arose she asked him. 'Why no photographs, David?'

He smiled. 'After my mother died I had to go through some papers for the solicitor and for some unknown reason I wanted to collect all the photographs and put them in a case. Why, do you want to see them?'

'No, I just wondered.' She thought she understood. For some it was comforting to look at photographs while for others it was upsetting. 'What would you like me to do, David?'

'Mum's bedroom, finish off there if you will?'

'Yes, I'll do that.'

Touching the clothes of someone no longer here gave her a funny feeling. Clothes told so much about a person. In the larger wardrobe which at one time must have held her husband's suits, were coats, two with fur collars and protected by a white cover was a full length fur coat. David would have to make up his mind what to do about it. Padded coat-hangers held a number of costumes and on the floor of the wardrobe in a neat row was an assortment of footwear. One of the costumes had a lovely brooch in the lapel and it reminded Lois that she must look through the pockets before the clothes went off to Mr Latimer and his band of helpers.

The other wardrobe held dresses, two looked to be ankle-length evening dresses and from them Lois gathered that David's mother must have been quite tall and slim. Skirts seemed to be most favoured. There were tweed skirts, tartan skirts, skirts in fine suiting, a folkweave skirt that was quite eye-catching and two lovely peasant skirts. They were very full and in glorious colours and what Lois might have chosen for herself. A skirt for any age, for the young at heart. Lois folded them neatly and placed them on top of the pile. As she did she had a picture of the woman wearing one and it swinging as she walked to the tram terminus to meet a little boy returning from school. The job completed she closed the door and contemplated the next task.

Why all of a sudden did she have this reluctance to clear out the drawers? Was it because it was too personal, an intrusion? If she didn't do it who else would? David would just heave the lot into a box which was unthinkable. Mrs McKenzie might have been called to do it but Lois thought the woman she had met would not relish the task. She went over to the dressing-table and knelt down ready to begin.

The long drawer in the centre held jewellery, most of it in velvet boxes. There were strings of pearls and amber beads and a gold chain but there were also cheap trinkets, the kind bought by a child. Lois's mouth twitched, very likely they had been purchased by a little boy out of his pocket money. Cherished gifts from her little boy, not her own little boy, a stepson but one who had become very dear to her. The rings, three of them very old-fashioned and in boxes falling apart with age, looked to be valuable and she would advise David to get them valued. There were three drawers at either side of the dressing-table. One held handkerchiefs, some still in their boxes. There were bottles of perfume, two powder compacts and a large box of loose powder some of which had spilled and left a pinkish stain on the paper lining the drawer. The others held belts, buckles, ribbons, hair slides, stockings, silk stockings and thicker ones suited to brogues. That completed, Lois went over to the chest of drawers and decided it was a useful piece of furniture that could be put in store.

She went down on her knees again and pulled out the first drawer. It glided out smoothly and held jumpers as did the one below. The bottom one came out smoothly too and the contents of this one was a surprise. Lying on tissue paper was a white matinée jacket beautifully knitted and finished off with white satin ribbon. Beside it was a pair of tiny bootees and hand-sewn gown of the purest cotton and so soft that it could almost have been silk.

Lois felt her eyes fill with tears. She could feel the love that had gone into making these exquisite garments, a baby's first size. Her first thought was that they must have been David's then she thought not. Perhaps he should have had a little brother or sister. Had the baby been stillborn or worse, Lois thought it would be worse, if the baby had clung to life for a little while? To lose a loved one was a deep sorrow but to lose a longed-for baby must be the worst pain of all.

Had David's mother come up here to touch her baby's clothes and draw some comfort from it? No one would ever know. Lois put the tiny garments on top of the drawers and wondered what to do with them. She was very tempted to keep them for the day when she . . . but perhaps that would be unlucky and she daren't risk it. Some other little one would wear them.

She was spending far too much time over this and David would be wondering what was holding her up. She pulled open the next drawer and drew out a package in a strong brown envelope, the kind used to keep important documents. Should she leave it for David? If it contained documents she would, but better to find out rather than bother David. Good thing she hadn't bothered him, all the envelope held were photographs and snapshots. She smiled. These must be of David as a baby. The top photograph was of an infant lying on a sofa. The baby was a little older in the next, but still wearing a gown so that it was impossible to tell whether it was a baby boy or girl. How odd that none of them showed the infant with a proud parent. Lois was becoming intrigued and then frankly puzzled as she went slowly through the bundle. When did it strike her? She didn't know, but when it did she gave a strangled cry. Her head was spinning and had she not been kneeling she would surely have fallen. Her heart was thudding painfully and her mouth had gone dry. She could feel the moisture on her skin.

David's step was on the stair. He called her name but she was incapable of answering.

'I've made tea – are you coming down for it?' he was saying as he opened the door wider. Then he saw her white face and the shocked look, and in an instant he was over beside her. 'Lois, what on earth is the matter? You look terrible. What is it?' Then his eyes fell on the baby clothes on top of the drawers. 'Have these upset you? I had no idea she had kept them.'

Lois had recovered her voice. 'You knew,' she said accusingly. 'All the time and you knew.'

'Yes, I knew,' he said bewildered. 'I meant to tell you but—'

'You decided against it?'

'There was no particular hurry.'

'No hurry at all,' she said sarcastically.

'Look, what is all this? I can't believe that you are getting yourself into a state over something that happened all those years ago, and for that matter it really has nothing to do with you,' he said coldly.

'Hasn't it?' she shouted. 'I would have said it had everything to do with me. The baby born to your stepmother before—'

'Oh, my God, I don't believe this, that it is really you talking. Do you find it so dreadful that a woman should give birth to a child outside marriage? Where is your compassion and how dare you judge my stepmother when you can't possibly know the circumstances. I don't know them myself and I don't particularly want to. Nothing, Lois, and I repeat nothing, could ever alter my feelings for her.'

'How touching, such depth of feeling for your oh-so-wonderful stepmother. What about the child, did anyone care what happened to it? No, you didn't give it a thought. In fact you felt positively cheated because she got the larger share when she was entitled to the lot. And even all that wouldn't have made up for being abandoned.' Lois was half sobbing and her breath was coming in odd little flutters.

Shocked as he was David couldn't tear his eyes away. In anger she was even more beautiful, the blazing eyes so vividly blue and the flushed cheeks. But a stranger, he no longer knew this girl. He turned away looking sad and defeated.

'No, don't go. Why David, just answer me that?'

'Why what?'

'How could I have been so wrong about you,' she said brokenly. 'I didn't think money mattered so much to you but I see now that it does.'

David's hand went through his hair in a gesture of hopeless despair.

'It doesn't.'

'You admitted to me yourself that you were dissatisfied with what you had been left or are you going to deny that?'

'Yes – no – I was disappointed,' he said slowly, 'but not about the money, though that came into it too. You don't seem to realise, Lois, that I didn't know of this girl's existence. I had always believed myself to be the only one and there I was hearing from the solicitor that I wasn't. That came as a big shock and I suppose I was jealous or hurt or both to find out that I hadn't come first with my stepmother. She had kept this secret from me. I wonder now if she had confided in my father or if he was unaware of what had happened. Of one thing I am sure it wouldn't have stopped him loving her.' He made to go.

'Not yet, not before you take a look at these.' She held out a bundle of photographs.

'Not now for God's sake. Why should I want to look at photos of a baby. Don't you think I've had enough for one day?'

'You have to see them, it is important.'

He took them from her with a show of irritability.

'Very nice baby photos, so what? We've established there was a baby and that baby is now a young woman.'

'Look at the others,' she said harshly.

He gave her a hard look then shrugged and began to go through the bundle. He stopped at one, studied it then moved on to the next. He looked at Lois then back at the photograph and there was a puzzled frown on his face.

'There is a slight resemblance, this one looks a bit like you—'

'It should. That isn't just a resemblance, David, that is a photograph of me. We have the very same ones at home,' she said unsteadily then added. 'Now I know why my father always insisted on taking snapshots of us singly.'

They were staring at each other. Lois had got to her feet and was holding on to the furniture as though for support.

'What I'm thinking isn't possible – you can't be—'

'Tell me your stepmother's Christian name.'

'Grace.'

She nodded. There was no mistake. She knew who had given birth to her.

David saw that she was shivering and he took her unprotesting body and held her close.

'It's a mess, but we'll sort it out. Right now it is too much for us to take in. We are both in shock and we are going downstairs. That tea should still be drinkable though something stronger would have done more good.' He led her downstairs and into the living-room where a good fire was burning. After settling her on to the sofa as though she were an invalid he added an extra log to the fire and pressed it down with his foot. Then he poured the tea and put the cup into her hands. She was shivering so much that when she raised the cup to her lips her teeth rattled against it.

'Thank you,' she said after she had managed to swallow some of the tea.

'Feel a bit better?'

She didn't, but she nodded.

'We need to talk, there is a lot to straighten out.'

'Yes, I know.'

'We have to be completely honest with each other and keep nothing back. Shall I begin?'

'I think you should,' she said coldly.

'Most of it you already know but I'll try and fill in the blanks. You have to remember that I had just met you about the time I went to see the solicitor.' He looked over to her and she nodded.

'The news had shocked me and I wasn't ready to talk about it. Then when things got serious between us I meant to tell you but you know how it is, one keeps putting off and' – he gave a half smile – 'you must have had your letter from the solicitor—'

'Mine got delayed.'

'You got it eventually?'

'Yes.'

'And kept it a secret which you were perfectly entitled to do although it would appear I wasn't.'

'I had my reasons, good reasons.'

'Since we are to be completely honest with each other shouldn't I be told the reason?'

'You talk about being shocked, well it was nothing to the shock I received. I had to try and come to terms with suddenly being informed that I was illegitimate.'

'That wasn't so very terrible,' he said gently. 'Did it upset you very much?'

'Yes, it did. It also explained a lot I hadn't understood.' The drained look had gone and a little colour was in her cheeks. 'I – I wanted to tell you but I didn't know how you would take it, and I couldn't tell you about my legacy without telling you the rest.'

'How could you have had such a low opinion of me? As if it would have made the slightest difference to my feelings for you,' he said reproachfully.

'I couldn't be sure.'

'What a lot we have still to learn about each other,' he said sadly.

She moistened her lips. 'Was – she happy with your father?'

'Yes, they had a good marriage and apart from being man and wife they were also friends. Thinking back I would say that my father was the one more in love but they were happy together. I imagine my father still thought of his first wife, I hope so, and it could be that my stepmother's heart belonged to someone else.'

'We'll never know.'

'No, we'll never know.'

Lois was staring into the fire. How cruel she had been, none of this was David's fault yet she had focused resentfully on the thought that he had enjoyed what should rightfully have been hers. She tried to hold back the words to be reasonable, but they tumbled out as memories overwhelmed her. It was like the bursting of a dam as she thought back to the hurts and slights that had been her lot all through childhood. At the moment she wasn't seeing David as the man she loved, but the one who had stolen what should have been hers.

'She was my mother not yours. All those years you were her darling boy, showered with love when her own child, her flesh and blood, was getting precious little. How do you think I feel about that?'

'Cheated perhaps but be fair, Lois—'

'Be fair, you have the nerve to say that to me. My father loved me but he didn't single me out for special treatment, we were all alike to him, he made no difference between us. Not so the woman I thought of as my mother.'

'It would seem that you weren't so well treated as your sisters, but, forgive me saying so, it couldn't have been an easy situation for Mrs Pringle.'

'I was a child, she was an adult. She couldn't but know the harm she was doing me.' Her voice broke. 'David, you can't even begin to understand, no one could unless they experienced it. Do you know this I honestly thought there was something wrong with me,

305

that I must be wicked, when my own mother didn't love me. Do you know what she said to me?'

He shook his head.

'I had asked her why she loved Marie and Winnie and not me and she said and this is true David, that I wasn't a very lovable person.'

'Surely not. That was cruel.'

'She was cruel to me and very good at hiding it. Mental cruelty is how it would be described. Dad wasn't unaware of what was going on,' she said sadly, 'but he never did much about it.'

'Not easy for him.'

'It wasn't easy for me.'

'Does it help knowing that Mrs Pringle isn't your natural mother?'

'In some ways it is a great relief but, given the choice, I wish I could have gone through life not knowing.'

'It hurts so much?'

'Being illegitimate? Yes I'm afraid it does. I feel different as though I didn't belong anywhere. I no longer have a proper family and Marie and Winnie are only my half-sisters.'

'That shouldn't matter so much now that you are grown up. You don't need a family, you have me.'

She bit her lip. 'David, I'm so sorry about the money, what I said—'

'I don't want to hear a word about that,' he said and his voice had gone cold.

'I didn't mean what I said.'

'I think you did.'

'No—'

'Leave it, Lois. Enough has been said.'

Too much, she thought sadly but it was too late for regrets.

'I think we should be getting on our way.'

'What about – I haven't finished—'

'Leave everything, most of it is done.'

'We can finish off next Sunday?'

'No, I'll come on my own. If I need any assistance I can call on the McKenzies.'

It was like a slap in the face and she knew she deserved it.

'I'm so sorry. Do you mind if I call her Grace to save confusion?'

'Why should I? She is your mother.'

Lois winced. 'Why did she cut herself off completely? There weren't so many miles between us yet not once did she send me a birthday card or come to see me.'

'I imagine it was forbidden.'

'The photographs – there had to be some contact for her to get them.'

'Your father may have sent them through a go-between. You should bear this in mind, Lois, twenty years ago an unmarried woman and her child would have had a difficult life. Many parents would have shown her the door rather than face the shame and you could have been singled out at school. Children can be unbelievably cruel.'

'You knew my mother, you knew Grace, would she have willingly abandoned me?'

'Lois, you can answer that yourself. Why would she have kept baby clothes all those years. Grace didn't abandon you, she parted with you to give you a better life. She would have trusted your father to look after you.'

'When I was old enough to understand why didn't he tell me?'

'You worshipped him didn't you?'

'Yes.'

'Then that could be the answer. He would be afraid of going down in your estimation and there was the shame too.'

'They sinned.'

'And paid for it. It all happened a long time ago and it is time to let the past go.'

'Not so easy.'

'Not so easy for Mrs Pringle either. Have you tried putting yourself in her shoes? To many she would come out best in this unhappy affair.'

The solicitor had said much the same, Lois remembered. Suddenly she felt dead tired and wearied.

'I thought we were going.'

'So we are but first I want you to promise me something.'

'What?'

'Go and see Mrs Pringle and talk it over with her.'

'Never.'

'You must. This is festering inside you and you won't be a whole person until you know the complete story.'

'What makes you think she'll tell me?'

'She might find it a relief to do so. There is her side of it you know.'

'I won't go, but even if I did she might not let me over the doorstep.'

'You will have tried. You might get a cautious welcome,' he smiled. 'Mrs Pringle must be very lonely with one daughter in London and the other in Edinburgh.'

'She has never had difficulty in filling her day.'

'If you won't do it for yourself, do it for me.'

She didn't answer.

'Try, please.'

'What would I say?'

'Tell her what you know.'

Her eyes swam. 'David, do you still love me after all this?'

'Even more if that is possible. We belong together and nothing is going to alter that.'

'Then let me say this. The money, the legacy, isn't mine it belongs to us.'

'No.'

'Yes,' she said firmly. 'It belongs to us and you should say the same about yours.'

He laughed. 'What is yours is mine but what is mine is my own.'

'Don't you dare,' and for the first time they were laughing together. Then he pulled her to him. 'All I have is yours,' he said softly.

'And all I have is yours.' She drew away a little to look into his face. 'I love you, David,' she said tremulously, 'never, never doubt that will you?'

'Why should I?'

'Because things happen.'

'They certainly happen to us.'

'No matter how long I live I'll never get over . . .' She shook her head amazement on her face.

'It will certainly take a while.'

'I do wish that Grace could have known about us,' Lois said wistfully.

'Perhaps she does. Who knows but that she had a hand in it.'

'Do you really believe in things like that?'

'Yesterday the question would have got a definite no. Now I'm not so sure.'

'This is all wrong, my own mother and I don't even have a photograph of her.'

'You soon will. Once I get my hands on that case we'll spend a whole evening going over them and I'll do my best to make her live for you.'

'Thank you, you are a dear. Tell me, please, am I like my mother, am I like Grace in appearance?'

'No, you aren't except in build. Grace was tall and slim and she wasn't nearly so dark. What you do have is her laugh. That really shook me the first time I met you.'

'Why didn't you say something?'

'Lois, be reasonable. I'd just been introduced to you—'

'I introduced myself I seem to remember.'

'So you did. Never mind, it comes to the same. What would you have thought if I'd blurted out – that laugh of yours reminds me of my late stepmother.'

'You wouldn't have said stepmother,' Lois said quickly.

'We are smart! You don't miss a trick. No, you are quite right I wouldn't. Does it bother you that I used to call her mother?'

'Not in the least, not now. I was being completely unreasonable before.'

'No, you weren't. In your position I might have felt the same.'

'I don't think so and it no longer matters. What I'm wondering is when we would have known if I hadn't come across those photographs.'

'Through the solicitor, I imagine, I can't think of any other way.'

'What a shock for both of us if we'd met in his office.'

'And a bigger shock when we discovered the reason.'

'It would have been awful.'

'Awful, yes, I agree but we would have handled it.'

'Better the way it happened?'

'I think so.' He grinned. 'Now I know what you look like when you are angry.'

'Not very nice I'm ashamed to say.' She was remembering the hurtful words she had hurled at David and his complete bewilderment.

'I'm in no hurry for a repeat performance I can tell you. But I have to say you looked magnificent standing there with flashing eyes and pink cheeks,' he teased.

'And you, David Sutherland, were coldness personified.'

'Was I?'

'Yes, you were, I hardly recognised you and I was frightened.'

'Frightened of me, surely not?'

'Frightened I would lose you.'

'Never, but it just shows what misunderstandings can do.'

'Don't let us ever quarrel, David, it is too dangerous.'

'We won't quarrel, my sweet, but we must have the occasional friendly argument. Life would be terribly dull otherwise.'

'No, it wouldn't, I'm all for a quiet life.'

'Poor darling, your life has been turned upside down but only one more hurdle for you.'

'What hurdle?'

He looked serious. 'Go and see Mrs Pringle and make your peace.'

'Why should I? I have nothing to apologise for,' she said sharply.

'I know that, Lois,' David said patiently. 'All the same I do wish you would make the effort and go. It could start the healing process.'

'Really, is that what you think?'

He ignored the sarcasm in her voice. 'Yes, it is but I'll say no more meantime and it is time we were getting on our way.'

Various shopping bags, a very nice wicker basket together with an assortment of cardboard boxes littered the sitting-room floor. Lois had to step round them to get to her coat and was buttoning it when she remembered the eggs in the kitchen. She gave a gasp and put her hand to her mouth. How awful, how absolutely dreadful, if she had left them behind. It would have seemed like carelessness and what would Mrs McKenzie have thought of her?

'What's the matter?'

'The eggs, David, I almost forgot them.'

'Hardly surprising in the circumstances, this has been quite a day.'

'Mrs McKenzie wouldn't have known that.'

'Neither she would but you did remember so no harm done.' He was looking around him and frowning. 'One thing is for sure, all this lot won't go in the car.'

Lois had come into the room with the eggs and heard him. 'The clock is a must, it has to go.'

'You and your clock, it wouldn't be so terrible if it was overlooked, we could get it on our next visit.'

'*Your* next visit, you'll be on your own,' Lois corrected him quietly.

David stopped what he was doing and looked up. 'I am going to pretend I didn't hear that.'

'You did say it.'

'We both said a lot of things we didn't mean.'

'I know we did but how could we have known – there was no way.'

'No way at all.'

Lois looked distressed, 'I wish with all my heart that I could take back the horrid things I said. Why in anger do we say things we don't mean?'

'A human weakness, most of us are guilty of it.'

'What if it had spelt the end for us.'

'No chance of that,' David said gently. 'There might have been a coolness for a day or two but it would have come all right. Certainly it is a lesson to both of us that we must not have secrets from each other.'

'I won't, I promise. David, I'll never keep anything from you.'

'Unlikely to be anything, not on this scale anyway.'

'I couldn't stand it.'

His face softened. 'Stumbling on the truth the way you did would have upset anyone and already you are coming to terms with it.'

'I'm not quite so shattered now about being illegitimate and that is because you don't think any less of me—'

David almost exploded. 'Any less of you? For heaven's sake, what do you take me for? How you came into the world is of no importance. I'm just very glad you were born.'

'A love child,' she smiled.

'That you were, no doubt about that. Silly to have let it bother you.' His face grew stern. 'Don't ever let it upset you.'

'I won't but I wish it could remain our secret.'

'Perhaps it can, I don't see how it need go any further.'

'I wasn't going to tell you this, David.'

'Why not?'

'This isn't a secret, nothing like that. I kept it to myself because I thought you might laugh.'

'Why should I do that?'

'Most people would.'

'I'm not most people.'

'Even so you would probably have said it was imagination.'

'I can't say if I don't know what it is.'

Lois was wishing now that she had kept silent, but David was waiting and she would have to go on. 'It happened, David, that first time I entered Viewfield House.' She moistened her lips. 'Don't think it was scary, it wasn't. It was just a strange feeling.'

'You should have said. Why didn't you?'

'I wanted to and I nearly did, then I thought you would laugh and somehow I knew that would upset me. I'm not an over-imaginative person.'

'Let me be absolutely honest. I might have laughed but I don't think I would.'

'Did you feel anything?'

'It was my home for as long as I can remember – no that isn't quite true I have a vague recollection of another house, but it is very hazy. For me Grace's presence is everywhere because—'

'Because everything in this house reminds you of her?'

'Yes, I suppose that is true.'

Lois tried not to be, but she couldn't help feeling jealous. She was picturing them in this room, Grace, Grace's husband and David. A happy family, a close-knit threesome. In those times did her own mother, the woman who had given birth to her, ever spare a thought for a little girl, an insecure little girl, growing up in another home? No, she wouldn't have, that was in the past. Mistakes had been made and those mistakes were better forgotten.

David was seeing the fleeting expressions crossing her face and leant forward in his chair earnest and anxious.

'We can talk about it.'

She shook her head. 'I don't think so.'

They had both completed what they had been doing and were sitting on chairs. David got up from his and held out his hand.

'Come on, we'll be more comfortable on the sofa, probably the last chance before it goes to the saleroom,' he smiled.

'Shouldn't we be getting everything in the car?'

'Another half an hour won't make much difference and I have a feeling you are keeping something back.'

'Nothing of importance.'

'Let me be the judge of that.'

David had been anxious to be on their way home by this time. They both had work to get up for and there was a particularly busy day ahead of him. Still he would cope with that and he had the feeling that if she said nothing now he would never discover what it was. His arm went round her shoulder and he felt her give a little shiver.

'Cold?' he asked, looking at the fire which was well down.

'No. I was just remembering the strange feeling was more pronounced in the bedroom, particularly when I was touching the clothes in the wardrobe.' She looked at him, her eyes huge. 'David, my own mother's clothes. They were hers, she had worn them and I didn't know.'

'I know, darling, all this has been too much for you.'

'I did feel something,' she said almost harshly.

'Perhaps it wasn't so very strange that you did,' he said gently, and gave her shoulder a reassuring squeeze.

'Do you believe in . . .' She didn't finish the sentence.

He knew what she wanted to ask and he was thoughtful. Lois wasn't herself, how could she be? She was still in a state of shock. The subject had never held any interest for him nevertheless he couldn't dismiss it lightly.

'To be honest I don't know what I believe in, darling.'

'Surely you don't put everything down to coincidence?'

'Before this I was inclined to.'

'But you aren't now?'

'Not after what we found out today.'

'What would you call it then? Fate?'

He shrugged. 'Who knows? Lois, I do believe there are

things in this life that we don't understand and are not meant to.'

She looked at him gratefully. 'You're not trying to humour me, you are taking me seriously?'

He nodded then smiled. 'I'll always take you seriously.'

'Thank you, and David,' she wanted to be generous, 'please go on calling her mother, I honestly won't mind, and it must be terribly difficult to stop.'

'Difficult or not that is what I am going to do. You have that right and I don't. As to calling her stepmother, that is out. She will be Grace to me from now on.'

'She will be Grace to both of us. It's a lovely name, I like it.'

'Me too, but I'm pretty fond of Lois.' He smiled. 'And before I forget,' he added, 'it might be a good idea to leave Grace's clothes and other belongings—'

'Not give them away you mean?'

'Not until you've had a chance to go over them. Wait until you feel up to it then decide what you would like to keep.'

Lois was grateful for David's thoughtfulness. Before she had been going over a stranger's possessions with no thought of keeping anything for herself. It was different now. Harriet used to say at spring-cleaning time, 'if in doubt don't throw out' or 'keep a thing for seven years and you'll get a use for it'. She would keep that in mind.

'Yes, I'll do that.' Lois was silent for a few moments then she said slowly. 'The woman I thought of as my mother did not treat me kindly and I won't sin my soul by saying otherwise. She did, however, bring me up. It was a cold upbringing but I suppose I have to show a little gratitude.' She paused and swallowed painfully. 'In a way I still want to go on calling her mother and that could be because I can't think of another way to address her.'

'Deep down, didn't you always long for her love?'

'Desperately. I would have done anything to have her treat me the way she treated Marie and Winnie. She knew that too which made it all the more hurtful. No wonder I felt insecure, I have her to thank for that.'

'My poor darling.'

'You don't really believe me, you think I am exaggerating and I'm not. Not that it matters, I have no need of her now.'

He shook his head and suddenly she laughed. 'David, stop looking for a happy ending or you are going to be disappointed.' She made a face. 'If I stopped calling her mother what in heaven's name would I call her? Mrs Pringle perhaps? That would be a hoot and don't you dare suggest Aunt Harriet or I'll hit you over the head.'

David burst out laughing. It was nice to see Lois almost herself again.

'I wasn't going to. This is a bit like the mother-in-law problem, what does one call her? Most get round it by calling the poor woman nothing at all.'

'That is usually solved when babies arrive, then she is just grandmother. Would you look at the time, David Sutherland, or are you contemplating staying the night here?'

'Now there's a bold suggestion.'

'It was nothing of the kind so don't be getting any wrong ideas. I do have my reputation to think about,' she said primly.

'Meaning mine doesn't matter?'

'You would get away with it, men get off with murder.'

'On your feet then, sweetheart, I'll get the guard for the fire though by the look of it it is hardly worth the bother,' he said looking at the dying embers.

'Better safe than sorry.'

They carried out what would go in the car and once the back seat was piled high, Lois made sure that the eggs and the clock were safely wedged so that they wouldn't come to grief as they bumped over the uneven surface.

Once he had the house locked up and Lois settled in the car David produced a tartan travelling rug from the boot and gave it to her to put round her legs.

'I'm not an invalid,' she protested.

'I know but you might feel the cold.' She did look a bit pale and he wasn't taking any chances. Going round to the driver's side he swung himself in and started up the engine. It fired first time and he sighed with relief. It wasn't always so obliging. The headlamps cut a strip of yellow light through the darkness and though he was familiar with the road David negotiated the tight bends with care and kept his speed well down until they were out onto Strathmartine Road.

Lois yawned, tiredness had crept up on her and though she tried to keep awake she lost the battle and sleep claimed her. Her head was back and hearing the regular breathing David glanced to his side and smiled when he saw that she was asleep. Poor darling, what a time she had come through. It had been pretty traumatic for him but so much worse for Lois. He wished they could be together always so that he could protect her. In a sense they were both free agents. Neither of them needed to worry about relatives, they could be married quickly and quietly. Still that was for the bride to decide and if Lois was set on an Easter engagement then so be it. What he could do, what he would do, would be to draw up the house plans and once Lois and he were satisfied and the legal side taken care of the builders could begin.

After about twenty minutes Lois awoke with a start.

'Did I doze off?'

'You have been dead to the world for at least twenty minutes.'

'Never!'

'I assure you it's true.'

'I'm sorry, David.'

'What for? Falling asleep?'

'I should have been company for you.'

'You were by just being there.'

She peered out at the darkness, looking for the outline of landmarks but unable to tell where they were.

'I'm lost, I have absolutely no idea where we are.'

'Good thing you weren't driving.'

'A very good thing. I'm hopeless, I have no sense of direction.'

'Grace was the same, Dad used to tease her about it.'

Lois smiled to herself. That was something else she had inherited from Grace.

In a remarkably short time or so it seemed to Lois after her nap, they were drawing up outside Glenburn.

'Home safe and sound,' he said as they both got out. 'Wonder how the eggs travelled?'

'I saw to them and the clock,' she said as he leaned in the back and handed her first the box of eggs and then the clock. 'David, I have the house key in my pocket, just you get away.'

'Nonsense, on you go and I'll follow.'

The hall light was on and showing through the casement window. David took the key from her and opened the door. They left it open but stood just inside.

'I'll share these with Miss Watt.'

He kissed her. 'Good night, darling,' he whispered, 'I hope that little nap won't have put you off sleeping.'

'I don't think so. Will you sleep?'

'I never have any trouble getting off, my problem is in the morning,' he grinned. 'Then I have to force myself. Incidentally the secret for getting off quickly is to empty your mind completely.'

'Easier said than done.'

'Takes practice that's all.'

'This has been the strangest day of my life,' she said softly, 'and you weren't just saying it, you do believe in fate?'

'When it brought me you – yes, I believe in fate.'

She smiled at that. 'Must go but I'll be round as usual.'

'I would rather you went to see Mrs Pringle.'

'There is no reason why I should.'

'There is every reason. I know it will take courage but you are not short on that.'

'I'm not prepared to risk a rebuff.'

'Perhaps you would be made welcome.'

'And pigs might fly. You are being ridiculous,' she said, annoyance creeping into her voice.

'I'm upsetting you?'

'You are as a matter of fact.'

'Let me just say this, then I'm going. If you don't do this you may come to regret it and by then, Lois, it could be too late. Mrs Pringle is your only link with the past.'

That struck home. Perhaps David was right, he certainly thought so. Would the day come when she would regret not trying to find out the truth?

'She may not want to talk about it, she probably won't.'

'That is a possibility, but on the other hand she may be anxious to give her side of it.'

'You don't give up easily.'

'Not with something as important as this.'

'Good night, David,' she said, turning away.

'Good night, sweetheart. I'll shut the door behind me.' He closed it making as little noise as possible and Lois went straight to the kitchen and got a bowl out of the cupboard. After removing the newspaper wrapped around each egg she placed them in the bowl and put the bowl in the pantry on the cold slab. That done she hung up her coat on the hallstand and carrying the clock went upstairs to her bedroom. The sleep in the car had taken the edge off her tiredness and she welcomed being alone with her thoughts. Putting the clock on the bedside table she felt a lump in her throat. Perhaps it had once been on Grace's bedside table. One thing was sure, even if it was beyond mending she would never part with it.

She shivered and realising the room was cold she put a match to the gas fire. A little heat would take the chill away and she would remember to switch it off before getting into bed. Drawing the chair nearer to the heat Lois sat down and let her thoughts take over. Knowing that her illegitimacy didn't bother David had come as a tremendous relief and she found that she wasn't thinking so much about it herself. What did trouble her was losing her position in the family. She still wanted to belong and not just as a half-sister to Marie and Winnie.

Her thoughts turned to what life would have been like if her own mother had defied her parents and kept her child. Would they have cut her off without a penny? How would they have managed? Andrew Pringle would have had to make some contribution and she didn't doubt that he would have done so and willingly. Not that it would have amounted to a great deal, not with a wife and child to support. Would the day have come when she might have blamed her mother for their predicament? Might she have been secretly ashamed? How could one tell?

Grace must have asked herself those same questions and then done what she thought best for her baby. She would know that Andrew's wife would have little or no affection for the baby, how could it be otherwise? Her only comfort would come from knowing that Andrew was there to protect his own daughter.

It was easy to understand now why she had been treated differently but it didn't explain why Harriet had accepted the responsibility in the first place.

If anything would take her to Laurelbank it would be to find out the answer to that question.

Chapter Twenty-Three

With her mind made up, Lois went straight from the office to the bus stop and after a few minutes' wait the bus came along and she got on. It seemed strange to her to be making this journey that had once been so familiar. She didn't expect changes and there weren't many. One shop that had changed hands had a new frontage and another had been given a fresh coat of paint. A canary yellow that stood out like a sore thumb between the more traditional green of its neighbour on either side.

It was ridiculous to feel nervous but she did and that was silly since all she had to do was get off at the next stop. Then she reminded herself that she was doing this for David and she didn't want to face his disappointment if she failed him. When her stop came she got off quickly and walked smartly along the road. Turning the corner the house came into view and she felt a lump come into her throat. It was so achingly familiar and despite all that had happened it was still home. The heavy curtains were hanging at the front windows, and would remain there until the end of March when they would be replaced by lighter weight curtains. Or would her mother bother now that she was on her own?

Lois opened the gate, went in, closed it behind her and began walking along the path. Then she wondered which door to use, the back or the front. The back door was for family and perhaps not for her, better to go to the front like a visitor which was what she felt like – an unwelcome one.

She pulled the bell at the front door and heard it ring. There were no hurrying footsteps, she waited and rang again. Still no answer, her mother wasn't at home. Lois felt an overwhelming relief that she had been spared the ordeal. She could try another time or better still put it off altogether. She was on the point of turning away when the door opened and her mother stood there.

'Hello, Mum,' Lois said awkwardly.

Mrs Pringle looked startled. 'What do you want?' The voice was sharp and Lois half expected to get the door shut in her face.

'May I come in?'

Harriet Pringle made no reply just turning on her heel and leaving Lois to do what she liked. After a moment's hesitation she stepped inside, closed the door and followed her mother into the sitting-room. The woman had seated herself in her usual chair and Lois stood in the middle of the floor waiting to be asked to sit down. When she wasn't she took the chair at the other side of the fire and since the room was so hot she took off her coat, put it over the back of the chair and sat down again.

'You're making yourself at home.'

'Do you mind?'

She didn't answer. 'This isn't a social visit, you've come for something?'

'In a way.' She took a deep breath. 'That letter,' she began, 'remember the one that slipped behind the clock and Winnie brought it over to me?'

'Vaguely. What about it?'

'The letter was from a firm of solicitors, Bryden & Edmondson of Dundee.'

'What has this to do with me?'

'Quite a lot I think. The solicitor informed me that I've been left some money.'

'Have you now? That'll please you.' The words were said lightly, but Lois thought her mother looked uncomfortable.

'The name Grace Melville, does it mean anything to you?'

Harriet stared staight ahead but the hands in her lap were clenching and unclenching.

'The money I take it was from her?'

'Yes.'

'She's dead?'

'Yes.'

'You know?'

'About Grace Melville being my natural mother? Yes, the solicitor told me.'

'The Lord works in mysterious ways, that's both of them gone, both of them dead.' She gave a twisted smile. 'I wonder if He will forgive them, I never could.' Her face was set in granite lines. 'Not short of money that family, left you a tidy sum did she?'

'Yes.'

'That is what you came to tell me. You shouldn't have bothered.'

'I came because there is so much I don't understand,' Lois said unsteadily.

'Better that way – leave it.'

'I can't and you are the only one who can tell me.'

'The pity was that you were ever born, that's what I can tell you.'

The words spoken in that voice shocked Lois. 'That is a terrible thing to say.'

'The truth is very often terrible.'

'I didn't ask to be born.'

'No, but if you hadn't put in your appearance my life could have been so different.'

'Different in what way? How can I understand when you won't tell me.'

'Why should I?'

'Don't you think I should know,' Lois said gently, 'and perhaps, Mum, you need to tell.'

'I don't, so you can rid yourself of that idea.'

'It concerns me and I have a right to know,' Lois persisted.

'Don't you dare talk about rights, my girl, I had those too or so I thought.' Her eyes glittered. 'The right of every wife to expect her husband to be faithful.'

'No one would dispute that.'

'Especially in my case with an infant to care for.'

'I don't know how Dad could have done that to you.'

'You thought him perfect. Well, you are about to find out that he wasn't.'

'None of us is perfect but Dad was always kind. He loved me which was just as well since I got precious little kindness from you.'

'I brought you up, wasn't that enough?'

Lois shook her head.

'And you would do well to remember what I saved you from –

a life of shame.' A spark from the fire had gone on the fireside rug and she quickly put her foot on it.

'Why did you bother saving me? That is what I want to know.'

Harriet shrugged.

'Why didn't you tell me or why didn't Dad? I had to know eventually that you weren't my mother.'

'Your father thought eighteen was time enough or before you were to be married was another suggestion of his. I was indifferent.' She got up. 'I'm having a cup of tea,' she said jerkily.

'Shall I make it?'

'If you want.' She sat down again. 'I suppose you remember where things are?'

Lois smiled. 'As if I could forget.' She went through to the kitchen, made the tea and brought it through with a plate of biscuits. Harriet had brought forward the small table and Lois set the tray down on it. She waited for her mother to pour then accepted her cup and sat down. Lois swallowed a piece of biscuit and drank some tea.

'Did you know that Dad was seeing someone?' Lois asked quietly.

'No.'

'It must have been a terrible shock?'

'Yes.'

'Did you – manage to forgive him?'

'I would have if you hadn't come on the scene.'

'May I ask you a personal question?'

'I would have thought that was what you were doing,' she managed a small smile.

'Did you love Dad?' Lois was surprised that she had managed to ask that.

Harriet was quiet for so long that Lois thought she wasn't going to answer then she spoke slowly, almost reluctantly.

'Yes, Lois, I loved your father and I could have forgiven him anything if only he hadn't loved her.'

'He must have loved you once,' Lois said gently.

'Never. He never loved me. Why did he marry me, that is what you want to know. Well. I was quite pretty.'

'Like Marie,' Lois smiled.

'Marie is prettier than I ever was. My mother wanted Andrew for a son-in-law and she made such a fuss of him. She was a first-rate cook and I gathered his mother was not – Sunday teas became an event in his life I think—'

Lois was laughing. 'Come on, it had to be more than that?'

'Of course there was an attraction on his part, but it wasn't love. He knew it and I knew it, but somehow the romance continued and we were engaged and then married. My mother said that if I was a good wife that love would grow.'

'Perhaps it did?'

'No. There was someone else for me and I should have married him. He was in love with me and it is easier for a wife to pretend love than a husband. What I am trying to say, Lois, I don't know what I am trying to say, except that I would rather be loved by someone I didn't love than the other way round.'

'I think I understand.'

'We were quite happy you see, we got on well and when Marie was born it seemed to me that life was perfect. Life can be very hard you know, Lois.'

'I do know, I've had first-hand experience,' Lois said bitterly.

'Nonsense you had nothing to complain about. You were well enough looked after.'

'I was fed and clothed but children need more than that. They need to be loved. I missed out, you can't deny that?'

'Why should I deny it?'

'If my presence upset you why did you agree to take me? That is what I can't understand. Was there some kind of pressure put on you to take me?'

Lois saw by the expression that she had hit home.

Harriet sounded wearied. 'There will be no rest for me until you hear the whole unhappy tale. To be honest I don't much care. What is left for me with Marie and Winnie both gone?'

'Winnie will be back.'

'She won't be the same girl who went away. She'll be changed.'

'I don't see Winnie changing.'

'Speaking of change have you heard the news about Stephen Hammond?'

'No, what about Stephen?'

'His engagement was in the paper.'

'That was quick. Who is the girl?'

'That one called Veronica?'

'Veronica! Wasn't that the name of Stephen's brother's fiancée?'

'One and the same, caused quite a stir.'

'I imagine it would. Did you write and tell Marie?'

'I did, but she didn't seem all that interested. What she did say was that she thought them well suited.'

'As long as they are happy.' Lois was anxious to get back to the story in case her mother changed her mind which was more than a possibility.

'What about your bus? Which one are you catching?'

'I'm not bothered as long as I don't miss the last one.'

Harriet sighed. 'It means going back to when Marie was an infant. None of this would have happened if my mother hadn't moved away from Dundee.'

'Why did she?'

'Montrose was where we spent our holidays and she always had a notion to live there. I wasn't in favour of her moving, chiefly I think because I had thought she would be on hand to help with the baby.'

'I'm sure you would have managed on your own.'

'Not on my own but with the help of a good neighbour. Where was I?'

'You were talking about your mother.'

She nodded. 'My mother took ill, she had not been enjoying good health for some time but this was serious and the doctor didn't give her long. Andrew and I talked it over and he agreed that my place was with my mother. He drove us there, saw the condition mother was in and said that I should stay until the end.'

Lois nodded. 'You couldn't do any other.'

'We were living in a tenement then and the good neighbour I mentioned was to look after Andrew. Hard for you to believe but he was quite good about the house at that time.'

Lois smiled. 'With four females in the house he would feel he didn't need to.'

'Mother improved, possibly because I was on hand and she was very taken with the baby. As for me, I was torn both ways wondering what I should do. It wasn't fair on Andrew leaving him so long on his own, but if I left Mother would choose that time to slip away.'

'Why wasn't she in hospital?'

'She wouldn't go, said she would die in her own bed. As it happened I had made up my mind to return home and had made arrangements for someone to see to Mother when she had a bad turn and died. Andrew came through for the funeral but I had to stay on to clear the house.'

'Why didn't Dad stay and help you?'

'He couldn't, he had his job to think about. I managed.'

'I'm sure you did.'

'Was I trusting or was I blind? When I returned home life went on as before or so I thought. There were nights when Andrew worked late but that wasn't unusual and I never gave it a thought.'

Lois was feeling sorry for this trusting young woman and anger against her father. David had said that we shouldn't judge a person until we knew all the facts and from all accounts her mother had had a shabby deal.

'This is all very upsetting for me and I'm going to make myself something to eat. Just a light snack, I've started taking my main meal midday.'

'I do too.'

'There's eggs and tomatoes and not much else. I only buy for one.'

'What shall I do?'

'Set the table. I'll make scrambled eggs.'

No more was said until they were sitting down to fluffy scrambled eggs.

'This is good, I'm enjoying it.' It was the truth. Lois was enjoying the meal with her mother. They weren't completely at ease but much of the tension had gone.

'Ready for the next instalment?'

'Yes, please.' It was a rare touch of humour from Harriet.

'That woman—'

Lois winced. 'Please don't call her that.'

'She'll never be anything else to me – dead or alive,' she ended viciously.

'For my sake, please call her Grace.'

'It won't be easy but very well I'll try. She – Grace must have got in touch with your father to tell him she was pregnant. Thinking back I can almost feel sorry for him. The poor man wouldn't have known what to do.' Then her face hardened. 'If it hadn't been for Marie he would have left me and gone to her.'

'You can't be sure of that.'

'There are a lot of things I can't be sure about,' she said tartly, 'but that isn't one. There was money on her side and money can solve a lot of things.' She pursed her lips. 'As it was he had to tread carefully. He was a young accountant with a well-respected firm and the disgrace might not have cost him his job but it would certainly have put paid to any chance of promotion. No, Lois, your father couldn't afford a scandal and this was one of the worst kind – a married man whose wife had recently given birth to a daughter getting a young girl pregnant.'

'I do feel sorry for what you went through. It must have been dreadful for you.'

'It was, I was nearly out of my mind. Poor Mother, I blamed her for dying at the wrong time. She wasn't there when I so desperately needed her and there was no one else I could trust not to gossip.' She grimaced. 'I am about to miscall your maternal grandparents.'

'Go ahead. What were they like? Dragons I expect?'

'It is as good a description as any. Cold. God-fearing folk they were. The minute they knew about their daughter's predicament they were making arrangements to send her away before she was showing or so I was led to believe. No doubt they had a plausible excuse ready to explain her absence.'

'Poor Grace, they wanted rid of their daughter.'

'Wrong. They didn't want rid of their daughter – just the child she was carrying. You have to remember she was their only child and they were depending on her to look after them in their old age.'

'How selfish.' Lois swallowed. 'What about—'

'What about you? You were to be adopted and the matter never again mentioned. No doubt they would have kept a firm hand on their daughter lest she strayed again.'

'Kept her a virtual prisoner.'

'Possibly. Only, as so often happens the best laid plans – you know the rest. They hadn't bargained on their daughter being so stubborn. She ignored all threats and refused to part with her baby even though those threats included being cut off without a penny.'

Lois felt a glow and her eyes shone. This was the best bit, to know that she had been wanted.

'That pleased you, hearing that?'

'Yes, more than you'll ever know.'

'Your mother—'

'Call her Grace, that's how I think of her.'

Harriet looked at her sharply. 'Very well. Grace was no fool, she would have had a good idea of the hardship ahead and you must remember that she had never known want.'

'Dad—' Lois began.

'Your father could only be expected to do so much. He wasn't highly paid at that time and the extra expense would have made it difficult for ends to meet. She must have thought it all out and decided that the only way she would give up her baby was if it went to the father to be brought up in his home.'

'She was right, Dad should have been shouldering some of the responsibility.'

'And what about me? Should that have included me?'

'It was a mess,' Lois said miserably. 'Was Dad prepared to do what she asked?'

'Of course, for him it was the perfect answer. I soon sorted him out. I told him in no uncertain terms what I thought of that suggestion.'

'Yet you agreed, why was that?'

'Don't rush me, I'm getting tired. Perhaps you don't realise it, but this is taking a lot out of me.'

'I'm sorry. I'll see to the fire, is there plenty of coal in?'

'Yes, I filled a bucket, it's behind the back door. Use what is in the scuttle.'

Lois emptied the rest of the coal out of the scuttle. 'Why did Mrs What-do-you-call-her not see to the coal?'

'She doesn't come now. Gave up a few weeks ago.'

'Haven't you been able to get a replacement?'

'Didn't try. There is only me and one person doesn't make a lot of work.'

Lois thought it might be a financial consideration, she might have done a lot of housework in her younger days but she hadn't been too keen in the last year or two.

'Why did I agree, you asked. Put it this way, I didn't change my

329

mind, I had it changed for me. Very astute grandparents you had. Looked for my weakness, found it and went to work on me.'

Lois leaned forward wondering what she was to hear. 'I can't imagine you with a weakness.'

'I was a young lass then.'

'Had you met Grace's parents?'

'Not until they arrived uninvited on my doorstep. Put me in a state I can tell you. Amidst all my worries I was still houseproud and I didn't like to be caught in a muddle . You see, I had been seeing to Marie and there was the clutter of baby things lying around that I hadn't had time to clear away. I flew to the door thinking it could only be a neighbour or maybe the boy with the messages.'

'A shock for you?'

'It was. They introduced themselves but it was unnecessary, I knew straight away who they were.'

'Can you describe them?' Lois wanted to learn as much as possible and she knew this would be the only opportunity.

'Very well turned-out, very posh. Not dressed to kill, nothing like that, but it was easy to see they were people of means.'

'Did they ask or did you invite them in?'

'I didn't want them in my house, but I was curious to know why they had come and at a time when they knew Andrew wouldn't be home.'

'To persuade you to take me. I would have thought that was obvious.'

'It wasn't to me, not after I had made it crystal clear to Andrew that nothing, absolutely nothing, would persuade me to have a bastard child in my house.'

'Did you have to use that word?' Lois said angrily.

'No use getting yourself in a state. Had I not taken you in that word would have been no stranger to you. Do I continue or do I not?'

'I'm sorry.'

'You've always been too sensitive, that has been half your trouble.' She paused. 'Your grandparents, I was talking about them, they came in and I got the pair of them seated. Mrs Melville was the nicer of the two. She said not to worry when I apologised for the state of the room, that it was only to be expected with a baby. Marie was asleep in her pram. I used to keep it in the corner of the room. She got up to look and said I had a beautiful baby and wasn't it a pity we didn't have a garden for her to play in. I told her we were lucky to have a park nearby but she shook her head and said that wasn't the same at all. Then for good measure she added that a tenement wasn't ideal to bring up a child and wasn't it a great inconvenience to get a pram up and downstairs.'

'I suppose she had a point, it must have been difficult.'

'Occasionally it was, but in a tenement there is usually someone available to give a helping hand.' She paused to clear her throat then went on. 'All this time her husband had been silent but his eyes were going round the room as though he was examining the furniture. Then he decided to have his say. Oh, but I forgot to say that I had let slip that we were hoping to buy our own house and then we would have a garden for Marie to play in. He gave a sort of sneer, I can see him yet, and said it would be a very long time indeed before my husband would be in a position to buy a house. Surely I must be aware of his responsibility, that he was to blame for his daughter's condition, that he had ruined her life – he said more but I can't recall it all. Suffice to say that Andrew had got her into this mess and it was his responsibility to pay maintenance.'

'He was right, but to say it like that must have made you furious.'

'At the time I think I was more frightened than furious, he had that effect on me. I do remember wanting to scream at him that none of it was my fault and why should I be made to suffer.'

'Was it true that Dad and you were thinking of buying your own home?'

'Yes, we had been saving to put down a deposit. Don't think I am doing down our tenement home, I'm not, we had a good house with a bathroom and scullery but I wanted something better.' She was silent for a long time and Lois kept quiet. It was as though she was letting the floodgates of memory open and Lois thought she had all but forgotten her existence. 'My face must have betrayed me because I remember his wife giving him a warning look and he must have taken the hint because he fell silent.'

'What happened then?'

'The offer came. Do what they wanted and there would be no waiting for our own home. A substantial sum of money would be paid into our bank account.' She gave a half smile. 'How could I resist that?'

'You had a good idea what they wanted of you?'

'A fair idea. I was willing to listen.'

'The means towards a home of your own if you would agree to take me, that was it, wasn't it?'

'Yes.'

'You accepted?'

'Not right away.'

'But you did?' Lois persisted.

'Yes.'

'What about Dad?'

'As you can imagine it was a great relief to him. In fact, as far as he was concerned it was the perfect solution.'

Lois was shaking, she couldn't help it. She was that baby being spoken of like a piece of merchandise, something to be got rid of. She almost choked on the words. 'You took their money gladly and agreed to bring me up as your own child, a sister for Marie.'

'Yes, that was what I did.'

'Only you didn't.'

'I beg your pardon.'

'You heard me well enough.'

'The agreement was that I should bring you up. I could hardly be expected to have any affection for you. Grow up, Lois.'

'A tiny baby, a tiny defenceless baby and you could spare no love for it. That was heartless,' she said and sniffed to hold back the tears.

'You might think so, but what about me? Can you imagine how much I suffered?'

'No matter how much you suffered you shouldn't have taken it out on me.'

'Did you expect me to give you the same loving care as I gave to Marie and Winnie?'

'Yes, that was what I expected.'

'You weren't mine.'

'But I didn't know that.'

'You began this not me,' Harriet said angrily.

'All right, we'll leave that but tell me this. Why Greenacre, why did you choose to come here?'

'There had to be no gossip and that meant moving away from Dundee to somewhere we weren't known. We broke off with the few friends we had and neither of us had close relatives who would have had to be told. Greenacre was ideal. You were our second child and then Winnie came along to complete the family. Are you satisfied now?'

'I know more, put it that way. You did rather well, Mum, in fact it was a very good bargain for you. A large sum towards the purchase of this house and when I was old enough you had the services of an unpaid maid.'

'What nonsense.'

'You can't deny that I was always the last to be considered.'

'Did you expect to be first?'

'No just to be treated the same. If I'd known the truth, that you weren't my mother, I think I would have found it easier. Certainly easier to understand.'

'Since we are both being honest I'll tell you this. I could hardly bear to look at you because when I did it was to see those two together—'

Lois heard the pain. 'Even after everything, you loved him?'

'I never stopped loving your father and I used to watch him when he was looking at you and knowing that he was longing to be with her.'

It was cruel to go on but she had to. 'Did they ever meet – I mean after?'

'Your father and Grace? No. Mr Melville thought of everything. He made them promise on the Bible that they would never see each other again or have any communication of any kind. Grace had to promise that she would make no attempt to see her baby or send anything to the child.'

'They took the oath, both of them?'

'They had no choice.'

'Do you think they kept their word?'

'Oh, I'm sure of it. Your father had his faults but he wouldn't have broken his word.'

Lois's thoughts went back to the photographs. How had they come to be with Grace? That was one question that would go unanswered. She would never tell how she had come across them.

'Your real mother broke her promise by leaving that money to you in her Will but then she wouldn't have expected to be taken so young.'

'Or she might have expected me to know about it by this time.'

Harriet shrugged. 'Perhaps.'

'I'm still puzzled why you didn't tell me after Dad died. I would have thought you would have been only too happy to inform me that I didn't belong to you.'

'Then you were wrong. To do that would have been to let Marie and Winnie know that their father had been unfaithful to me.'

'Do you still want it kept from them?'

'I would much prefer it, but the decision rests with you.'

She smiled at her mother. They were in agreement about this. 'I don't want Marie and Winnie to think of me as a half-sister.'

'Then leave things as they are for as long as you can.'

'Mum, there is no reason why they should ever know.'

'You don't have to go on calling me Mum you know, not now you know that I'm not.'

'Grace is my natural mother but she is only a name to me,' Lois said quietly. 'I have to go on thinking of you as Mum.'

Harried nodded and Lois thought she looked pleased. Then Lois's face changed when she saw the time.

'For heaven's sake, I had no idea it was anything like that time. Mum, I'll have to dash.'

Harriet had gone over to the window and moved the curtain to look out.

'You can't go out in that, it's coming down in sheets.'

'I'll have to, it's the last bus.'

'You'd be pushed to get it.'

'What am I going to do?'

'Will anyone miss you?'

'Not until tomorrow morning. I come and go as I please.'

'Then you'll just have to spend the night here.'

'You don't mind?'

'Why should I?'

'I thought you might.' This was a far cry from what Lois had expected.

'Better make up your mind.'

'Thanks,' she said awkwardly, 'I'll stay and I'm sorry to put you to all this inconvenience.'

'No inconvenience,' she said briskly, 'you can see to yourself. The bed will need sheets and better fill a hot-water bottle before you retire to take the chill away. You'll mind it is a while since the bed was slept in.'

'That last bus is ridiculously early, don't you think so?'

'There's a move to get a later one but you know the time it takes for these things to be decided. No use standing, sit yourself down, you can't make a better of it.'

Lois sat down. 'I must get the early bus, Mum, and if you let me have an alarm clock I'll see myself out without disturbing you.'

'You won't disturb me and why the early bus? Why not the one you used to get?'

'That would mean going straight to the office and Mrs Barlow would wonder. She's Miss Watt's housekeeper and we usually have a cup of tea together when she gets in.'

'Do what you want.' She was frowning. 'I have a horrible feeling that by tomorrow morning I am going to regret all this.'

'Don't, it has helped me. Mum—'

'What now?'

'Did you ever meet Grace?'

'No and I had no wish to.'

'Who brought me?'

'A nurse.'

'I was handed over, just like that?'

'Yes, how else could it have been done?' She sounded amused.

'I don't know but it seems so cold and unfeeling.'

'You were an infant for God's sake,' Harriet said in exasperation, 'you wouldn't have known what was going on. And if I were you, my girl, I would be counting my blessings. She would have left you a tidy sum I fancy.'

'Yes, I won't want, but I wasn't the only beneficiary.'

Harriet looked surprised. 'I understood she was an only child.'

'She was but Grace married a widower with a small boy.'

'Is he, the husband I mean, still alive?'

'No, he died a few years ago.'

'And the small boy?'

Lois smiled. 'The small boy is now well over six feet.'

'You've met him?'

'Yes, Mum, I've met him,' Lois said softly and Harriet looked at her quickly.

'Am I missing something?'

'Better I tell you now. His name is David Sutherland and he is the other beneficiary,' she said slowly and distinctly then added. 'And, Mum, I'm in love with him.' She waited but could see that the words hadn't registered.

'What about Tim? Does this mean that you have given him the go by?'

'That was never serious, we were just very good friends – we still are.'

Harriet frowned. 'And this new lad of yours, what does he do?'

'David is a qualified vet and has his own practice in Muirford, actually just round the corner from where I am staying.'

'That should be handy.' Was there a hint of sarcasm? Lois couldn't be sure.

'Yes, very convenient.'

'Wait a minute – you can't mean—'

'You aren't usually so slow on the uptake, Mum. I wondered when the penny was going to drop.' She was smiling broadly. 'David Sutherland happens to be Grace's stepson. I'm not surprised you are looking shocked, I know it takes a bit of getting used to.'

There was shock, but a strange look had come over Harriet's face. 'Who would have believed it? And this is serious you say?'

'Yes, I am going to marry David.'

'Your own mother's stepson?' She shook her head in disbelief.

'David is quite sure that Grace would have approved.'

'Maybe she would at that.'

'Did he know that Grace had a child outside marriage?'

'No, I was a complete surprise to him and he to me for that matter. It took a bit of sorting out but we managed it eventually.'

'More a shock than a surprise.'

'You'd better know that I'm here because David pleaded with me to come. He said there were always two sides to a story and you had the right to tell yours.'

'Sounds like a nice lad.' She paused. 'Handsome like Tim?'

'Handsome but not like Tim. David is sort of ruggedly

336

handsome if you can imagine that.' Describing David, Lois thought, didn't do him justice. When you looked into his face you saw kindness and strength and honesty. He was her rock, steady and true and with David beside her she would never again feel insecure.

'I'll give you this, you seem to be able to pick nice lads. Tim would have been my choice for a son-in-law, I was very fond of him. What went wrong between you two?'

Nothing went wrong. Tim was a darling and we had some lovely times but we weren't in love. Tim is reunited with his first love and David is to be best man at the wedding. I'll be there too of course.'

'Marie and Tim, that was what I wanted and not so far-fetched, so don't think it was. Given a chance that would have developed and I had the feeling she was tiring of Stephen.'

'Where do I come in or where did I come in in this scheme of things?'

'Stephen admired you, I saw that.'

'Dangerous to try and pair people and I thought you were so keen for Marie to marry into the Hammond family.'

'I was and a lot of good it did me. That silly, stupid girl throwing herself away,' she said viciously. 'All my hopes and dreams were set on her and look what she did.'

'It was a shabby way to treat you, Mum, but I honestly believe that Marie is happy with Harry.'

'Just now, but it won't last.'

'I think it will.'

'Well I don't and I know my daughter.' She paused and pursed her lips. 'Went off without a thought of what it would do to me, gave me no consideration. Well I'll tell you this, Lois, I've stopped worrying about her, in fact I've stopped worrying about the three of you.'

Lois could have answered that, but what was the point, what would it have gained? The hurts of the past didn't seem to matter so much.

She nodded.

'One thing it did, it saved me the cost of the wedding.'

'That's true, the money can stay in the bank.'

'Some of it. I've made up my mind to be good to myself

and if I see something that takes my fancy then I'll have it.'

'That is just what to do.' She paused. 'Winnie sounds happy in her letters and this is a wonderful experience for her.'

'I'm not so sure. All this is going to change her.'

'No, not Winnie.'

'Time will tell. Am I allowed to ask what plans you have for your inheritance?'

'A lot of it, David's and mine, will go on the house we hope to have built and, later on, David has plans for an extension to the practice.'

'You won't pay any attention to what I say, but I would advise not rushing at things. You can't have known him long.'

'Long enough to know that he is the only one for me.'

'You sound sure enough,' she said, a little sourly.

'What about your committees, Mum, do you still do as much?'

'No, I've cut down. It took me a while to discover it but it is true that the more you do the more is expected of you.'

'Be honest, you enjoyed being needed.' She could have said bossing everybody about but she didn't.

'Being needed yes, but not being taken advantage of.'

Her mother needed to get out of the house and Lois persisted. 'You need an interest to keep you occupied.'

'I didn't say I'd stopped completely, just cut down.'

Lois yawned.

'You look as though you could do with your bed.'

'I am tired.'

'I'll make a cup of tea and you go up and see to your bed.'

'Which bedroom?'

'Either, it doesn't matter.'

'My old room I think. Is there a spare nightie?'

'Bound to be one – take a look in the drawers.'

Chapter Twenty-Four

Lying in bed cuddling Winnie's hot-water bottle, Lois was remembering the past but it didn't hurt nearly so much. She knew that she could never completely forget the hurts and slights that she had suffered throughout her childhood but it didn't do to dwell on them. She had matured enough to realise the futility of that. Going over it all in her mind it had been an amazing conversation to have had with her mother. Harriet had been surprisingly open about answering her questions. Maybe she had needed to unburden herself as David had suggested. David was right about a lot of things.

She fell asleep thinking about David. A gentle giant was how one little old lady had described him and Lois had thought that very apt. He wasn't soft, far from it, but he cared. He cared about people and he cared about his four-legged friends. There was compassion and a ready sympathy and it was small wonder that so many came to him from far and near with their pets. David was dependable, someone to trust and she was just so lucky to have found him.

Lois got up in plenty of time to catch the early bus and was surprised and curiously touched to find her mother already in the kitchen with the kettle on and cutting the bread for toast. She was wearing a very pretty pink quilted dressing-gown that was obviously new.

'Sleep well, did you?'

'Like a top and I didn't expect to. Mum, you shouldn't have got up, there was no need, I would have got myself out.'

'I don't doubt it. Two slices do you?'

'Yes, thank you.' She drew out the chair and sat down at the table.

'Makes a change having company for breakfast. Were you warm enough?'

'Yes and that reminds me I meant to bring down Winnie's hot-water bottle.'

'Never mind it, I'm not rushing anywhere. I've the whole day ahead of me.'

'You've changed,' Lois said.

'So have you.'

'In what way?'

'Not so prickly, not so sensitive. You've turned out not bad-looking since you were such a plain skinny wee thing. One thing you did have was lovely black curly hair and folk weren't slow to remark on it. Made such a contrast—'

'The three of you being so fair?'

She nodded and pushed the marmalade dish over to Lois. 'Marie envied you those curls I can tell you. Must have got those from Grace.' She raised her brows in a question.

'I don't know.'

'Hasn't this David of yours told you if—'

'I haven't seen a photograph of Grace, I will when David finds them. He did say Grace was tall and slim and apparently I have her laugh but otherwise no close resemblance.'

'Funny us talking like this and none of it seems important.' She put a scraping of marmalade on her toast and took a small bite. 'This is a big house to keep up,' she said suddenly.

'Would you consider going to a smaller house?'

'One day I'll think seriously about it. Want that filled up?' she said touching the teapot.

'No, thank you, I'll have to watch my time.'

'You've still a few minutes.'

Lois got up from the table, she didn't want to miss the bus. 'Thanks, Mum, thanks for everything.'

Harriet got to her feet. 'You'll be welcome if you want to come again. We should get on better now that you know the situation.'

'Yes, it has given me a lot to think about and, thank you, I'd like to come occasionally.'

'If you want you can bring that young man of yours. I won't hold it against him that he's Grace's stepson,' she added with a smile.

'I'll ask him and I'm sure he'll be delighted.'

Lois was smiling as she let herself out of the house and sprinted for the bus. She had arrived uncertain of the welcome she would receive. Indeed to have the door shut in her face wouldn't have surprised her. It had all been so different to what she had expected. Life was very strange.

Mrs Barlow, always glad of that early cup of tea, sank into the chair before taking off her coat.

'Thanks, lass, I'd miss this.' She looked across the table and nodded. 'That's more like it, you've been looking real down in the mouth this past while so whatever was troubling you must have sorted itself out.'

Yes, she thought, it has all sorted itself out. 'Thank you, everything is fine, Mrs Barlow.' How nice to know that people cared, genuinely cared, and not just curious.

Because she wanted it to finish the day seemed to drag. There was so much she wanted to tell David but she kept smiling so he must know. At last the door closed finally and David held out his arms. It was where she belonged and Lois went into them with a sigh of pure happiness.

'I told you it was wise to face your devils,' he smiled.

'Yes, you told me that and you were right.'

'Aren't I always?'

'No but this time you were. I feel lightheaded with relief and there is so much I have to tell you.'

'Over a meal or shall we have coffee first?'

'Coffee I think.' They went through to make it and once it was ready sat down together.

'Save the details until later just tell me that you and your mother have put the bad old days behind you.'

'Maybe she has and I'm trying to, but it isn't as easy as all that. I think I have forgiven her, then I remember something—'

'You will go on doing that for a while then it will fade altogether.'

She thought David was right. It would take time. But then she had plenty of that. David and she had a whole future together and one day there would be children – a little Grace and a little Andrew.

'You are smiling.'

'I'm happy that's why.'

'And that is the way it is always going to be. Your happiness is what I want above all else. My turn, let me tell you my bit of news. I've set the wheels in motion and plans for our future home will soon be forthcoming.'

'Marvellous.'

'There's more. Things are doing well, very well and I intend advertising for a qualified vet which should give us more time together.' He paused. 'The wedding—'

'A quiet wedding, I don't want a lot of fuss.'

'Gretna Green?' he said, tongue in cheek.

'Absolutely not. David I don't want to leave Miss Watt and go home—'

'Why not?'

'She has been very good to me and she was there when I needed her, but the main reason is that I can come round here every night and I couldn't do that if I went back to Greenacre.'

'How very true. Heavens! how would I survive?'

'You'd manage but you won't have to. David if Mum is agreeable and I have a feeling she will be, then I would like to be married from Laurelbank. I feel it is still my home.'

'Time I met Mrs Pringle since the woman is going to be my mother-in-law. Will she want a say in the wedding?'

'No, I'll be paying for everything or rather Grace will,' she said mischievously.

'And so she should. The mother of the bride.'

'Mum's big worry about Marie's wedding or rather the one that didn't come off was finding someone to give the bride away.'

'Have you anyone to fill the bill?'

She nodded happily. 'I think so. Mr Latimer is my boss but as well as that he is a friend. I think he might oblige.'

'Be honoured, I imagine.'

Lois got up to rinse out the cups. 'Where are you taking me?'

'Where we had our first meal together.'

'The Stag's Head, that was the place I was going to suggest.'